A Guide to Programs for Parenting Children
with Autism Spectrum Disorder, Intellectual
Disabilities or Developmental Disabilities

of related interest

A Complete ABA Curriculum for Individuals on the Autism Spectrum
with a Developmental Age of 7 Years Up to Young Adulthood
A Step-by-Step Treatment Manual Including Supporting
Materials for Teaching 140 Advanced Skills
Julie Knapp, PhD, BCBA-D and Carolline Turnbull, BA, BCaBA
ISBN 978 1 78592 988 5
eISBN 978 0 85700 890 9

A Complete ABA Curriculum for Individuals on the Autism
Spectrum with a Developmental Age of 4–7 Years
A Step-by-Step Treatment Manual Including Supporting
Materials for Teaching 150 Intermediate Skills
Julie Knapp, PhD, BCBA-D and Carolline Turnbull, BA, BCaBA
ISBN 978 1 78592 987 8
eISBN 978 0 85700 889 3

A Complete ABA Curriculum for Individuals on the Autism
Spectrum with a Developmental Age of 3–5 Years
A Step-by-Step Treatment Manual Including Supporting
Materials for Teaching 140 Beginning Skills
Julie Knapp, PhD, BCBA-D and Carolline Turnbull, BA, BCaBA
ISBN 978 1 78592 996 0
eISBN 978 0 85700 888 6

A Complete ABA Curriculum for Individuals on the Autism
Spectrum with a Developmental Age of 1–4 Years
A Step-by-Step Treatment Manual Including Supporting
Materials for Teaching 140 Foundational Skill
Julie Knapp, PhD, BCBA-D and Carolline Turnbull, BA, BCaBA
ISBN 978 1 78592 983 0
eISBN 978 0 85700 887 9

A Guide to Programs for

PARENTING CHILDREN with AUTISM SPECTRUM DISORDER, INTELLECTUAL DISABILITIES or DEVELOPMENTAL DISABILITIES

Evidence-Based Guidance for Professionals

Edited by KATE GUASTAFERRO
and JOHN R. LUTZKER

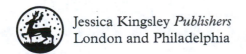
Jessica Kingsley *Publishers*
London and Philadelphia

First published in 2018
by Jessica Kingsley Publishers
73 Collier Street
London N1 9BE, UK
and
400 Market Street, Suite 400
Philadelphia, PA 19106, USA

www.jkp.com

Library of Congress Cataloging in Publication Data
A CIP catalog record for this book is available from the Library of Congress

British Library Cataloguing in Publication Data
A CIP catalogue record for this book is available from the British Library

ISBN 978 1 78592 735 5
eISBN 978 1 78450 440 3

Printed and bound in the United States

Contents

INTRODUCTION

Kate Guastaferro and John R. Lutzker

Intellectual and developmental disabilities (IDD) are limitations in intellectual functioning, adaptive behaviors, and delays in cognitive, physical, or emotional development occurring before the age of 18. IDD includes, but is not limited to, autism spectrum disorder (ASD). Individuals with IDD are an increased risk for early mortality, morbidity (e.g., obesity, chronic health problems, poor mental health), and social isolation (Emerson, 2012; Heller *et al.*, 2014; Taggart & Cousins, 2014). A higher rate of adverse health conditions among people with IDD is coupled with disparities in access to preventive care and utilization of health promotion activities (Krahn & Fox, 2014). The lifetime indirect and direct cost of supporting an individual with IDD exceeds $2.4 million dollars (Buescher *et al.*, 2014). In high-income countries, the prevalence of intellectual and developmental disabilities among children is estimated as being 3–4% (Emerson, 2012). In the United States, approximately 1 in 6 children is diagnosed with a developmental disability (Boyle *et al.*, 2011) and 1 in 68 is identified to have an ASD (Christensen *et al.*, 2016). Prevalence estimates of IDD vary for a variety of reasons, including inconsistent terminology and changing diagnostic criteria, but overall the consensus is that the prevalence of IDD, and notably ASD, is rapidly increasing. Although higher rates may appear disconcerting, they may actually be a positive indication of increased awareness and improved screening and diagnostic capabilities (McKenzie *et al.*, 2016). With more children with IDD identified than ever before, there is a compelling need for effective and efficient interventions to improve the quality of life for individuals with IDD.

Evidence-based intervention

A number of support approaches have been developed for individuals with IDD, the majority of which have strong roots in applied behavior analysis (ABA). To ensure that practices delivered to individuals with IDD are in-line with the highest quality of evidence available, there is a movement toward the use of evidence-based programs (EBP). By definition, EBP have been empirically evaluated in several efficacy and effectiveness trials, the most rigorous of which is the randomized controlled trial (RCT). Practices that lack this most rigorous level of evidence may be labeled evidence-informed or a promising practice.

Early intervention is particularly important for individuals with IDD: it may improve the developmental trajectory of a child at-risk for or diagnosed with IDD (Guralnick, 2005). In other words, the earlier that strategies are introduced, the greater the likelihood that children and their families develop skills to alleviate stress, reduce burden, and improve outcomes. As parents or primary caregivers spend the most time with a child, one promising and strongly supported intervention approach includes parents (or primary caregivers) in treatment or intervention implementation and engaging in treatment or intervention early (Matson, Mahan, & LoVullo, 2009). The support for parent or primary caregiver inclusion is twofold: (1) to maximize generalization of skills at home or in other settings; and (2) to reduce parent stress. Including parents as intervention mediators is critical to maintenance, and generalization of newly taught skills is critical to success in improving child behavior and children learning new skills (Matson *et al.*, 2009). The direct association between parental stress and having a child with IDD is complex and not well understood (Hastings, 2002); however, one study indicated that high levels of parental stress counteracted the effect of an early intervention strategy for children with autism spectrum disorders (Dempsey *et al.*, 2009). In addition, it is known that some parental reactions to children's behavior can reinforce problem behaviors (Hastings, 2002). Therefore, there is strong evidence for the importance of training parents in behavior management tools.

History of evidence-based parent training and support

According to most evidence, humans have been around for approximately 200,000 years. Modern habits appeared around 50,000 years ago. Despite this long tenure on this planet, until the late 1940s, help in parenting came mostly from Biblical and other religious/spiritual written or oral guides. Yet, somehow, great figures emerged very successfully from their childhoods and most people learned culturally accepted toileting habits, social mores, communication skills, and a host of other necessary interactive skills without the benefits of their parents having exposure to parenting manuals and books, videos, internet advice, or evidence-based parenting programs. Until World War II, in developed countries, extended families often lived together or in close proximity for most of their lives. Thus, communal/familial child-rearing support and care was often available from family and friends. After the war, families became increasingly dispersed. And, by the late 1950s, in the US and UK, the nuclear family began some significant changes that have accelerated and morphed in recent decades.

The first major bestselling book for parents appeared in 1946, *Baby and Child Care*, authored by Dr Benjamin Spock. Nine English editions have been published, as well as editions in other languages. It is a basic guide for medical issues and on being a parent. Thus, in addition to covering feeding, vitamins, diet, and schedules, daily health care, predictable infant illnesses, development and developmental changes, foods, illnesses of older children, clothing and equipment needs, and first aid; it also covered what today we would call behavioral challenges. This included considerable child-rearing advice, the role of the extended family, crying, behavioral expectations for age groupings, traveling with children, and special situations such as divorce and separation, prematurity, disabilities, and other challenges. It sold millions of copies because its coverage was what parents wanted: a one-stop shop for answers to parents' questions and concerns about their babies and older children. It was updated frequently enough that the medical advice was trustworthy and was an easy source for parents to judge what course of action to take for a host of common medical problems of their children.

The "behavioral" advice, however, was based mostly on old unsupported theories of child development and behavior and clearly also based on Spock's experience and beliefs. Between 1946 and the mid-1960s, the book was also the "Gospel" on behavior because there were no evidence-based parenting approaches. This changed with the advent of ABA that will be described below. With the plethora of parenting advice in print today, along with media, internet, blogs, and videos that parents crave, more advice than ever is available. Some is reputable, much is not; that is to say, much has no scientific foundations.

New directions: A scientific approach to parenting

Behavior modification is a seldom-used term today, but between 1964 and 1968, it was used to describe the use of operant conditioning procedures that came from the animal laboratories of B.F. Skinner and others that were applied to a scientific, systematic set of techniques to change human behavior. The term and the field had mixed reactions from practitioners, journalists, and the public. On the one hand, some striking positive changes were achieved that had never occurred in areas such as schizophrenia, and with children with various disorders. On the other hand, the name itself, "behavior modification," sparked Orwellian images for many people, and proponents of older theories, particularly Freudian, Jungian, others, and newer nondirective Rogerian practices. It was believed that behavior modification, with its focus on measureable behavior change through systematic changes in the patient's environment and mostly direct observations of behavior in its natural setting, was manipulative and in the long-run not able to produce enduring results. Despite the critics, the field expanded rapidly and published peer-reviewed journal articles were reporting new strides in teaching skills and reducing or eliminating seriously challenging behaviors with autistic children, adults and children with intellectual and developmental disabilities, and strategies for teachers to improve classroom decorum and improve students' academic skills.

Soon thereafter, ABA was showing success in many other areas of human development, such as, but not limited to, environmental and community issues, industrial safety, problems of seniors and other gerontology issues, medical and prescription compliance, and athletic skills (Lutzker & Martin, 1981). In 1968, the first issue of the *Journal of Applied Behavior Analysis* was published and quickly became the standard of rigorous research in what had been formerly called behavior modification and was soon to be called ABA. In the first issue, three of the pioneers of ABA, Donald Baer, Montrose Wolf, and Todd Risley, laid out the basic precepts of the field, and those precepts endure (Baer, Wolf, & Risley, 1968). The term "applied," these pioneers noted, required that behaviors that would be measured and changed or skills taught needed to be of social significance. Thus, for example, teaching an autistic child to name state capitals would not be considered socially significant for that child until other, more important, basic academic skills were taught. "Behavior" referred primarily to being able to directly observe and measure that which was to be changed, to define the behavior(s) in an operational way so that more than one observer could agree on the rate or frequency the behavior occurred, and the sufficient operational description of procedures used to promote behavior change such that techniques could be replicated. By "analysis," it was meant that to be published and replicated there must be sufficient evidence that the behavior change observed was, in fact, a function of the techniques applied and not chance or random social environment or physical environment reasons.

In other words, the scientific community needed to have confidence that there could be few or no other explanations for the behavior change other than the procedures applied. Prior to the development of ABA, such confidence was only possible with group research requiring, at minimum, an "experimental" group receiving a treatment group and a control group that did not receive the treatment and a statistical test conducted to demonstrate that any positive results were not due to chance. With a rapidly growing field of novel techniques, new designs were needed that would also allow confidence, but without having to have groups large enough to be able to show statistical significance and would also have the ability to modify research procedures in real time should an initial attempt to produce behavior change not show any favorable results. These new designs had to be able to examine the nuances of techniques during any given research. Thus, part of the development of ABA was a set of new research designs referred to as "single-case research design." These designs could be applied with one participant or a group of participants without needing statistical analysis because the designs could visually show that changes in behavior only occurred only when the treatment procedures were in effect and not when they were not in effect, in a design such that other explanations for the behavior change could be ruled out.

Using the single-case research design, it is possible for interventionists to see what treatment or intervention procedures produce the desired effect. An RCT can add external validity to evidence-based single-case research designs.

Parent training in practice

One of the earliest applications of behavior modification with a child was described by Williams (1959). A 22-month-old boy who had a history of medical problems in his young life was brought to attention when his parents and aunt could not control what were described as violent tantrums when put to bed for the night or for a nap. After medical causes for the tantrums were ruled out, observations revealed that contingent upon a tantrum to calm the child down, the parents or aunt would read to the child in bed. While reading to children is a highly recommended practice, in this case it was contingent upon tantrums thereby likely inadvertently providing positive reinforcement for the tantrums. Thus, the parents were instructed to ignore the tantrums. By the second time that the tantrums were ignored, they virtually disappeared. Williams reported that at age 3½, the child had no other behavioral problems and was developing well. Although this "extinction" procedure is replete with possible adverse side effects because of inadvertent misapplications by parents, in this case it was effective and was the first in the literature showing how parents could be taught to apply evidence-based procedures to help manage their children's behavior.

Making use of a procedure called "reciprocal inhibition," loosely based on the principles of classical conditioning, Bentler (1962) described a case study of what appeared to be a developing water phobia in an 11½-month-old girl who displayed considerable anxiety around washing and baths. The intervention first consisted of placing the child in a bathtub that contained toys, but no water. Then, the child was placed on a table by the sink in which water was running with toys in it, but the child was not put in the water. The third step was placing toys on the other side of a basin such that if the child wanted to play with them, she would have to walk through the basin that had some water in it, and the mother began washing the child in the sink during diaper changes. Finally, diaper changes occurred while being in the sink with water running. These steps eliminated the child's water fears. This case study and the Williams (1959) study were primitive in that they lacked single-case research designs and that the procedures were very simple. Nonetheless, they were among the first to show that child behavior change could occur by teaching parents simple behavioral procedures.

The truly seminal study of the 1960s that produced a sea change was published by Wolf, Risley, and Mees (1964), describing remarkably successful results with an autistic child, Dicky. Intervention with Dicky began when he was 3½ years old. At nine months old, Dicky was diagnosed with rare childhood cataracts on his eyes. Concurrent with that, despite typical development to that point, Dicky began to display severe tantrums and sleep disorder. He also began displaying problematic food preferences and was not showing typical social and verbal repertoires, common in children showing increasing signs of autism. To that point, there had never been a successful intervention with an autistic child reported in the scientific literature. Though the term "autism" had appeared in the literature, Dicky was referred to a mental hospital under the common inaccurate diagnosis of the time for these "symptoms," childhood schizophrenia. The cataracts created an especially difficult complication in that surgical removal of them was necessary to prevent blindness and it would be necessary for Dicky to wear glasses after surgery. Without such he would also not be able to see.

The interventions designed for Dicky took place at the hospital and at home when he returned there. The intervention for tantrums was similar to the "extinction" procedure described by Bentler (1962), that is, tantrums were ignored and Dicky was placed in his room with the door closed and carefully supervised by the researchers. Further, an important additional procedure, differential reinforcement for non-tantrum behavior, was introduced. His door was opened when he was not having a tantrum. This was presumed to act as reinforcement for calm behavior. His parents were taught the procedures at the hospital and later carried them out at home. Both severity and frequency of tantrums decreased dramatically.

Shaping is a critically important tool in ABA. It involves reinforcement of successive approximations toward desired target behavior. For Dicky, this was used to get him to wear glasses, which he initially refused by taking them off and throwing them. Numerous pairs of empty glasses frames were placed around his hospital room and a hospital attendant was taught to conduct three shaping sessions each day. During these sessions, Dicky received small bites of desirable edible reinforcers, paired with a conditioned reinforcer, each time he moved closer to the frames. Eventually, he was shaped to pick up the frames and to wear them for increasing amounts of time until he wore them throughout his waking hours. After his surgery, prescription glasses were introduced.

Within this comprehensive and novel set of interventions, these pioneering behavior analysts also taught Dicky language and social skills and helped the parents with teaching Dicky to eat a balanced diet by using positive reinforcement and timeout. Todd Risley kept in touch with Dicky throughout his young adulthood, at which time he lived in semi-independent living accommodation, had a part-time job, and expressed an interest in working with autistic children and other disabilities. He remembered parts of his intervention and referred to the days "when I was autistic."

Every practitioner who successfully uses ABA, every parent whose loved one has benefitted from an ABA intervention, and every child or adult who received and benefitted from ABA can tie their success directly back to this seminal 1964 work. In the ensuing 50-plus years, the field has evolved with much more sophisticated techniques and assessment strategies, as well as a more sophisticated approach to a participant's social ecology and a focus on teaching relevant skills that will help maintain success in natural environments. Some of this further development of behavioral parent training will be covered in this chapter as well as a review of the other chapters and the programs they describe. The chapters reflect a variety of innovative programs, some with a history of a long evidence base and some in exploratory but very promising nascent efforts.

Early more developed parent training and support programs

Hall (1984) described a more advanced group parent training program for middle-class suburban families that used more behavioral procedures than the earlier efforts for everyday parenting issues such as chore compliance and whining. Parents were taught some behavior recording techniques and how to use descriptive praise and planned ignoring procedures. Descriptive praise involves praising the child upon the desired behavior and letting the child know exactly for what behavior the praise is occurring. Thus, for example, rather than telling the child, "You're being a good boy," the parent would say, "Nice job setting the table." Planned ignoring involves teaching parents how to ignore minor misbehavior without inadvertently reinforcing behavior targeted for reduction. Every parent was provided the *Responsive Parenting Manual*, a tool for reference between group meetings and to keep after the program had finished so as to help maintain behavior change and for parents to be able to use with other child behaviors.

The Portage Project (Shearer & Shearer, 1976) was one of the earliest home-based family support programs aimed at preschool services for children with IDD and their parents. The project's efforts were empirically supported: activity charts and behavior logs for parents to keep at home, teaching parents to become "home teachers" through learning many behavioral teaching strategies, teaching verbal and nonverbal communication techniques for the children, and helping parents find other needed social services.

The work with Dicky, the autistic boy treated by Wolf, Risley, and Mees (1964), was conducted at the University of Washington, which, in the 1960s, was a hotbed of the developing field of ABA. Also at the University of Washington in that era was O. Ivar Lovaas, who pioneered intensive treatment for autistic children, focusing on eliminating challenging and self-injurious behavior, and most importantly, teaching language skills. Referred to as "discrete trail training," positive reinforcement was used along with shaping, prompting, and teaching eye contact. Initially, all child training took place in laboratory settings conducted by highly skilled subdoctoral therapists. Later, a parent-training component was added (Lovaas *et al.*, 1973).

Robert L. Koegel and his colleagues advanced the laboratory and parent training approach of Lovaas and studied countless nuances of skills and how to teach children with autistic children. Koegel and colleagues (1982) initially showed the advantages of parent training over clinic only training and Koegel and colleagues (1984) expanded on the positive effects on children from systematic parent training. They laid out basic critical steps for parent training: (1) use of teaching children clear discriminative stimuli (so that a child knows when to respond and that a consequence is forthcoming); (2) giving instructions and asking questions; (3) providing prompts; (4) shaping and chaining (stringing skills together). Chapter 1 of this volume details the most recent work of the Koegels in parent training.

An "ecobehavioral" approach to in-home parent support services for children with IDD and autism was described by Lutzker and Campbell (1994). They described services that were all conducted *in situ*, mostly at home, where parents were taught a host of procedures wherein interventionists modeled skills, parents role-played the skills and then were provided feedback. Before moving onto any next step or new technique, the parents had to master performance criteria such that they could display the skill with no prompting from the interventionist. This approach included teaching strictly positive behavior management techniques, increasing language and other communication skills as dictated by behavioral assessments, and other challenges posed by particular children. For example, a young child with IDD was referred by a pediatric neurologist from a major university teaching hospital because the child was facing draconian brain surgery for seizures that were not successfully being managed by medication. The physician was familiar with the ecobehavioral program and expressed a hope that behavioral procedures might offer an alternative. Direct observations of the child were conducted at home and at school. The observations revealed that hyperventilation almost always preceded the seizures and that hyperventilation was preceded by a situation change (i.e., transition). For instance, at home, if the child was quietly playing and his mother told him that it was time to get ready for dinner, this transition would cause hyperventilation and then a seizure was likely to occur. Similarly, at school, a change of tasks or settings (e.g., classroom to the individual teaching room) would produce a similar sequence, leading to a seizure. The intervention consisted of first teaching the child behavioral relaxation through posturing, initially in a beanbag chair. He was taught to put his body in relaxed positions known to correlate with typically developing people when they receive progressive muscle relaxation training and indicate that they are very relaxed. Once he was proficient at being able to position himself such, his mother was taught to say to him "relax" and he would demonstrate relaxed posturing while sitting or standing. In order to prevent the transition/hyperventilation sequence, the mother was taught to always give the child a clear oral indication that a transition was about to occur and then she held up a finger indication to the child to show her his relaxed position. Using a single-case research design known as a multiple baseline across settings, once there was a considerable decrease in hyperventilation and seizures at home, the teacher was taught the same procedures and there was another significant drop in the hyperventilation/seizure sequence. No surgery was subsequently needed (Kiesel, Lutzker, & Campbell, 1989).

Some other studies exemplify the diversity of successful efforts using the ecobehavioral approach to parent training with children with IDD/autism. Harrold and colleagues (1992) demonstrated that timeout was not necessary to reduce challenging behavior when planned activities training (Lutzker & Campbell, 1994) was used. Planned activities training involves teaching parents to prevent challenging behaviors by making sure that their children are engaged with their parents, in solitary activities, or in shared activities. Parents are taught to prepare for activities, state rules to the children regarding the activities, apprise children of what reinforcers will be available for their appropriate engagement with the activities, use descriptive praise, and incidental teaching where parents always require expanded language or use teaching moments to make sure that learning is involved in all activities. Huynen and colleagues (1996) showed that mothers and their children were able to apply the planned activities training that they had been taught to use at home to community settings without needing any additional training.

Current parent training approaches

The 21st century has seen a variety of "packaged" parent training programs for families with autistic children or children with IDD. Some have an evidence base, some use evidence-based procedures without any solid program evaluation, and a few have no evidence base. Researchers, providers, and parents should continue the movement toward the exclusive use of EBP. This book provides a comprehensive overview of parent training programs for parents with children with IDD, including ASD. Each chapter in this volume describes evidence-based and promising programs, the evidence base for the program, and offers a discussion of implementation and dissemination efforts. The programs serve families with children in infancy through adolescence and are delivered by a range of different providers with varying educational backgrounds. The chapters are ordered by strength of their evidence-base, including the scope of their historical research, as a nod to the importance of using EBP. The evidence for the models and programs presented in this volume is a combination of rigorous research on the model specific to the IDD population as well as the prior amount of research on the model not specific to the IDD population. Programs currently lacking high levels of rigor but that are highly promising and should be considered for future research are also included.

Chapters 1 and 2 describe parent training programs for parents of children with IDD that have undergone the highest level of rigorous evaluation, an RCT. In Chapter 1, Koegel, Koegel and Koegel describe Pivotal Response Treatment (PRT) for individuals with ASD in which motivation is seen as an essential element of behavior change, which can produce rapid improvements in target behaviors and related behaviors. PRT is a seminal behavioral intervention that has informed many of the other programs included in this volume. Chapter 2, by Durand, Clarke, and Strauss, describes the Positive Family Intervention, in which parents are taught to use optimism in order to overcome obstacles to successful parenting. Chapters 3 to 5 are focused on programs with an ongoing RCT. In Chapter 3, McIntyre and Brown discuss the adaption of Incredible Years® Parent Training Program for parents of children with IDD. Mello, Talbott, and Rogers describe the parent-mediated Early Start Denver

Model (P-ESDM) in Chapter 4, which adds a specialized approach to developmental topics only when the needs of a child with ASD are known to be different from that of typical development. Chapter 5, by Magaña, Machalicek, Lopez, and Iland, describes Padres en Acción, a parent education program designed for Latino parents of children with ASD, an increasingly needed effort. In Chapter 6, Timmer, Hawk, and Urquiza describe the tailored delivery of Parent–Child Interaction Therapy (PCIT), a well-established evidence-based parent training program on its own, to newer efforts with children on the autism spectrum and diagnosed with IDD. Chapters 7 and 8 describe very promising programs that are currently lacking the highest level of rigor. The Infant Catch-Up Program, described in Chapter 7 by Molko-Harpaz and Guastaferro, is an individually delivered parent-education program designed to enhance developmental growth, or alter the developmental trajectory, of infants at-risk for or diagnosed with ASD. Fung, Steel, Bryce, Lake, and Lunsky in Chapter 8, present Acceptance and Commitment Therapy for parents of children with ASD, in which parents are taught mindfulness strategies to enhance psychological flexibility and acceptance.

The presentation of these parent programs collectively is designed to provide the reader—a researcher, provider, or parent—with enough detail to decide whether a program might be relevant to their specific needs, but not enough to deliver the program without further training. It provides a resource to inform providers, agencies, professors, students, and advocates.

Future directions

Technology remains the easiest prediction for the future of most behavioral interventions as well as for assessment, particularly in assessing autism. Advances in testing for biomarkers and for eye contact in infants will make very early intervention likely. The use of video games and virtual reality in teaching a host of skills to children with IDD and autism will become ever more available. Intervention programs that use data portals and data collection from tablets when home visiting is conducted will allow for the accrual of important data as well as for easier program evaluations. Interactive videos and virtual reality training for parents will become the status quo in services for parents with children with IDD and autism. Hopefully, researchers and service providers will collaborate to braid or blend the kinds of programs described in this volume to create best assessment and intervention fits for families. Advocacy has improved geometrically in the 21st century and this will continue. The future holds much promise for families, their training, and their children.

References

Baer, D.M., Wolf, M.M., & Risley, T.R. (1968) "Some current dimensions of applied behavior analysis." *Journal of Applied Behavior Analysis 1*, 91–97.

Bentler, P.M. (1962) "An infant's phobia treated with reciprocal inhibition." *Journal of Child Psychology and Psychiatry 3*, 185–189.

Boyle, C.A., Boulet, S., Schieve, L.A., *et al.* (2011) "Trends in the prevalence of developmental disabilities in children, 1997–2008." *Pediatrics 127*, 6, 1034–1042.

Buescher, A.V.S., Cidav, Z., Knapp, M., & Mandell, D.S. (2014) "Costs of Autism Spectrum Disorders in the United Kingdom and the United States." *JAMA Pediatrics 168*, 8, 721–728.

Christensen, D.L., Baio, J., Braun, K.V., *et al.* (2016) "Prevalence and characteristics of Autism Spectrum Disorder among children aged 8 years – Autism and Developmental Disabilities Monitoring Network, 11 Sites, United States, 2012." *MMWR Surveillance Summaries 63*, 2, 1–23.

Dempsey, I., Keen, D., Pennell, D., O'Reilly, J., & Neilands, J. (2009) "Parent stress, parenting competence and family-centered support to young children with an intellectual or developmental disability." *Research in Developmental Disabilities 30*, 558–566.

Emerson, E. (2012) "Deprivation, ethnicity, and the prevalence of intellectual and developmental disabilities." *Journal of Epidemiology & Community Health 66*, 218–224.

Guralnick, M.J. (2005) "Early intervention for children with intellectual disabilities: Current knowledge and future prospects." *Journal of Applied Research in Intellectual Disabilities 18*, 313–324.

Hall, M.C. (1984) "Responsive Parenting: A Large-Scale Training Program for School Districts, Hospitals, and Mental Health Centers." In R.A. Dangel & R.A. Polster (eds) *Parent Training*. New York: Guilford Press.

Harrold, M., Lutzker, J.R., Campbell, R.V., & Touchette, P.E. (1992) "Improving parent–child interactions for families of children with developmental disabilities." *Journal of Behavior Therapy and Experimental Psychiatry 23*, 89–100.

Hastings, R.P. (2002) "Parental stress and behaviour problems of children with developmental disability." *Journal of Intellectual and Developmental Disability 27*, 3, 149–160.

Heller, T., Fisher, D., Marks, B., & Hsieh, K. (2014) "Interventions to promote health: Crossing networks of intellectual and developmental disabilities and aging." *Disability and Health Journal 7*, 1, S24–S32.

Huynen, K.B., Lutzker, J.R., Bigelow, K.M., Touchette, P.E., & Campbell, R.V. (1996) "Planned activities training for mothers of children with developmental disabilities: Community generalization and follow-up." *Behavior Modification 20*, 406–427.

Kiesel, K.B., Lutzker, J.R., & Campbell, R.V. (1989) "Behavioral relaxation training to reduce hyperventilation and seizures in a profoundly retarded epileptic child." *Journal of the Multihandicapped Person 2*, 179–190.

Koegel, R.L., Schreibman, L., Britten, K.R., Burke, J.C., & O'Neill, R.E. (1982) "A Comparison of Parent Training to Direct Child Treatment." In R.L. Koegel, & A.L. Egel (eds) *Educating and Understanding Autistic Children*. San Diego, CA: College-Hill Press.

Koegel, R.L., Schreibman, L., Johnson, J., O'Neill, R.E., & Dunlap, G. (1984) "Collateral Effects of Parent Training on Families with Autistic Children." In R.A. Dangel & R.A. Polster (eds) *Parent Training*. New York: Guilford Press.

Krahn, G.L. & Fox, M.H. (2014) "Health disparities of adults with intellectual disabilities: What do we know? What do we do?" *Journal of Applied Research in Intellectual Disabilities 27*, 431–446.

Lovaas, I.O., Koegel, R.L., Simmons, J.Q., & Long, J.S. (1973) "Some generalization and follow-up measures on autistic children in behavior therapy." *Journal of Applied Behavior Analysis 6*, 131–166.

Lutzker, J.R. & Campbell, R.V. (1994) *Ecobehavioral Family Interventions in Developmental Disabilities*. Pacific Grove, CA: Brooks/Cole Publishing Co.

Lutzker, J.R. & Martin, J.A. (1981) *Behavior Change*. Monterey, CA: Brooks/Cole.

Matson, J.L., Mahan, S., & LoVullo, S.V. (2009) "Parent training: A review of methods for children with developmental disabilities." *Research in Developmental Disabilities 30*, 961–968.

McKenzie, K., Milton, M., Smith, G., & Ouellette-Kuntz, H. (2016) "Systematic review of the prevalence and incidence of intellectual disabilities: Current trends and issues." *Current Developmental Disorders Reports 3*, 2, 104–115.

Shearer, D. & Shearer, M. (1976) "The Portage Project: A Model for Early Childhood Intervention." In T. Tjossen (ed.) *Intervention Strategies for High-Risk Infants and Young Children*. Baltimore, MD: University Park Press.

Spock, B. (1976) *Baby and Child Care* (3rd ed.). New York: Pocket Books.

Taggart, L. & Cousins, W. (eds) (2014) *Health Promotion for People with Intellectual and Developmental Disabilities*. New York: McGraw-Hill Education.

Williams, C.D. (1959) "The elimination of tantrum behavior by extinction procedures." *Journal of Abnormal and Social Psychology 59*, 269.

Wolf, M.M., Risley, T.R., & Mees, H. (1964) "Application of operant conditioning procedures to the behavior problems of an autistic child." *Behaviour Research and Therapy 1*, 305–312

Chapter 1

PIVOTAL RESPONSE TREATMENT AND PARENT EDUCATION

Lynn Kern Koegel, Brittany Lynn Koegel, and Robert L. Koegel

ABSTRACT

Pivotal Response Treatment (PRT) is a naturalistic motivation-based behavioral intervention developed for individuals with autism spectrum disorder. It is based on the identification of motivation as a key pivotal area in autism that, when treated, can produce very rapid and widespread improvements in thousands of individual target behaviors as well as in the condition of autism as a whole. Specific evidence-based procedures have been combined as a package to improve "motivation" in terms of responsiveness, correct responses, affect, interest, and engagement, which produce a rapid learning curve in individuals with autism spectrum disorders. As well, when these procedures are applied, positive improvements in untreated areas occur. This chapter will discuss the theory behind the need for motivational procedures, pivotal areas, fidelity of implementation, and the importance of parent education. We include a discussion of scholarly published research studies as well as a table that includes a body of literature, published within our research clinics and replicated in other research clinics, supporting the positive effects of PRT in a variety of areas. We conclude with areas in need of future research.

Keywords: Pivotal Response Treatment (PRT); parent education; motivational procedures; trainer-of-trainers; fidelity of implementation

This chapter discusses Pivotal Response Treatment (PRT), an especially powerful intervention technique for autism that was developed through the research analytics of applied behavior analysis (Koegel & Koegel, 2012). There is widespread consensus that behavioral interventions (often referred to as Applied Behavior Analysis or ABA) are the most empirically validated methods for the treatment of autism spectrum disorders (ASD). Compared with an eclectic approach with many different types of interventions combined, outcomes are significantly higher when ABA treatments alone are consistently provided (Eikeseth et al., 2007; Howard et al., 2005). This is also true with respect to long-term outcomes following early intervention using ABA, with the most optimistic studies suggesting that as many as 49% of children will achieve typical intellectual and educational functioning and will participate in regular education, compared with 2% of children who do not receive early intensive behavioral interventions (EIBI). Further, without EIBI, most children with autism will test as having severe intellectual impairments and will remain, or be placed, in special education classes for children with autism throughout their school years (Lovaas, 1987). Thus, the benefits of early ABA intervention are well-documented and result in improved outcomes, compared to control groups in a wide variety of areas (Cohen, Amerine-Dickens, & Smith, 2006).

The initial effective ABA therapies that focused on teaching children with autism were conducted in highly controlled environments (Baer, Wolf, & Risley, 1968). These techniques removed all distractions and taught individual behaviors using external reinforcers (e.g., tokens or candy) as well as punishers if children engaged in inappropriate behaviors or did not respond correctly in the context of a strict shaping paradigm (Lovaas, 1987). Within the context of ABA, Discrete Trial Training (DTT) was developed (Hewett, 1965; Lovaas et al., 1966), which consisted of teaching small, measureable units of behavior systematically in these carefully controlled environments (Lovaas & Smith, 1989). This focused on an antecedent (A), wherein the interventionist provided an instruction to the child; a behavior (B), wherein the individual with ASD emits a response after the antecedent instruction; and a consequence (C), in which the interventionist provides either a reward or a punisher, depending on the child's response. In this ABC format (which is one discrete trial), each behavior was taught to the individual by presenting a specific cue (or by use of prompts) in a one-on-one situation. Children who received this type of therapy made slow and steady progress, learning individual behaviors. Generally, a child first began DTT treatments focused on learning to imitate nonverbal behaviors and later communication skills (Lovaas, 1987). For communication, shaping and chaining were used, wherein the interventionist first taught individual phonetic sounds, and then used shaping and chaining (i.e., rewarding only successive approximations) to combine sounds into word approximations until they very closely approximated the adult word. Many other behaviors were also taught using this format, which used repeated drill-like procedures until the child perfected the expected response. While these interventions resulted in steady improvements, the children often engaged in disruptive behaviors, which were punished or placed on extinction (e.g., the removal of reinforcement). During the structured sessions, the children appeared to lack the motivation to engage in the intervention. In fact, when they were not being disruptive, they often appeared lethargic.

From a theoretical point of view, the children appeared to be responding similarly to participants in learned helplessness experiments. That is, learned helplessness theorizes that exposure to events that are uncontrollable or noncontingent consequences leads individuals to behave as if behaviors and outcomes are independent, which produces a negative effect on the subject's motivation (Maier & Seligman, 1976; Seligman, 1972). Specifically, study participants fail to respond to stimuli (such as trying to escape an aversive event) and after experiencing situations where their behaviors do not have an effect on the stimulus, often have difficulties with other correct responses even when their behaviors could result in having an effect on their environment. Put simply, they seem to give up and stop trying. With regard to autism, it is likely that, very early on, the children have difficulty with many behaviors. If they do attempt behaviors, they frequently fail, but may sometimes accidentally make a correct response. Additionally, well-meaning adults may attempt to help the children with communication, self-help skills, socialization, and other behaviors. For example, if a child with autism is having difficulty getting dressed or putting on a jacket, and the adult needs to leave the house quickly, the adult may dress the child. While this would seem to be innocuous, repeated failure, occasional accidental correct responses, and "assistance" with communication, self-help, and other areas may contribute to extensive noncontingent reinforcement and eventual learned helplessness, and the child may give up on attempting these activities. Over time, the child may appear to give up altogether and seem very unengaged.

Early studies focusing on improving motivation of a child with autism attempted to remediate the learned helplessness phenomenon and assessed whether contingencies could be manipulated to emphasize the response-reinforcer relationship and potentially create a more responsive and active learner. For example, Koegel and Egel (1979) implemented a multiple baseline design with three children with autism (ages 6 to 12), wherein they assessed the enthusiasm of the children while attempting to complete a fine motor task (e.g., putting shaped blocks into a toy puzzle, dressing themselves, etc.). Children who had low levels of responding or inconsistent responses tended to receive noncontingent rewards for their attempts to respond (decreasing their motivation). However, children who were reinforced for their attempts to respond ("Nice job," "Keep trying!") and/or were unobtrusively prompted to make a correct response had increased levels of positive emotion and steadily higher levels of responsiveness as the session continued.

The research also showed that the improved emotions were not merely a function of obtaining increased reinforcers; it was only when the reinforcers were contingent that motivation and emotions improved. Further, because the children were so often incorrect, it was important to reinforce attempts at correct responses even if they were not fully correct. By reinforcing attempts to respond, rather than relying on the previous ABA procedures that had focused on a strict shaping paradigm, wherein only responses that were equal to or better than the previous response were rewarded (Lovaas *et al.*, 1966), the child's level of responsiveness and enthusiasm (rated on a Likert scale) improved. This appeared to be "pivotal" to the child's progress in that, when motivation improved, many nontargeted child behaviors began to improve. Thus, the concept of motivation to respond to environmental stimuli appeared to be a key area for increasing task acquisition and child affect. Other similar research related to the delivery of rewards, identified that reinforcing a child's attempts rather than using a strict shaping paradigm was also effective for teaching verbal communication in previously nonverbal children (Koegel, O'Dell, & Dunlap, 1988). This is in contrast to early attempts at teaching expressive verbal communication that only reinforced correct responding, focused on teaching phoneme discrimination, and used a strict shaping paradigm to improve phoneme production. As noted above, while the strict shaping procedure was effective, the intervention was incredibly labor and time intensive and many children needed to be provided with thousands of trials before they learned even a single word (Lovaas, 1966). In addition, valuable time was wasted dealing with disruptive behavior as the children attempted to escape the intervention environment. In contrast, when motivational variables such as reinforcing the child's attempts were implemented, the children's affect improved, as did their level of responsiveness and correct responding to the target stimuli, with the children very rapidly acquiring new words, sometimes as many as five or more words in a single session.

Encouraged by this initial research, the idea emerged that developing intrinsic motivation in children with autism was a possible key area that could be pivotal to increasing other untreated areas for a child with autism. As such, a motivated child might dramatically improve or possibly even overcome the symptoms of autism (Koegel & Koegel, 2012). Thus, there was a push to find additional components that would lead to motivating these children. This was a major change from the previous use of extrinsic reinforcers (e.g. candy or a sticker, that, although they were rewarding, bore no direct relationship to the target behavior being reinforced) to focusing on intrinsic reinforcers (which was not only reinforcing, but also bore a direct relationship to the target behavior being reinforced, e.g. giving the child the preferred item that was requested). Thus, in the 1980s, we attempted to decrease what we hypothesized was a core, pivotal area of learned helplessness by studying potential interventions that may improve motivation and dramatically improve the overall condition of autism.

Introduction to the model

Koegel and Mentis (1985) hypothesized that learned helplessness may have developed as a condition in autism due to the difficulty that the children with autism experienced in learning the relationship between their responding and the consequences of their responses, which meant that they failed to understand the response-reinforcer contingency. This would then lead to a lack of motivation to respond at all. Additional research which also focused on emphasizing response-reinforcer contingencies showed that using natural reinforcers that were related to the task itself, rather than an unrelated "artificial" reinforcer, improved the responsiveness of children with autism (Williams, Koegel, & Egel, 1981). That is, if the reward became a functional part of the activity, for example if a child got access to a desired toy after verbally requesting it, the reward was inherently related to the child's response and the response-reinforcer contingency was emphasized. Williams, Koegel, and Egel (1981) used functional items, such as teaching children with autism the expressive verbal word "cup." When the child requested a cup, either a different cup with juice in it was handed to them in one condition, or the specific cup they were labeling (also with juice in it) was given to them in the other condition. The children who received the natural reward of obtaining the specific cup with juice they were labeling learned much better than when the unrelated cup with juice was handed to them. While this concept may seem logical, most of the ABA interventions in the 1980s used far less related antecedent stimuli and rewards, such as flash cards with a picture of a tree vs. a horse as stimuli and edible foods as rewards. So, there was no intrinsic connection between the behavior and the reward, and within the context of a theory of learned helplessness, it is not surprising that learning was slow and motivation was low.

In addition to efforts on understanding the role of reinforcement contingencies, other studies focused on variables relating to antecedent variables during instruction. For example, Dunlap and Koegel (1980) used a multiple baseline design (with reversals) across participants in order to identify the area of task variation as another key component in motivating children with autism. In this study, children had a higher percentage of correct responses on an individual task when the interventionist frequently varied the task, rather than repeatedly drilling on a single task until the child reached criterion. When target trials were varied, blind observers rated the children as more enthusiastic, more interested, happier, and better behaved. Again, this helped lead to an understanding of specific teaching variables that could reverse the effects of learned-helplessness and produce a motivated learner. An important concept in these studies is that the intervention is executed in a manner that improves intrinsic enjoyment, thereby resulting in lower escape and avoidance motivated behavior. It is also interesting to consider these antecedent variables as preventative such that they may reduce or eliminate the need for responsive interventions to address problem behavior.

In a related study, also focused on antecedent manipulations, Dunlap (1984) found that interspersing "maintenance" or easy tasks that the child had previously mastered with "acquisition" targeted tasks that the child had not yet learned increased the child's responsiveness and correct responding. This study evaluated three different conditions: one where only acquisition tasks targeting a single target behavior were presented (until the child reached criterion), another where 10 different acquisition tasks were presented during each session until the child reached criterion, and a third where an even split of maintenance and acquisition tasks were presented during the session. Of great interest, the children in the condition that included the maintenance tasks performed significantly better than the children in the other two conditions, even though they had few acquisition trials. Further, naïve observers rated the children's attention and affect higher during the sessions that included maintenance tasks. Thus, when interspersing the previously acquired tasks, the children exhibited faster acquisition, greater engagement, and more positive affect on Likert scales.

Another line of research focused on antecedent manipulations related to curriculum issues. Specifically, Koegel, Dyer, and Bell (1987) found child choice of the stimulus materials and activities to be another key component in motivating children with ASD to engage in nontargeted social behaviors. In a multiple baseline reversal design, children were either prompted to complete teacher-chosen tasks or complete a task of their own choice (with the same target behavior). The children's social avoidance behaviors decreased when they were provided with child choice. Many subsequent studies have supported this finding, emphasizing the importance of child choice with children with autism, or following the child's lead (Yoder *et al.*, 1993). Of great importance was the fact that widespread areas of improvement occurred well beyond the specific target behavior being trained, including nontargeted social behavior that had been considered to be a particularly concerning area for children with autism.

Following the discovery of these individual variables, Koegel, O'Dell, and Koegel (1987) found that combining all of these components as a package resulted in an especially powerful effect; individuals with ASD were able to learn faster and their responses were more likely to generalize, which addressed common problems with the structured ABA interventions. These motivational components as a package were first shown to be effective with improving the acquisition of first words (Koegel *et al.*, 1987) as well as with learning language structures and improving the use of multi-word combinations (Koegel, Koegel, & Surratt, 1992), Because much of this initial research on improving motivation for ASD focused on improving verbal communication, the package of procedures was originally named the Natural Language Paradigm (NLP). Later research found that these motivational components could be incorporated into a variety of other areas resulting in the same positive learning effects, as well as improvements in untargeted areas, and therefore the Natural Language Paradigm was renamed Pivotal Response Treatment (PRT).

Other areas that have been shown to improve when the motivational components are incorporated include symbolic play (Stahmer, 1995), sociodramatic play (Thorp, Stahmer, & Schreibman, 1995), academics (Koegel, Singh, & Koegel, 2010), self-help (Koegel & LaZebnik, 2014), socialization (Robinson, 2011), and many others. It appeared as if motivation to engage was such an important pivotal area, that the entire learned helplessness problem might be able to be eliminated. Thus, as a whole, the focus on improving motivation to engage and respond creates a general climate that is likely to produce a motivated learner. It was also possible to define this motivated responding so that it was amenable to research and measurement. This more abstract notion of motivation in the PRT intervention could be behaviorally defined when scoring areas such as engagement, responsiveness, rate of responding, correct responses, and affect, resulting in the possibility of large amounts of subsequent productive research.

Age range and diagnosis of children

Our initial research focused primarily on preschool and elementary school-aged children, but, more recently, we have found that modified components of PRT may be very effective with infants during the first year of life (Koegel *et al.*, 2014). In a multiple baseline design, we selected infants, aged four, seven, and nine months, who demonstrated low affect, low social engagement, avoidance of eye contact, and low responsiveness to their names being called. Because of their young age, we attempted to influence social engagement with selected components of PRT that may be relevant to preverbal infants.

Specifically, we videotaped the children during parent–child interactions to assess for activities that evoked higher levels of affect, such as smiling and eye contact. Most of the children demonstrated very low or neutral affect during the majority of activities (e.g., peekaboo, patty cake, parents talking to the child, singing), however, each child had three or four activities (e.g., silly faces, nibbling on toes, tickles), which individually and reliably produced higher affect. Then, these "child choice" activities were implemented for brief periods of time (approximately 10 seconds). We incorporated task variation by rotating through the preferred activities for five to seven minutes. Following a group of rotations through the activities, we took the infants on a walk as a natural reinforcer for their improved responding. Following several sessions where the infants were engaging in high affect because of the child choice activities, task variation, and natural reinforcers, the activities that previously elicited neutral affect were gradually and systematically interspersed (interspersal of acquisition and maintenance tasks). This intervention, implemented by the parents, resulted in improving and stabilizing levels of affect (e.g., happiness and interest) as measured on five point Likert scales. The ratings of low, neutral, and high interest and happiness were made by observers, who scored video-clips of the infants and were blind to the experimental condition. In addition to improved affect, response to name improved for all three infants. It was hypothesized that motivation was a pivotal area for these infants, and that these PRT motivational variables were effective in a classical conditioning paradigm to produce the same widespread areas of improvement as were obtained in the operant motivational paradigm described above.

Obtaining such rapid large improvements with a different (infant) population and using a different intervention paradigm (classical conditioning) suggests that there is considerable external validity to motivation being a pivotal area in the treatment of autism.

In addition to applying PRT to infants, we have also shown that motivational components can be effectively used with adolescents. During the adolescent years, many individuals with ASD do not readily fit into a peer clique. Adolescents with ASD are often more focused on a restricted interest than in engaging with peers. Therefore, we assessed whether we could use child choice by tapping into their restricted interests as the theme of a school club to improve their social engagement. In a multiple baseline design across seven high school students (Koegel *et al.*, 2013), we developed school lunch clubs (e.g., computer graphics club, comic book club, young inventors club). Following the start of the club, the adolescents with ASD interacted at a much higher frequency and demonstrated improved pragmatics, social responsiveness, and asking questions. That is, prior to starting the clubs, the students spent far less time than the typical students in social engagement with peers, with some students spending many of their lunch periods completely alone. After the introduction of lunch clubs, all of the students' social engagement improved to be within the range of their typical peers—socially engaging most of the lunch periods. Similar methodologies have been effective with older elementary and middle school students (Baker, Koegel, & Koegel, 1998; Koegel, Fredeen *et al.*, 2012).

Adults also benefit from focusing on the motivational component of choice. For example, during weekly intervention sessions, college students with ASD who engaged in no social activities were assisted with planning social events around their interests. The adults had three options: (1) to remain alone without going to any events; (2) to attend social events around their interests without a peer mentor; or (3) to attend social events with a peer mentor. Interestingly, all requested to attend social events and activities around their interests with a peer mentor. Of most importance is that, following intervention, all of the adults demonstrated increases in the number of social events they attended. Further, all participants reported improved levels of satisfaction and confidence. In addition, following the intervention, all of the students' grade point averages improved and employment improved. As a whole, these studies suggest the importance of social interaction for well being and stress the significance of assuring that the intervention considers the pivotal area of motivation in order to increase success.

In keeping with our goal of finding "pivotal" areas that have a widespread positive effect on other untreated behaviors in order to increase the learning process, we have identified other areas that also appear to be pivotal for development in individuals with ASD. For example, we noted that teaching children to initiate interactions through asking questions resulted in greatly improved long-term outcomes (Koegel, Koegel, et al., 1999). That is, an initial retrospective study using archival data showed that preschool children who do not initiate interactions tend to have poorer long-term outcomes as adolescents or adults. In contrast, preschool children who verbally or nonverbally initiated had better long-term outcomes as adolescents or adults. In a follow-up study, we found that using the aforementioned motivational components, children who initially do not initiate can be taught to initiate and maintain interactions through asking questions, and such an intervention resulted in these children also having improved long-term outcomes. Thus, the results suggest that a critical part of an intervention program should include the teaching of initiations as a pivotal area.

Another area that seems to be pivotal is self-management wherein children, adolescents, or adults learn to manage their own behaviors. This intervention can be used to target social responsiveness (Koegel et al., 1992), disruptive behavior (Koegel & Koegel, 1990), repetitive ritualistic behaviors (Koegel & Koegel, 1990), and a myriad of other behaviors. While some self-management programs rely on the presence of verbal communication, pictorial self-management can be used for nonverbal individuals (Pierce & Schreibman, 1994). Self-management can be used to create independence from an inter-ventionist in classroom and community settings (Dunlap, Dunlap, Koegel, & Koegel, 1991), and is therefore very helpful throughout the intervention process and, in particular, during the final phases of an intervention program.

Two other areas that appear to be pivotal are responsiveness to multiple cues and empathy. With regard to responding to multiple cues, some individuals with autism respond on the basis of a limited, and often irrelevant, number of cues (Koegel & Wilhelm, 1973; Lovaas *et al.*, 1971). This was a considerable problem in the past when we used flash cards that were not interesting to the children. The children often responded to an irrelevant cue, such as a bend or dirt speck on the card or a part of the picture that was not relevant to the behavior being taught. Although we have not specifically researched it yet, anecdotally, it appears as though, once the motivational components of PRT are incorporated, the children tend to become more engaged and more responsive to multiple cues without the need for specialized intervention. However, a considerable amount of research has shown that, if the individual seems to be responding to only a limited number of cues, it is possible to teach responsiveness to multiple cues (e.g., Schreibman & Koegel, 1982). Currently, we usually accomplish this clinically by providing instructions using multiple cues in a motivational context. For example, if the child enjoys using markers, the interventionist may provide a number of different sized and colored markers. Then, the interventionist can say, "Color the tree with the big green marker." The child will have to distinguish both the size and color cues before being given an opportunity to color as a natural reinforcer. Similarly, when a child is getting ready to go to the zoo, the parent may ask the child to put on his blue shirt. The drawer has various colored pants and shirts, so the child will have to discriminate both the item and the color. If the child pulls out the blue pants, he is only responding to one of the cues (color). Similarly, if the child puts on a red shirt, the child is responding to only one of the cues (clothing item). Again, some children may benefit from specific focused practice in this area, while others pick it up without specialized intervention during PRT general motivation sessions.

Finally, empathy seems to be an important pivotal area. In a study focusing on young adults who did not show empathy during social conversation, Koegel, Ashbaugh, Navab, & Koegel (2016) taught verbal individuals with ASD to respond to a conversational partner's statement with expressive understanding and then to ask a question. For example, if the conversational partner said "I'm not feeling well today," then the individual was taught to respond with an expression of understanding, such as "I'm sorry you're not feeling well" and then to ask a question, such as "Have you been to the doctor?" Many such trials were employed in order to teach generalized empathic communication. Following intervention, which used a combination of video feedback and a visual schematic guide, all participants improved in both their expression of understanding and their empathetic questions. As well, participants reported improved confidence and their tested empathy quotient scores improved. Targeting empathy may result in greatly improved social conversational skills. As can be noted, teaching empathic skills appears to also have a positive effect on other psychological areas, such as decreasing social anxiety and improving socialization.

Evidence for the model

Well over 200 rigorous single-case research design studies as well as randomized clinical trials have been published that support the efficacy of PRT. Table 1.1 shows some of the studies that support the use of PRT. This table includes some studies that were implemented in our clinics, as well as replications of PRT in other independent clinics. This controls for any possible experimenter bias, and it demonstrates the replicability of the intervention approach on a widespread scale throughout the world.

Table 1.1 Treatment (PRT) interventions

Study	Design	Treatment/ independent variable	Dependent variables	Treatment outcome
Original PRT studies				
Koegel, O'Dell, & Koegel (1987)	Within-subject design: multiple baseline across participants	Traditional discrete trial vs. PRT (called analogue treatment vs. NLPa)	• Imitative child utterances • Spontaneous child utterances • Generalization	• Children produced more imitative and spontaneous utterances in PRT condition. Generalization of treatment gains occurred only in PRT condition.
Koegel, Koegel, & Surratt (1992)	Within-subject design: repeated reversal design with counterbalancing	Traditional discrete trial vs. PRT (called analogue treatment vs. PRT) for teaching of target sounds and words	• Disruptive behavior • Target language responses	• Increased responding and less disruptive behaviors occurred during PRT condition compared with analogue condition.
Koegel, Koegel, Shoshan, & McNerney (1999), Phase 1	Retrospective analysis of archival data	High vs. low child-initiated social interactions in PRT treatment	• Language age • Number of initiations • Pragmatic ratings • Social/community functioning • Adaptive behavior scale scores	• Children with poor and favorable outcomes had comparable language ages and adaptive behavior scale scores at preintervention. Children who exhibited high levels of spontaneous initiations at preintervention had more favorable outcomes.
Koegel, Koegel, Shoshan, & McNerney (1999), Phase 2	Clinical replication	PRT teaching of child-initiated spontaneous interactions	• Language ages • Number of initiations • Pragmatics ratings • Social/community functioning • Adaptive behavior scale scores	• Following initiation training, children's adaptive and pragmatic scores increased to near chronological age level. They did not retain diagnosis of autism or special education placements. Social/academic functioning was comparable to typically developing peers.

Study	Design	Intervention	Measures	Findings
Koegel, Carter, & Koegel (2003)	Within-subject design: multiple baseline across participants	PRT to teach self-initiated queries as method to access verbs together with temporal morpheme	• Number of verb productions • Number of queries • Use of correct tense • Mean length of utterance (MLU) • Number/diversity of verbs • Generalization	• Children were successfully taught to use the queries "What happened?" or "What's happening?" during intervention. Both children generalized the use of "-ing" and "-ed" to other verbs and increased MLU and verb diversity.
Independent replications of PRT effectiveness with original lab collaboration				
Schreibman, Kaneko, & Koegel (1991)	Group design with random assignment	Traditional Discrete Trial vs. PRT (called individual target behaviorsa vs. PRT)	• Parental affect (scored by naïve observers)	• Parents in PRT condition displayed significantly more positive affect than parents trained in Discrete Trial.
Koegel, Bimbela, & Schreibman (1996)	Group design with random assignment	Discrete Trial vs. PRT (called individual target behaviorsa vs. PRT)	• Ratings of happiness, interest, stress, communication style during dinnertime probes	• Discrete Trial condition resulted in no significant influence on interactions, whereas PRT resulted in positive parent–child interactions.
Koegel, Camarata, Koegel, Ben-Tall, & Smith (1998)	Within-subject design: ABA with counterbalancing to control for order effects	Traditional discrete trial vs. PRT (called analogue Treatmenta vs. PRT) for teaching target sounds	• Correct production of target sounds in language samples • Intelligibility ratings	• Significant gains in correct production of target sounds and speech intelligibility during PRT intervention.

Study	Design	Treatment/ independent variable	Dependent variables	Treatment outcome
Bryson *et al.* (2007)	Clinical replication	Large-scale community training in PRT for interventionists, clinical supervisors, clinical leaders, parents	• Fidelity of implementation • Intervals with functional verbal utterances	• Preliminary data show that treatment providers maintained fidelity of implementation across time and increased functional verbal utterances of the participant children.
Mohammad-Zaheri *et al.* (2014)	Randomized clinical trial design	Traditional ABA vs. PRT for language	• Verbal communication and generalization to pragmatic areas	• The PRT groups significantly outperformed the traditional ABA group on MLU and pragmatic areas.
Hardan *et al.* (2015)	Randomized clinical trial Design of group-delivered PRT	Psychoeducation vs. PRT	• Fidelity of Implementation and communication	• PRT resulted in significantly greater improvements than the psychoeducational group on Fidelity of Implementation and child communication gains.
Mohammad-Zaheri *et al.* (2015)	Randomized clinical trial design	Traditional ABA vs. PRT for language	• Disruptive Behavior	• The PRT group had significantly lower levels of disruptive behavior compared to the traditional ABA group.

Independent replications of effectiveness of PRT

Laski, Charlop, & Schreibman (1988)	Within-subject design: multiple baseline across participants	Parent training in PRT (called NLPa) at home and in a clinic setting	• Parent verbalizations • Child vocalizations • Frequency of echolalia	• Post-treatment increases in parent requests for vocalizations. Increases in children's verbal responsiveness during intervention and generalization.
Pierce & Schreibman (1995)	Within-subject design: multiple baseline across participants	Peer-implemented PRT to increase social skills	• Intervals with peer interaction • Conversation initiations • Play initiations • Attention behaviors	• Following peer-implemented PRT, children increased interactions to high level of intervals and increased play and conversation initiations. Both children exhibited increases in coordinated and supported joint attention behaviors after treatment.
Thorp, Stahmer, & Schreibman (1995)	Within-subject design: multiple baseline across participants	PRT teaching of sociodramatic play	• Language assessments • Play behaviors (role playing, make-believe, persistence, social behavior, verbal communication)	• All three children increased in all play behavior measures. Play behavior gains maintained during generalization.
Stahmer (1995)	Within-subject design: multiple baseline across participants	Modified PRT using symbolic play as a target behavior	• Symbolic play • Complexity of play • Creativity of play • Generalization across toys, settings, play partners	• Increase in symbolic play and play complexity after PRT play training. Maintenance of treatment gains during generalizations.

Study	Design	Treatment/ independent variable	Dependent variables	Treatment outcome
Sherer & Schreibman (2005)	Clinical replication	PRT administered to groups with two distinct profiles (predicted responders vs. nonresponders)	• Language (echolalia, cued speech, spontaneous speech) • Play (functional, symbolic, and varied play measures) • Social measures (interaction, social initiations)	• Children in the responder profile exhibited increases in language, play, and social behavior after PRT intervention.
Ventola et al. (2014)	Clinical replication	Short duration (4-month) treatment program	• Social communication and adaptive skills	• Large social communication improvements in participants with generalized gains in adaptive behaviors.
Baker-Ericzen, Stahmer, & Burns (2007)	Clinical replication	12-week PRT parent education program	• Vineland Adaptive Behavior Scales domain scores	• After parent education in PRT, all children showed significant improvement in adaptive behavior scale scores regardless of gender, age, child/family race/ethnicity.
Vismara & Lyons (2007)	Within-subject design: applied behavior analysis with counterbalancing and alternating treatments in final phase	PRT with child's perseverative interests vs. nonperseverative interests	• Number of joint attention initiations • Contingencies to joint attention initiations • Child affect ratings	• Using child's perseverative interests in PRT model increased joint attention initiations.

Gillett & LeBlanc (2007)	Within-subject design: multiple baseline across participants	Parent-implemented PRT (called NLPa) to target language and play skills	• Frequency of vocalizations • Spontaneous vocalizations • Appropriate play • Social validity questionnaire	• Increases in overall rate and spontaneity of utterances for all three children. Children also showed an increase in appropriate play. Parents rated intervention as simple to implement and endorsed continued use of PRT.
Harper, Symon, & Frea (2008)	Within-subject design: multiple baseline across participants	Peer-implemented PRT to increase social play	• Attempts at gaining peer's attention • Turn-taking interactions • Play initiations	• After peer implementation of PRT, both children increased initiations and turn-taking initiations. Results were maintained during generalization.

a. Historically, various terms have been used synonymously in these empirical articles. For example, PRT has been called the natural language paradigm (NLP) when intervention focuses on language. Similarly, Discrete Trial Training has been labeled the "individual target behavior condition" or the "analogue treatment condition" in some publications.

The model: Settings, dosage, and training of trainers

PRT should be implemented in natural settings using natural stimuli. To the maximum extent possible, the PRT model advocates full inclusion. When children with ASD are placed in segregated classrooms and not allowed to participate in community events, they have difficulty learning to socialize appropriately and do not have role models for social communication and behavior. If the end goal is to have the children fully participating as employed adults with satisfying social lives, they need to learn the behaviors that they need to use in everyday settings, and this starts early on. The social and social communicative difficulties displayed by these children have serious long-term health implications, and excluding them from natural settings exacerbates the problem. Typically developing children spend about 20 hours a week interacting with their peers outside of the classroom, but children with ASD often spend few or no hours socializing with their peers. This can result in extreme negative effects on their mental health, such as low levels of self-esteem and self-evaluation (Ladd & Troop-Gordon, 2003), as well as putting them at a high risk for developing the comorbid disorders of depression and anxiety (Spence, Donovan, & Brechman-Toussaint, 1999). Within the context of a regular education classroom, the children can partially or fully participate in all aspects of the typical curriculum (Ferguson & Baumgart, 1991) and can socialize with support and proper programming during lunch and after school activities (Baker et al., 1998; Koegel et al., 2005).

With regard to dosage, individuals with ASD need a constant therapeutic environment throughout their waking hours. For this reason, a key component of PRT is parent involvement (to be discussed in greater detail in the following section). As individuals with ASD improve, self-control procedures may be taught so that they are, in a sense, responsible for their own intervention. However, during the early years, particularly for the children with ASD who do not initiate interactions or attempt to engage, teaching opportunities will need to be provided throughout the day. These can be created in the context of everyday activities and routines (Koegel, Bimbela, & Schreibman, 1996).

Proper training is also critical. PRT has developed a training model which begins with teaching the trainees to understand the basic procedures and then proceeds to teach methods for improving various pivotal areas (e.g., motivation, initiations, socialization, self-management). All trainees must submit videotapes or be observed *in vivo* by an individual who has already met Fidelity of Implementation (FoI) in PRT. This person will score the session to assess whether the trainee is competent with regard to FoI. Finally, in this trainer of trainers (ToT) model, trainees are provided with feedback in training others through presentations as well as in how to provide feedback to their new trainees. In a large-scale study of the effectiveness of a ToT model in Nova Scotia, Canada, staff who were skilled in PRT from the university where PRT was developed (University of California, Santa Barbara) trained an initial cohort of team members providing early intervention with 27 (mostly preschool) children. Teams included parents, clinicians, and one-on-one interventionists, and supervisors. The training consisted of two to three days of oral presentation, then 30 hours of individualized feedback through videotape analysis (adults brought in tapes of themselves working with children daily) implemented in small groups. Trainees did not meet the minimum 80% criteria for FoI prior to the training but all met FoI following the trainings. Importantly, not only did the trainees show acquisition of the intervention techniques, but all the children showed gains following the PRT training for their therapists (Bryson *et al.*, 2007). Our preliminary data suggest that FoI in PRT is not likely to be met unless the trainee has specific feedback regarding their skills. That is, simply attending a workshop is not sufficient. Thus, the spread of effect for serving children with autism can be realized through a ToT model, with an important part being feedback on implementation of the procedures.

Parent education

There is no doubt that parents play an important, if not critical, role in the habilitation of ASD. Many decades of research have consistently shown that, without parent education, children are unlikely to maintain or generalize newly learned skills (Koegel, Glahn, & Nieminen, 1978). In contrast, when parent education is provided in partnership with skilled clinicians, significant gains can be seen in measured IQ (Sheinkopf & Siegel, 1998), communication, daily living skills, socialization (Sallows & Graupner, 2005), and so on. For PRT, parents or guardians are required to participate in sessions and are provided with "practice with feedback." That is, the parents work with their child, are scored in specific areas, and are then provided with feedback on their performance in each area. Feedback is provided in a supportive and helpful way: if the target behavior is first words, and a child is playing with a ball while the parent redirects the child to a musical toy, the clinician might say, "You're doing a great job of finding fun toys, but since he's playing with the ball, let's see if we can give him an opportunity to try and say 'ball' since that seems to be what he's interested in right now." Our research shows that if parents are required to sit down and provide designated practice with their children, stress levels increase. In contrast, if intervention is provided throughout the day in the context of everyday activities and routines, parent stress decreases (Koegel *et al.*, 1996). Thus, every preferred activity is designed to promote learning. For example, if the child is learning to use two word utterances and likes to ride in the car, we might have the parent prompt "Car key," or "Open door," or "Turn key" or "Buckle up," after which the child is naturally rewarded with a ride in the car. These naturally occurring opportunities throughout the day provide a continuous learning environment, while teaching the child that appropriate responding and communication must occur all day long.

Measures and Fidelity of Implementation (FoI)

Data are important. Teachers who consistently collect data have better student outcomes. Data collection is a regular part of our program, but we do not get overwhelmed by it. Some children do not need every response recorded. Sometimes, regular probe data collected as infrequently as once per day, or even once per week or once per month, will be sufficient. This can be determined by assessing the individual's goal, considering how long it may take for a goal to be met, and how often the individual is seen. For example, if an adult is being provided with sessions once weekly, monthly probes may be sufficient. In contrast, if a child is being seen for many hours daily and is exhibiting rapid progress, data may need to be collected weekly, or even daily. That is, the goal is to collect enough data to make sure that the individual is making the most progress possible with the program and to be able to quickly tweak the program if the child is not responding. Sometimes, that requires trial-by-trial data recording, but at other times monthly probes are sufficient. In addition, we collect regular FoI data when we are training parents or professionals. We require an 80% criterion on several different areas. Table 1.2 shows an FoI scoring sheet for the motivational components of PRT. Each area is scored in one-minute intervals such that parents and professionals can be given specific feedback regarding their correct implementation of each variable.

Table 1.2 PRT fidelity sheet

1-Minute intervals	Child attending	Clear opportunity	Maintenance tasks	Multiple cues	Choice	Contingent	Natural	Contingent on attempts
1								
2								
3								
4								
5								
6								
7								
8								
9								
10								
%								

INSTRUCTIONS

- Fidelity is scored in 10 one-minute intervals. Pause the video-clip after each one-minute interval to score each of the eight PRT components.
- Score each category either as:
  * + (plus): The interventionist utilized this component of PRT
  * – (minus): The PRT component was not demonstrated
  * N/A (not applicable): The child is not at an appropriate level for this PRT component (i.e., multiple cues) or the scorer is not familiar with the child (i.e., maintenance tasks).
- Performance should be independent of child's response.

- Intervals that have no opportunities are scored "–" in all categories. The interventionist must be actively seeking out opportunities.
- To meet fidelity participant must score 80% (8 out of 10) in *each* category.

DEFINITIONS

Child attending: The interventionist must have the child's attention prior to presenting an opportunity.

Clear opportunity: The question/instruction/opportunity (S^D) to respond must be **clear** and appropriate to the task.

Maintenance tasks: The interventionist should be interspersing tasks the child can already perform with acquisition (new) tasks. Do not score unless you are familiar with the child.

Multiple cues: If appropriate to the developmental level of the child, the question/instruction should involve the use of multiple cues (i.e., asking if a child wants the "blue ball" or the "red ball" if the child is at an appropriate level to begin learning colors).

Child choice: To a large extent, the interventionist should follow the child's choice with tasks and activities. However, the interventionist must always assume control should the child engage in hazardous (i.e., self-injury) or inappropriate (i.e., self-stimulation) activities. If child is not showing interest in the current task, interventionist should attempt to change the activity.

Contingent: Reinforcement must be contingent upon child's behavior. The interventionist's response (i.e., giving the child a toy) must be dependent upon the child's response (i.e., saying "toy").

Natural: Reinforcement should be **natural** or directly related to the desired behavior.

Contingent on attempts: Any goal-directed **attempt** to respond to questions, instructions, or opportunities should be reinforced. Although an attempt does not necessarily need to be correct, it has to be reasonable.

Implementation and dissemination efforts

We have developed training levels that include direct observations so that we can be assured that the interventions are being implemented correctly and with fidelity to the model. Dissemination efforts have been implemented on a large scale and through small group and individual trainings. In addition to the ToT study discussed above, many single-subject design studies have shown that parents, as well as school personnel, can learn to implement PRT. Robinson (2011) taught paraprofessionals to implement PRT on a playground setting. Following the training, the students improved their social interaction with typical peers. The paraprofessionals reported that they enjoyed the training and met fidelity after a brief period of time. Similarly, research shows that parents can reach FoI and their stress is reduced after PRT parent education programs in comparison to other programs that require sit down one-on-one time with the child (Koegel *et al.*, 1996). In a randomized clinical trial, Hardan and colleagues (2015) showed that parent education could be provided in groups and, following the education, most reached FoI. The children with ASD whose parents received the PRT education scored significantly higher than the control group. Another study showed that speech therapists could easily implement PRT in public schools, and following the intervention the students showed significantly greater language gains and lower levels of disruptive behavior than the control group (Mohammad-Zaheri *et al.*, 2014, 2015). While we have focused on dissemination, there is often a gap between research and practice, and many children and adults with ASD are not receiving "state of the art" interventions. Despite the fact that empirically validated methodologies exist for the treatment of ASD, many parents use non-evidence-based interventions (Green *et al.*, 2006), and school personnel often lack the training to provide scientifically validated interventions (Lerman *et al.*, 2004). Thus, there is still a great need for dissemination of research findings.

Conclusions

PRT is an intervention model with considerable scientific support. Parent participation is an important component of the PRT model, and parent education is provided in the context of practice with feedback until FoI is met. Intervention in the natural environment is also important. As studies have continued to accumulate, the model has evolved and more pivotal areas have been recognized in addition to the original area of motivation. However, additional research is warranted in areas such as teacher training, adolescents and adults, parent stress, inclusion, and dissemination. While the last few decades have seen considerable improvements in the treatment of ASD through behavioral interventions, there is still a paucity of information in many areas. As the population of individuals diagnosed with ASD continues to rise, interventions, community involvement, parent support, and improved and refined treatment options continue to warrant research.

With this type of continued progress, the future looks very promising. PRT has many research articles supporting the effectiveness of the procedures, and has also been shown to be effective as a service program. That is, parents can be educated in the PRT procedures and can effectively implement the intervention with positive results in their children. Research has also shown that paraprofessionals hired by the schools can also learn to implement PRT procedures with FoI, resulting in social improvements in their students (Koegel, Matos-Fredeen et al., 2012).

However, dissemination is always a challenge. Many community programs use structured, drill-like, less effective procedures. Preliminary research suggests that it takes some time to teach the more flexible PRT procedures to someone who has already been trained in a very structured drill practice type of intervention. Nevertheless, a variety of training techniques have been successful in teaching people how to implement PRT. Professionals and parents have been successful when they are trained in a one-to-one format. Similarly, group trainings and distance learning have been helpful with dissemination of PRT. In addition, with regard to research needs, there is still a small percentage of children with ASD that progress slowly and about 5% of young children who are unable to learn to use expressive verbal communication even with intervention. Rather than saying that such children are a lost cause, PRT focuses on using research analytics to further develop the approach so that it can become effective with such children as well. Another area that may benefit from further research is the area of applying PRT to older populations. While many of the PRT procedures have been effectively applied to adolescents and adults, there are fewer research studies with older individuals with ASD. Developing enhanced and new PRT interventions for the more challenged learners and scientifically documenting the applicability of the procedures for older individuals are a few directions that will likely be addressed in the future. We expect that like the other areas that have developed rapidly and successfully, these new areas will also benefit dramatically from future research.

References

Baer, D.M., Wolf, M.M., & Risley, T.R. (1968) "Some current dimensions of applied behavior analysis." *Journal of Applied Behavior Analysis 1*, 1, 91–97.

Baker, M.J., Koegel, R.L., & Koegel, L.K. (1998) "Increasing the social behavior of young children with autism using their obsessive behaviors." *Research and Practice for Persons with Severe Disabilities 23*, 4, 300–308.

Baker-Ericzén, M.J., Stahmer, A.C., & Burns, A. (2007) "Child demographics associated with outcomes in a community-based pivotal response training program." *Journal of Positive Behavior Interventions 9*, 1, 52–60.

Bryson, S.E., Koegel, L.K., Koegel, R.L., Openden, D., Smith, I.M., & Nefdt, N. (2007) "Large-scale dissemination and community implementation of pivotal response treatment: Program description and preliminary data." *Research and Practice for Persons with Severe Disabilities 32*, 2, 142.

Cohen, H., Amerine-Dickens, M., & Smith, T. (2006) "Early intensive behavioral treatment: Replication of the UCLA model in a community setting." *Journal of Developmental & Behavioral Pediatrics 27*, 2, S145–S155.

Dunlap, G. (1984) "The influence of task variation and maintenance tasks on the learning and affect of autistic children." *Journal of Experimental Child Psychology 37*, 1, 41–64.

Dunlap, G. & Koegel, R.L. (1980) "Motivating autistic children through stimulus variation." *Journal of Applied Behavior Analysis 13*, 4, 619–627.

Dunlap, L.K., Dunlap, G., Koegel, L.K., & Koegel, R.L. (1991) "Using self-monitoring to increase students' success and independence." *Teaching Exceptional Children 23*, 17–22.

Eikeseth, S., Smith, T., Jahr, E., & Eldevik, S. (2007) "Outcome for children with autism who began intensive behavioral treatment between ages 4 and 7: A comparison controlled study." *Behavior Modification 31*, 3, 264–278.

Ferguson, D.L. & Baumgart, D. (1991) "Partial participation revisited." *Research and Practice for Persons with Severe Disabilities 16*, 4, 218–227.

Gillett, J.N. & LeBlanc, L.A. (2007) "Parent-implemented natural language paradigm to increase language and play in children with autism." *Research in Autism Spectrum Disorders 1*, 247–255.

Green, V.A., Pituch, K.A., Itchon, J., Choi, A., O'Reilly, M., & Sigafoos, J. (2006) "Internet survey of treatments used by parents of children with autism." *Research in Developmental Disabilities 27*, 1, 70–84.

Hardan, A.Y., Gengoux, G.W., Berquist, K.L., Libove, R.A., Ardel, C.M., Phillips, J., Frazier, T.W., & Minjarez, M.B. (2015) "A randomized controlled trial of Pivotal Response Treatment Group for parents of children with autism." *Journal of Child Psychology and Psychiatry 56*, 8, 884–892.

Harper, C.B., Symon, J.B., & Frea, W.D. (2008) "Recess is time-in: Using peers to improve social skills of children with autism." *Journal of Autism and Developmental Disorders 38*, 815–826.

Hewett, F.M. (1965) "Teaching speech to an autistic child through operant conditioning." *American Journal of Orthopsychiatry 35*, 5, 927.

Howard, J.S., Sparkman, C.R., Cohen, H.G., Green, G., & Stanislaw, H. (2005) "A comparison of intensive behavior analytic and eclectic treatments for young children with autism." *Research in Developmental Disabilities 26*, 4, 359–383.

Koegel, L. & LaZebnik, C. (2014) *Overcoming Autism.* New York: Viking Penguin.

Koegel, L., Matos-Fredeen, R., Lang, R., & Koegel, R. (2012) "Interventions for children with autism spectrum disorders in inclusive school settings." *Cognitive and Behavioral Practice 19*, 3, 401–412.

Koegel, L.K., Ashbaugh, K., Navab, A., & Koegel, R.L. (2016) "Improving empathic communication skills in adults with autism spectrum disorder." *Journal of Autism and Developmental Disorders 46*, 3, 921–933.

Koegel, L.K., Camarata, S.M., Valdez-Menchaca, M., & Koegel, R.L. (1998) "Setting generalization of question-asking by children with autism." *American Journal on Mental Retardation 102*, 346–357.

Koegel, L.K., Carter, C.M., & Koegel, R.L. (2003) "Teaching children with autism self-initiations as a pivotal response." *Topics in Language Disorders 23*, 2, 134–145.

Koegel, L.K., Koegel, R.L., Hurley, C., & Frea, W.D. (1992) "Improving social skills and disruptive behavior in children with autism through self-management." *Journal of Applied Behavior Analysis 25*, 2, 341–353.

Koegel, L.K., Koegel, R.L., Shoshan, Y., & McNerney, E. (1999) "Pivotal response intervention II: Preliminary long-term outcome data." *Research and Practice for Persons with Severe Disabilities 24*, 3, 186–198.

Koegel, L.K., Singh, A., & Koegel, R. (2010) "Improving motivation for academics in children with autism." *Journal of Autism and Developmental Disorders 40*, 9, 1057–1066.

Koegel, L.K., Singh, A.K., Koegel, R.L., Hollingsworth, J.R., & Bradshaw, J. (2014) "Assessing and improving early social engagement in infants." *Journal of Positive Behavior Interventions 16*, 2, 69–80.

Koegel, R.L., Bimbela, A., & Schreibman, L. (1996) "Collateral effects of parent training on family interactions." *Journal of Autism and Developmental Disorders 26*, 347–359.

Koegel, R.L., Camarata, S., Koegel, L.K., Ben-Tall, A., & Smith, A.E. (1998) "Increasing speech intelligibility in children with autism." *Journal of Autism and Developmental Disorders 28*, 3, 241–251.

Koegel, R.L., Dyer, K., & Bell, L.K. (1987) "The influence of child-preferred activities on autistic children's social behavior." *Journal of Applied Behavior Analysis 20*, 3, 243–252.

Koegel, R.L. & Egel, A.L. (1979) "Motivating autistic children." *Journal of Abnormal Psychology 88*, 4, 418.

Koegel, R.L., Fredeen, R., Kim, S., Danial, J., Rubinstein, D., & Koegel, L. (2012) "Using perseverative interests to improve interactions between adolescents with autism and their typical peers in school settings." *Journal of Positive Behavior Interventions 14*, 3, 133–141.

Koegel, R.L., Glahn, T.J., & Nieminen, G.S. (1978) "Generalization of parent-training results." *Journal of Applied Behavior Analysis 11*, 1, 95–109.

Koegel, R., Kim, S., Koegel, L., & Schwartzman, B. (2013) "Improving socialization for high school students with ASD by using their preferred interests." *Journal of Autism and Developmental Disorders 43*, 9, 2121–2134.

Koegel, R.L. & Koegel, L.K. (1990) "Extended reductions in stereotypic behaviors through self-management in multiple community settings." *Journal of Applied Behavior Analysis 23*, 1, 119–127.

Koegel, R.L. & Koegel, L.K. (2012) *The PRT Pocket Guide: Pivotal Response Treatment for Autism Spectrum Disorders*. Baltimore, MD: Brookes.

Koegel, R.L., Koegel, L.K., & Surratt, A. (1992) "Language intervention and disruptive behavior in preschool children with autism." *Journal of Autism and Developmental Disorders 22*, 2, 141–153.

Koegel, R.L. & Mentis, M. (1985) "Motivation in childhood autism: Can they or won't they?" *Journal of Child Psychology and Psychiatry 26*, 2, 185–191.

Koegel, R.L., O'Dell, M., & Dunlap, G. (1988) "Producing speech use in nonverbal autistic children by reinforcing attempts." *Journal of Autism and Developmental Disorders 18*, 4, 525–538.

Koegel, R.L., O'Dell, M.C., & Koegel, L.K. (1987) "A natural language teaching paradigm for nonverbal autistic children." *Journal of Autism and Developmental Disorders 17*, 2, 187–200.

Koegel, R.L., Werner, G.A., Vismara, L.A., & Koegel, L.K. (2005) "The effectiveness of contextually supported play date interactions between children with autism and typically developing peers." *Research and Practice for Persons with Severe Disabilities 30*, 2, 93–102.

Koegel, R.L. & Wilhelm, H. (1973) "Selective responding to the components of multiple visual cues by autistic children." *Journal of Experimental Child Psychology 15*, 3, 442–453.

Ladd, G.W. & Troop-Gordon, W. (2003) "The role of chronic peer difficulties in the development of children's psychological adjustment problems." *Child Development 74*, 5, 1344–1367.

Laski, K.E., Charlop, M.H., & Schreibman, L. (1988) "Training parents to use the natural language paradigm to increase their autistic children's speech." *Journal of Applied Behavior Analysis 21*, 391–400.

Lerman, D.C., Vorndran, C.M., Addison, L., & Kuhn, S.C. (2004) "Preparing teachers in evidence-based practices for young children with autism." *School Psychology Review 33*, 4, 510–526.

Lovaas, O.I. (1966) "A program for the establishment of speech in psychotic children." *Early Childhood Autism*, 115-144.

Lovaas, O.I. (1987) "Behavioral treatment and normal educational and intellectual functioning in young autistic children." *Journal of Consulting and Clinical Psychology 55*, 1, 3–9.

Lovaas, O.I., Berberich, J.P., Perloff, B.F., & Schaeffer, B. (1966) "Acquisition of imitative speech by schizophrenic children." *Science 151*, 3711, 705–707.

Lovaas, O.I., Schreibman, L.E., Koegel, R.L., & Rehm, R. (1971) "Selective responding by autistic children to multiple sensory input." *Journal of Abnormal Psychology 77*, 3, 211–222.

Lovaas, O.I. & Smith, T. (1989) "A comprehensive behavioral theory of autistic children: Paradigm for research and treatment." *Journal of Behavior Therapy and Experimental Psychiatry 20*, 1, 17–29.

Maier, S.F. & Seligman, M.E. (1976) "Learned helplessness: Theory and evidence." *Journal of Experimental Psychology: General 105*, 1, 3.

Mohammad-Zaheri, F., Koegel, L.K., Rezaei, M., & Bakhshi, E. (2015) "A Randomized Clinical Trial Comparison Between Pivotal Response Treatment (PRT) and Adult-Driven Applied Behavior Analysis (ABA) intervention on disruptive behaviors in public school children with autism." *Journal of Autism and Developmental Disorders 45*, 9, 2899–2907.

Mohammad-Zaheri, F., Koegel, L.K., Rezaee, M., & Rafiee, S.M. (2014) "A randomized clinical trial comparison between pivotal response treatment (PRT) and structured applied behavior analysis (ABA) intervention for children with autism." *Journal of Autism and Developmental Disorders 44*, 11, 2769–2777.

Pierce, K.L. & Schreibman, L. (1994) "Teaching daily living skills to children with autism in unsupervised settings through pictorial self-management." *Journal of Applied Behavior Analysis 27*, 3, 471–481.

Pierce, K. & Schreibman, L. (1995) "Increasing complex social behaviors in children with autism: Effects of peer-implemented pivotal response training." *Journal of Applied Behavior Analysis 28*, 285–295.

Pierce, K. & Schreibman, L. (1997) "Multiple peer use of pivotal response training to increase social behaviors of classmates with autism: Results from trained and untrained peers." *Journal of Applied Behavior Analysis 30*, 157–160.

Robinson, S.E. (2011) "Teaching paraprofessionals of students with autism to implement pivotal response treatment in inclusive school settings using a brief video feedback training package." *Focus on Autism and Other Developmental Disabilities 26*, 2, 105–118.

Sallows, G.O. & Graupner, T.D. (2005) "Intensive behavioral treatment for children with autism: Four-year outcome and predictors." *American Journal on Mental Retardation 110*, 6, 417–438.

Schreibman, L., Kaneko, W.M., & Koegel, R.L. (1991) "Positive affect of parents of autistic children: A comparison across two teaching techniques." *Behavior Therapy 22*, 479–490.

Schreibman, L. & Koegel, R.L. (1982) "Multiple-cue responding in autistic children." *Advances in Child Behavioral Analysis & Therapy 2*, 81–99.

Seligman, M.E. (1972) "Learned helplessness." *Annual Review of Medicine 23*, 1, 407–412.

Sheinkopf, S.J. & Siegel, B. (1998) "Home-based behavioral treatment of young children with autism." *Journal of Autism and Developmental Disorders 28*, 1, 15–23.

Sherer, M.R. & Schreibman, L. (2005) "Individual behavioral profiles and predictors of treatment effectiveness for children with autism." *Journal of Consulting and Clinical Psychology 73*, 525–538.

Spence, S.H., Donovan, C., & Brechman-Toussaint, M. (1999) "The treatment of childhood social phobia: The effectiveness of a social skills training-based, cognitive-behavioural intervention, with and without parental involvement." *Journal of Child Psychology and Psychiatry and Allied Disciplines 41*, 6, 713–726.

Stahmer, A.C. (1995) "Teaching symbolic play skills to children with autism using pivotal response training." *Journal of Autism and Developmental Disorders 25*, 2, 123–141.

Thorp, D.M., Stahmer, A.C., & Schreibman, L. (1995) "Effects of sociodramatic playtraining on children with autism." *Journal of Autism and Developmental Disorders 25*, 3, 265–282.

Ventola, P., Friedman, H.E., Anderson, L.C., Wolf, J.M., et al. (2014) "Improvements in social and adaptive functioning following short-duration PRT program: A Clinical Replication." *Journal of Autism and Developmental Disorders 44*, 11, 2862-2870.

Vismara, L.A. & Lyons, G.L. (2007) "Using perseverative interests to elicit joint attention behaviors in young children with autism: Theoretical and clinical implications to understanding motivation." *Journal of Positive Behavior Intervention, 9*, 214–228.

Williams, J.A., Koegel, R.L., & Egel, A.L. (1981) "Response-reinforcer relationships and improved learning in autistic children." *Journal of Applied Behavior Analysis 14*, 1, 53–60.

Yoder, P.J., Kaiser, A.P., Alpert, C., & Fischer, R. (1993) "Following the child's lead when teaching nouns to preschoolers with mental retardation." *Journal of Speech, Language, and Hearing Research 36*, 1, 158–167.

Chapter 2

POSITIVE FAMILY INTERVENTION

Using Optimism to Overcome Obstacles to Successful Parenting

V. Mark Durand, Shelley Clarke, and Julia Strauss

ABSTRACT

Advances in our understanding of the nature of severe behavior problems continue to spur meaningful research in function-based intervention strategies, and positive behavior support in particular. Along with documenting these accomplishments, it is time that researchers turn their attention to those circumstances that serve as obstacles to these successes. This chapter describes research that identifies parental pessimism as a potential barrier to optimum outcomes with behavioral parent training. In other words, one of the more significant obstacles appears to be a lack of confidence either in the person's ability to carry out these plans or skepticism that the child will benefit. Data from a multi-site randomized clinical trial indicate that the addition of a cognitive-behavioral intervention for pessimistic parents who are resistant or reluctant to commit to and use interventions can enhance the effectiveness of behavioral parent training (this approach is called Positive Family Intervention). We may be able to help families who have difficulty carrying out our treatments by focusing on the attitudinal barriers that interfere with their ability to successfully implement behavioral interventions with their children.

Keywords: behavioral parent training; cognitive behavior therapy; parental stress; parental self-efficacy

Challenging behaviors—including aggressive, disruptive, and socially inappropriate behaviors—are highly prevalent among children with autism spectrum disorder (ASD) and intellectual disabilities. Research suggests that problem behavior in general is three to four times more frequent in these populations than among children without disabilities and that as many as 50% of children with disabilities display frequent and severe challenging behaviors (Aaron *et al.*, 2011). These behaviors are among the most frequently cited obstacles to efforts to place students in community settings (Emerson & Einfeld, 2011) and they increase recidivism significantly for those individuals referred to crisis intervention programs from community placements (Shoham-Vardi *et al.*, 1996). Challenging behavior interferes with such essential activities as family life (Hassiotis *et al.*, 2008; Hassiotis *et al.*, 2011), educational activities, and employment (Emerson & Einfeld, 2011).

In one of the largest studies of its kind, Byrd and Weitzman (1994) examined almost 10,000 children and found that the single best predictor of early school failure was the presence of behavior problems compared to other factors such as poverty, speech and hearing impairments, and low birth weight (Byrd & Weitzman, 1994). Gilliam and Shahar determined that almost 40% of preschool teachers reported expelling a child each year due to behavior problems (2006; US Department of Health and Human Services and US Department of Education, 2014). Additionally, such behaviors can pose a physical threat to these individuals and those who work with them. The impact of restricted opportunities for young children due to their challenging behavior, as well as the possible consequences of suspension and expulsion from community settings, have great effects not only on the child, but also on the parents and the entire family unit. It is recognized that parents are essential and responsible for insuring the educational and social success of their children. Yet, the stresses associated with caring for a child with a significant disability—especially one who also presents behavioral challenges—can interfere with parenting at home and can also limit the support schools need in areas such as behavioral intervention (Emily, Andrew, & Fiona, 2006; Hayes & Watson, 2013; Plant & Sanders, 2007). Parental stress has been shown to significantly increase when caring for a child with problem behavior (Floyd & Gallagher, 1997; Hastings, 2002; Saloviita,

Italinna, & Leinonen, 2003). Mothers of children with disabilities tend to have higher rates of depression and depressed mothers are more likely to have a child with behavior problems (Feldman *et al.*, 2007). These mothers report less parental self-efficacy and they relied on escape-avoidance coping strategies (e.g., hoping a problem will go away, giving in to demands) compared to non-depressed mothers. Behavior problems increase strain on families and the responses to this stress (e.g., not intervening or "giving in") may serve to increase child misbehavior.

Parenting a child with ASD, in particular, results in a great deal of stress (Abbeduto *et al.*, 2004; Hoffman *et al.*, 2009; Rao & Beidel, 2009). Rao and Beidel (2009) studied reports of stress by parents of 15 children (8–14 years of age) with high-functioning autism (HFA) and parents of 15 matched control children. The results indicate that parents of children with HFA experience significantly more parenting stress than parents of children with no psychological disorder and the higher intellectual functioning in children with HFA did not compensate for stress associated with parenting children with ASD. Meirsschaut, Roeyers, and Warreyn (2010) studied the stress of mothers, comparing their perceptions of their children with ASD with their perceptions of their typically developing (TD) children. Mothers differentiated in parenting cognitions, with strong associations between mothers' symptoms of stress and depression about their child with ASD as compared to cognitions associated with their TD child.

Although a variety of factors influence levels of stress among parents of children with ASD, problem behavior is routinely highly correlated with reports of elevated stress levels in these families (Hastings, 2002; Lecavalier, Leone, & Wiltz, 2006). There is a growing body of research demonstrating that when children with ASD engage in more problem behaviors, their parents are also likely to report more stress and other psychological symptoms, such as anxiety and depression (Dumas *et al.*, 1991; Hastings, 2002; Hastings & Johnson, 2001; Lecavalier *et al.*, 2006; Seltzer *et al.*, 2010). In addition to self-reported levels of stress, some research is now finding biological markers that support these verbal reports. Several important studies have begun to measure levels of cortisol (a hormonal marker for stress) among mothers of children with ASD who also displayed challenging behavior (Seltzer *et al.*, 2010; Smith *et al.*, 2010).

The pattern of reaction to stress observed in these studies is striking, and comparable in levels to findings on other groups experiencing chronic stress, including parents of children with cancer, combat soldiers, Holocaust survivors, and individuals suffering from PTSD (Seltzer *et al.*, 2010). And, as quoted by Smith *et al.*, "It is likely that these stressors accumulate over years of caregiving, potentially taking a cumulative toll on the wellbeing of mothers of individuals with ASD and further highlighting the need for appropriate family services" (quoted in Seltzer *et al.*, 2010, p.177).

Behavioral parent training

Improving challenging behavior in children with ASD is one of the major priorities in the effort to improve academic and social achievement among these students. Fortunately, our knowledge of the origins of these behaviors has increased over the past several decades along with our ability to respond to these behaviors in a positive, constructive way (Fox *et al.*, 2002; Hieneman, Childs, & Sergay, 2006). As a result, work on interventions with persons exhibiting severe challenging behavior has increased in a multitude of areas such as environmental/curricular changes (Dunlap *et al.*, 1991; Evans & Meyer, 1985; Meyer & Evans, 1989) and teaching replacement skills (Durand, 1990; Fox *et al.*, 2011; Durand & Moskowitz, 2015).

Behavioral parent training typically employs the principles of applied behavior analysis (ABA) in order to help families develop the skills that they need to support and manage their child(ren)'s behavior (Dangel *et al.*, 1994; Gimpel & Collett, 2002; Kazdin, 2008). In general, behavioral parent training (BPT) has been demonstrated to be effective (Maughan, Christiansen, & Jensen, 2005; Serketich & Dumas, 1996). However, the effectiveness of this approach to intervention may vary with the stressors being experienced by the family, the specific features of the intervention protocols, and the adjunctive supports being provided to the family (Aman *et al.*, 2009; Drew *et al.*, 2002; Johnson *et al.*, 2007; Ozonoff & Cathcart, 1998; Whittingham *et al.*, 2009). The range of intervention approaches—from interventions for single behaviors to comprehensive and multimodal interventions across a range of life-style changes—is referred to as positive behavioral supports (Horner *et al.*, 1990). The federal government codified these approaches through the reauthorization in 1997 of the Individuals with Disabilities Education Act (IDEA).

Attitudinal obstacles to successful parent education

Research suggests that an individual's optimistic or pessimistic outlook on the world affects numerous outcomes, such as health (Aspinwall & Brunhart, 2000) and the motivation to achieve goals (Carver & Scheier, 1990). The influence of parental characteristics on children's behavioral treatment may be greater than previously noted; in a review of the literature on child and adolescent treatment, Morrissey-Kane and Prinz (1999) noted that parental cognitions and attributions were found to influence three aspects of treatment: help-seeking, treatment engagement and retention, and treatment outcome.

The research on the impact of parental attitudes in treatment participation and outcomes points to an important consideration that has not been adequately addressed in behavioral parent training. Further, there is reason to believe that interventions may only be effective with the portion of our population that has the ability and motivation to complete all aspects of the intervention (Durand, 2001, 2011). If so, it only makes sense that interventions may be developed to overcome such barriers. Some preliminary research on the development of challenging behavior among young children suggests that the attitudes of family members may play an important role in treatment outcome. Fortunately, this research may also open up a new avenue for understanding the obstacles to successful intervention.

Evidence for the model

In an effort to demonstrate the impact of a parent targeted intervention implemented to address how perceptions and thoughts affect child behavior and outcomes, a three-year longitudinal prospective study was completed to examine factors that might contribute to later behavior problems in young children (Durand, 2001). One hundred and forty 3-year-old children identified with a cognitive and/or developmental disability who also displayed behavior problems were identified and followed for up to three years. A number of factors were measured to assess their role in predicting which children would later display more severe behavior problems. These included measures of IQ, DSM-IV diagnosis, child behavior problems, child adaptive skills (communication and social skills), and a variety of family indicators (e.g., stress, attitudes, etc.). Surprisingly, the most significant factor in predicting later behavior problems was not the severity of the child's problems at age 3, nor was it the extent of cognitive or adaptive behavior deficits initially displayed by the children. Rather, the best predictor of which children would have more severe problems at age 6 was a measure of parental optimism/pessimism; parents who had limited confidence in their ability to influence their child's behaviors by the time the child was 3 years old were most likely to have children with more difficult behaviors later in life. For example, if parents resisted placing demands on their child for fear of escalating behavior problems, then children were more likely to develop severe behavior problems as they became older. This finding was true despite the fact that some of the children with more optimistic parents initially had more severe deficits and behavior problems. It appeared that parental optimism may have served as a protective factor for these children and parental pessimism may put a child more at risk for developing severe behavior problems. If an important obstacle to successful behavioral parent training is the pessimistic attitudes of some family members, the logical next question is: Can we intervene with these families in a way that will help them feel more optimistic about their abilities to work with their children? In turn, if we can successfully intervene with these families to assist them with this attitudinal barrier, will it help them continue in and complete behavioral parent training and will this lead to improvements in child behavior? The answers to these questions have been tested in a study of children with behavior problems and their families.

Full description of the model

The Positive Family Intervention Project is a multi-site study designed to develop and assess the effectiveness of a treatment package that integrates cognitive-behavioral intervention with function-based behavioral parent training (i.e., positive behavior support); this approach is referred to as Positive Family Intervention (PFI). PFI is a clinically-based approach to provide family members with the skills they need to cope with the stressors associated with everyday life along with the added stress of having a child with significant challenges.

More specifically, we adapt cognitive-behavioral intervention techniques to meet the specific needs of these families and combine this approach with the components of Positive Behavior Support (PBS). Fortunately, there is work underway addressing pessimism—through "learned optimism"—and the need for some people to address feelings of being out of control, and this research appears to be an invaluable addition to our traditional approaches for helping these families. Seligman (1998), for example, outlines a treatment protocol that focuses on the way in which people view events, and attempts to provide them with more adaptive styles. Research on this cognitive-behavioral therapy approach suggests that significant improvements can be observed in persons with pessimistic styles, which, in turn, results in improvements in such areas as depression.

PFI is an adaptation of PBS, integrating a version of Seligman's work for use with families of children with disabilities and challenging behavior. In our preliminary work, we found that parents who score high on a measure of pessimism might describe a child's difficult trip to the supermarket this way: "Shopping with my child is a disaster." On the other hand, parents scoring high on optimism might describe it this way: "My child is not ready yet for long shopping trips." The former pessimistic description suggests that the problem is pervasive (all shopping is a problem) and permanent (shopping may never get better), while the latter optimistic view is local (it is just long shopping trips that are a problem) and temporary (someday he will be ready). Presenting families with their styles of describing situations and having them practice more adaptive optimistic styles—referred to as positive family intervention—is proving to be quite successful. We assessed the effectiveness of PFI through a multi-site randomized clinical trial assessing the effects of adding a cognitive-behavioral intervention to positive behavior support (PBS). Families from throughout the Tampa Bay region in Florida (through the University of South Florida St. Petersburg and the University of South Florida Tampa) and the Capital region in New York (through the University at Albany, State University of New York) participated in this project. Our experience to date is that more than 80% of the families referred to our project meet criterion for pessimism. This number is higher than expected and may, in part, represent an ascertainment issue; that is, families may be more likely to be referred to this project if they express reservations about their ability to intervene with their child.

Participants for this study were recruited through various referral sources (e.g., schools, physicians, therapy groups), fliers at conferences (Annual Conference for the Center for Autism and Related Disabilities, Conference for Family Network on Disabilities, Exceptional Children's Conference), and local media at two research sites (university centers in Florida and New York) over a five-year period from 2005 to 2009. Eligibility for inclusion was assessed using predetermined selection criteria: (1) The parents or legal guardians could not have participated in previous parent training or received in-home assistance in behavioral parent training; (2) parents needed to score a 6 or above on the pessimism scale (1–11) of the Questionnaire on Resources and Stress–Short Form (QRS-SF; Friedrich, Greenberg, & Crnic, 1983); and (3) the target child needed to be between the ages of 3 and 6, have a diagnosed developmental disability, and exhibit serious problem behavior as evidenced by a score of −20 or below on the General Maladaptive Behavior Index (GMI) of the Scales of Independent Behavior–Revised (SIB-R; Bruininks et al., 1996). Typical problem behaviors reported by parents of the children targeted included tantrums, aggression, noncompliance, elopement, and stereotyped behaviors. Of the 257 families assessed for eligibility, 203 were excluded due to not meeting the inclusion criteria (e.g., age of child, less severe behavior, low score on the measure of pessimism; $n = 165$) or for reasons such as moving out of area, not wanting to be videotaped, or having participated in previous parent training programs or supports ($n = 38$).

Institutional Review Board approved consent forms (from both participating universities) were used in order to obtain and document consent to participate in study as well as consent for videotaping in training sessions as for family and child observations at home. The eligible and consented families ($n = 54$) were randomly assigned to either the PBS only group (PBS) or the PFI group (PFI). A randomized control design (Durand & Wang, 2011) with two conditions: (a) PBS and (b) PBS plus optimism training (PFI) was utilized. All therapists administered both interventions. Measures were administered prior to initiating intervention and within two weeks of completing intervention. Research assistants administered all assessments and a separate group of assistants videotaped parent-selected target daily home family routines at a separate time. None of the assistants participated in delivering the interventions. Although instruments were administered to both parents when possible, only the data from the primary caregivers were analyzed. In regards to demographics, all parent participants were over the age of 18 and under the age of 60. Parents involved in the study represented all education levels and socio-economic status.

We evaluated if the PFI would: (1) increase family participation in training; and (2) if it would successfully prevent child behavior problems from escalating into more severe problems. We also sought to assess whether a cost effective approach, a clinic-based intervention just for parents, would result in significant changes in child behavior at home. Follow-up of the children was conducted up to two years after the initial intervention.

For both experimental conditions, eight weekly individual sessions, lasting 90 minutes each were provided within a small conference room, with only the parent and therapist present. All families received PBS training, which included how to identify problem behaviors, how to assess the function of these behaviors, prevention strategies, managing consequences, and replacing behavior problems with communication (Durand, 1990; Hieneman et al., 2006). For those families receiving PFI, the cognitive-behavioral intervention component was integrated into the same sessions. Through this project, we developed standard protocols for both PBS alone and PFI. (The PFI protocol for interventionists and an accompanying parent manual are published; see Durand & Hieneman, 2008a, 2008b.)

The PBS process began with an assessment that involved identification of goals and specific behaviors of concern, and the collection and analysis of information through interviews and observations to determine the purposes problem behaviors serve. Based on the assessment, a team (including parents, teachers, and other support providers, under the guidance of someone trained in PBS) designed a behavior support plan for the child. The multi-component intervention included strategies designed to:

1. prevent problems through modifications to the physical and social environment

2. manage consequences to maximize reinforcement for positive behavior rather than problem behavior

3. develop and teach skills to replace problem behavior (e.g., via functional communication training (FCT)).

The optimism training component was integrated into the sessions for the parents assigned to that condition (PFI). The sessions varied by parent, but typically began with a discussion of the recent successes and challenges with the child with a disability. Parents were encouraged to speak freely (which is why these sessions occur individually and not in groups) and the therapist's role was to be supportive but also to note how the parent described situations. For example, if a parent made a statement such as "Shopping with my child is a disaster" or "I will never have my own life," then these were brought up later in the session for discussion. The overall goal was to reduce pessimistic beliefs by learning to: (1) identify them when they occur; and (2) develop coping skills (Seligman, 1998). Thus, for example, the previous statements would be mentioned along with a discussion of how to dispute them. Pointing out that not all shopping has been problematic and that there are times when the parent may have opportunities for activities just for her/him would start the discussion. Parents were asked to identify such self-statements over the next week, and to practice disputing them.

Measures
QRS-SF

The QRS-SF is a 52-item true–false instrument measuring four factors: parent and family problems, pessimism, child characteristics, and physical incapacities (Friedrich et al., 1983). The 11-item pessimism factor measures the parent's pessimism about immediate and future events associated with the child's prospects of achieving self-sufficiency and was used as the measure of parental pessimism in this study. The pessimism scale ranges from 1 to 11; based on prior research (Konstantareas, Homatidis, & Plowright, 1992; Hayes & Watson, 2013), a score of 6 or higher was used for inclusion in this study (this is consistent with previous research indicating that this score represents a high level of pessimism (Hodapp, Fidler, & Smith, 1998). Several studies have supported the reliability and validity of the QRS-SF (e.g., Scott et al., 1989).

SIB-R (GMI)

The SIB-R is a comprehensive, norm-referenced assessment used to measure the skills required for the child to function independently in home, social, and community settings. The problem behavior section yields a General Maladaptive Behavior Index (GMI). The scores on the GMI (used in screening and as an outcome measure) indicate the degree of seriousness of the following behaviors: hurtful to self, hurtful to others, destructive to property, disruptive behavior, unusual or repetitive habits, socially offensive behavior, withdrawal or inattentive behavior, and uncooperative behavior. The seriousness of the child's problem behaviors is summarized on the GMI as falling within the following categories: normal = +10 to –10; marginally serious = –11 to –20; moderately serious = –21 to –30; serious = –31 to –40; and very serious = –41 and below. A score of –21 or below (moderately serious to very serious) was required criteria for inclusion in this study. The SIB-R manual (Bruininks et al., 1996) reports adequate test–retest reliability, interrater reliability, construct validity, and criterion validity for the GMI.

Behavioral observations

Project staff developed a task analysis of home routines identified as most problematic by the family. Common routines included transition periods, demand situations, mealtimes, incidents when parental attention was removed, and other typical but stressful daily situations. The expectations for the child (e.g., putting away toys, going to bed at night) were written out to promote consistent target routines for analysis. The children were videotaped during 20–30-minute probes in the home, interacting with their parents during these identified natural routines prior to and following intervention. The videotaping was conducted unobtrusively at the same time of day on three separate days during a two-week period at each assessment point until there was a stable trend, or until the taping needed to be terminated due to parental concerns. At no time did data collectors who videotaped routines provide any feedback to parents on how to intervene with their child and they did not interact with the child in any manner.

The videotapes were scored using a 10-s partial-interval time-sampling procedure using a pencil-and-paper method of data collection. Each video recorded home routine was viewed and scored by observers who had experience with young children and data collection features. Specific target challenging behaviors were individually identified and operationally defined for each target child prior to the observers scoring home routine videos. The categories of problem behavior included aggression, destruction, opposition, stereotyped behavior, and inappropriate vocalizations. An audio cue was provided during the videotape viewing, which provided a signal for each 10-second interval that was scored. If the defined target child behavior occurred within a specific 10-second interval, then a check was marked next to the corresponding interval number on a data collection sheet. Behaviors were displayed as percentage of intervals with challenging behavior. Percentage of challenging behavior was calculated by dividing the number of intervals with challenging behavior from the total overall intervals for each home routine session. Interobserver agreement was also completed, in which two observers coded each target child's home routine videotape independently in order to ensure that data was being collected accurately and as intended. Interobserver agreement was conducted for a minimum of 33% of the videos. The mean for the interobserver agreement data (calculated as agreements/agreements + disagreements) was 92% for problematic behavior for pre-observations and 95.3% for post-observations. Because the original observers were not naïve to condition, an additional observer who was not aware of the experimental conditions scored one pre-session and one post-session for each child. These observations were then compared with the original data, and the mean for the interobserver agreement data (calculated as agreements/agreements + disagreements) was 86% for problematic behavior for pre-observations and 88.1% for post-observations. Kappa was also calculated from these observations and was 0.64 (suggesting substantial agreement). These data suggest that there were no apparent biases in the original observations.

Attrition

Data were maintained on the parents' attendance of sessions to evaluate their rate of completion and/or attrition from the program. Therapists recorded sessions, indicating dates and duration of sessions and whether the sessions were completed as scheduled. Duration of session was used to ensure comparable session duration for both treatments. A family was considered as a noncompleter if they refused to continue or failed to attend three consecutive sessions or respond to scheduling attempts. To ensure consistency in the data, specific procedures for providing reminders and follow-up after missed sessions (i.e., no more than three attempts to contact the parent) were maintained.

Parent Satisfaction Questionnaire (PSQ)

We created a questionnaire with five items used to assess satisfaction with the skills taught through the project (e.g., "I have a greater understanding of what affects my child's behavior") and five items used to assess satisfaction with the outcomes (e.g., "My child's problem behavior has decreased"). Questionnaire items were rated on a 5-point Likert-type scale, ranging from 5 (strongly agree) to 1 (strongly disagree). This questionnaire was administered immediately after the last intervention session.

Intervention conditions

PBS

In the PBS condition, parents were provided with eight weekly sessions lasting 90 minutes each based on principles of applied behavior analysis and PBS (Durand, 1990; Hieneman et al., 2006). The sessions were formally outlined using a therapist protocol and adhered to following an eight session sequence (Table 2.1).

Table 2.1 PBS eight-session sequence

Session 1	Introduction and goal setting
Session 2	Gathering information on challenging behavior
Session 3	Analyzing data and plan design
Session 4	Using prevention strategies
Session 5	Using consequences
Session 6	Replacing challenging behavior with appropriate alternatives
Session 7	Implementing the strategies
Session 8	Monitoring the results

Parents were guided to establish a support team (e.g., of family members and service providers) with whom they would work throughout the process. The first session focused on identifying short- and long-term goals for the family and child, and then went on to identify and define operationally specific behaviors of concern within typical family routine. In the second session, the parent(s) were guided on how to collect information about the occurrence and nonoccurrence of challenging behavior, and provided materials to collect data, gain information from others, and complete Antecedent–Behavior–Consequence forms. This process was designed to collect information from multiple sources to assist with the third session, in which the Functional Behavioral Assessment (FBA) was facilitated by the therapist to synthesize all the information gathered by the parent(s). The therapist helped the parents to analyze patterns surrounding their child's behavior throughout the FBA process in order to determine the function or purpose of behavior and to be able to link the assessment outcomes to hypotheses statements as to why the behavior is occurring and what is motivating behavior (i.e., escape/attention) in order to develop interventions linked to function of behavior.

Sessions 4–6 addressed the strategy development and description of how to implement specific types of strategies, with session 7 generating a comprehensive behavior support plan and developing all the steps necessary to implement consistently. The final sessions focused on: ensuring that the interventions fit the family circumstances and needs; monitoring implementation with data collection; and relapse prevention. Although therapists adhered strictly to the written protocols, their primary goal was to help parents apply the principles of PBS to understand and resolve their own problems, rather than just teaching them procedures. This was accomplished through questioning (e.g., "What could you do to respond differently given this pattern?") instead of just presenting solutions.

An example of this process involved Jeff, a 3-year-old boy identified with autism who exhibited challenging behavior during his daily bath time routine. His mother was the primary person to complete the FBA process. Her identified goal was to reduce aggression during Jeff's daily bath/grooming routine and reduce the length of time that the routine took to complete. The target behavior for Jeff was "aggression," defined as any attempt, successful or otherwise, to hit, kick, and/or pull his mother's hair, as she facilitated the bath/grooming routine daily. Results of the FBA gleaned the following information about Jeff's strength and difficulties and what circumstances were associated with challenging behavior. It was identified that Jeff liked to help with chores, and "liked to do things in certain way." Difficulties for Jeff in which aggression was more likely to occur included transition activities, stopping preferred activities, lack of predictability or changes in schedule, as well as a sensitivity to loud noises. His parents typically responded to aggressive behavior by using consequences such as bribing with M&Ms, coaxing, reasoning, and/or removal of demands. During very difficult bath routines, the demands were reduced, including eliminating the steps of hair washing and brushing teeth. Based on the summary of the FBA, it was hypothesized that Jeff engaged in aggression during the bath routine in an effort to escape from demands that were nonpreferred, unpredictable, and were associated with loud noises (the reverberation echo of the water running against the porcelain of the tub).

Intervention strategies were developed that were linked to the "escape" function of behavior and included components related to prevention strategies, skill building, and modifying consequences. For the prevention strategies, the following intervention components were implemented during the bath routine: visual cues/schedule; a choice chart; having all materials ready to go; easy access to preferred items; modified materials (using a cup for rinsing hair instead of using faucet); and removal of distractions. Skill-building strategies include: having Jeff actively participate in completing routine; walking independently instead of being carried to the bathroom; teaching him to choose preferred items; and teaching him to gesture for a hug. Parent responses were modified to help Jeff have a better understanding of expectations. Instructions were clear and concise, no more coaxing and reasoning, when he started to engage in challenging behavior, his parents would redirect and ignore, as well as when he was following expectations they would provide specific praise throughout the bath routine in order to promote Jeff's understanding of expectations. Using these strategies improved the bath time activity, as aggression was reduced; the full routine and all steps were now completed, as well as improvement in the quality of life for family reported anecdotally.

PFI

In the PFI condition, each family also received eight weekly sessions lasting 90 minutes each. The outline and content of the sessions were identical to the PBS condition with the addition of an adaptation of optimism training. Therefore, in addition to teaching parents how to identify patterns in their child's behavior and develop intervention strategies, they were also helped to identify patterns in their own thoughts and feelings and taught strategies for cognitive restructuring. Practice on identifying thoughts and feelings associated with their child's behavior (e.g., "I feel out of control" and "I must be a bad parent") along with strategies for looking at these situations in a more objective and constructive perspective were incorporated into these sessions. Table 2.2 provides two parent examples describing scenarios of self-talk across the sequence of optimism training.

Table 2.2 Positive Family Intervention session sequence and examples

Situation What happened (success or difficulty)?	Beliefs What did you think or feel (self-talk)?	Consequences What happened as a result (actions)?	Disputation Was this a useful or accurate belief?	Substitution What is a more positive belief (affirmation)
The family takes Nick to a relative's birthday party. Before all the guests arrive, Nikolas sees the cake and starts whining and trying to grab at it, demanding a piece now.	"Nick has a disability and therefore doesn't understand and can't help misbehaving. We should just let him have what he wants."	Nick's father talks the host into cutting him a small piece of the cake before he really gets out of control. Although he apologizes, his father still thinks it was the best thing to do.	Nick's disability does affect his understanding of situations; however, he could learn to respond to limits. Getting what he wants only makes his behavior worse.	"Nick is capable of learning limits. We will do our best to anticipate problems when we can and avoid giving in to unreasonable demands."

Lilly's siblings need school supplies by the next day, so her mother reluctantly ventures out to the store with all the kids. As they walk into the store, Lilly begins to pull away and cry.	"Going out in public with Lilly is always a disaster. Lilly's tantrums and everyone looks at me like I'm doing something wrong. It's easier to just not go, even if it means the other kids don't get what they need."	The next time Lilly's mother needs to do an errand, she arranges for a babysitter or waits for her husband to get home instead. Having to use babysitters or do all the errands this way limits the time that the parents spend together as a couple.	Many outings have been difficult, but there have also been successes— especially when we are prepared for the outing and complete it quickly. Arranging for sitters and taking turns staying with the children are not good options for our family. Lilly needs to learn to go out.	"I will plan ahead to make shopping trips as successful as possible. When problems do occur, I will ignore the reactions of others and do what I need to do to manage the situation— without giving up."

Parents were taught to complete and maintain a self-talk journal throughout their participation in the study and bring it to sessions each week to address and review it with the therapist. The therapist guided the parents sequentially through each step of optimism training protocols. During the first week of training, the self-talk journal was introduced, along with the purpose for collecting this information on thoughts and feelings. Parents were taught about how perceptions influence actions, and how we can change responses that are ineffective through the use of: examining situations, beliefs, and the consequence of those beliefs; intentionally disputing those beliefs; and substituting them with a more a positive belief to impact behavior. During session 1, the parent was asked to identify and record situations that they encountered with their child reflecting one "challenge" and one "success." During the training session, the therapist would guide parents to articulate their thoughts and feelings in response to targeted situations and determine what they were saying to themselves. This helped to build rapport and understanding, and introduce the premise that thoughts are linked to reactions (i.e., to the child's behavior). Over the next two sessions, this homework assignment was completed and reviewed during the session, and the therapist introduced the tools for how to learn to identify the consequences of thoughts and feelings.

Table 2.3 Positive Family Intervention session objectives and therapist training procedures

	Session objective	Example

Session 1	Identifying situations and associated self-talk
	
	What happened (success or difficulty)?
	
	What did you think or feel (self-talk)?
		• Identify triggers to negative thinking (what happens that upsets you?).
		• Think about situations that are successful and difficult. For a particular situation that was difficult:
		   ○ Identify what exactly your child (and/or someone else) does or says that triggers your negative thoughts and feelings.
		   ○ Identify unproductive thought patterns: What do you say to yourself?
		   ○ What are you thinking (e.g., anger, frustration, sadness) and feeling (e.g., "It's never going to get better")?

Session 2	Determining consequences of beliefs *What happened as a result (actions)?*	• Identify consequences of negative thinking (what happens as a result of these negative thoughts and actions?). • How do you respond when these situations occur? • What do you get out of these reactions (e.g., attention, control)? • What do you avoid as a result (e.g., responsibility, disappointment)?
Session 3	Disputing current thinking *Was this a useful or accurate belief?*	• Challenge the accuracy and usefulness of their perceptions. • Is what I am thinking true? • What is the evidence to support that belief? • What are the alternative explanations for this problem? • Is what I am thinking helpful? • Are the consequences of this perspective beneficial?
Session 4	Using distraction to interrupt negative thinking *What can you say to yourself or do to stop unproductive thinking in its tracks?*	• Distraction involves shifting our attention away from any pessimistic thoughts during activities such as a meeting at school, a behavior problem, or a stressful workday. Distraction should be used during times or situations when it is not an ideal time to dispute belief. • When you are stating some negative ideas or thoughts, how can you recognize that they are occurring and stop them from continuing? • Select an easy cue to remind yourself not to think negative thoughts (e.g., singing to self, choosing a mantra, touching a bracelet).

Session 5	Substituting pessimistic thoughts with positive, productive thoughts *What is a more positive belief (affirmation?)*	• If the perception is unproductive, create a new belief. • What is a more accurate appraisal of what is going on? • What is a more productive way of thinking? • Replace negative thoughts with positive self-talk—known as substitution or reattribution. • Develop an affirmation (e.g., "This is a difficult situation, and I am handling it well"). • Affirmations should be stated in present tense, focus on solutions, be both specific and comprehensive (clear and relate to various situations in which pessimistic beliefs are likely to arise). • Replace negative thoughts with positive affirmations during challenging circumstances.
Session 6	Practicing skills to recognize/modify self-talk	• Ask the participant to consider one or more events recorded in self-talk journal and work through all the steps of using positive self-talk. • Encourage them to use disputation and/or distraction and substitute pessimistic thoughts with positive affirmations.
Session 7	Practicing skills to recognize/modify self-talk	• Ask the participant to consider one or more events recorded in self-talk journal and work through all the steps of using positive self-talk. • Encourage them to use disputation and/or distraction and substitute pessimistic thoughts with positive affirmations.
Session 8	Maintaining positive changes in self-talk	• Ask the participant to review their self-talk journal, identifying situations in which they were successful and areas in which they are having difficulty. Focus on those areas, and determine ways in which to maintain positive self-talk (e.g., continue to keep a journal, complete a weekly review of thoughts and feelings).

Table 2.3 outlines each week's training objectives and the procedures and descriptions of how therapists facilitated the optimism training and skill building. The therapist would guide the parents to start thinking about why thoughts and feelings are important, focusing on the outcomes of how we interpret situations around us and how those interpretations may influence how we perceive life and how we react and behave. Those identified consequences (behavior and their results) have a purpose or function for the parent, allowing them to get/obtain or escape/avoid events. The process of distraction was then introduced

in session 4 as a method to temporarily set aside pessimistic thinking in the moment and return to the thoughts later when it is more comfortable to process them. This step involved establishing a brief statement in order to shift attention away from pessimistic thoughts when it is not possible to address the beliefs (such as saying "stop" or "refocus," singing to oneself, making a note, or saying to oneself to "think about this later"). The next step of the optimism protocol was to incorporate the action of disputation. This involves acknowledging and being aware that inaccurate or unproductive thoughts can have a detrimental effect on actions and outcomes.

The final step of the five-part optimism training was taught during session 5, in which the process of substitution was introduced. Substitution involved replacing pessimistic ideas with positive thoughts or affirmations, allowing parents to take active control over negative thoughts and activate positive thoughts instead of simply accepting pessimistic thinking imprinted through past experiences. This step also allows a parent to be more effective when responding to the child's behavior. The parent's self-talk journal was reviewed during the remaining sessions, and in addition to teaching and practicing the five-step process of optimism training, evaluation and maintenance of the optimism process was addressed to help to ensure that parents had the tools needed for continually evaluating and addressing their thinking, as well as establishing a more positive orientation to life. This was completed by teaching participants to assess overall use and effectiveness of optimism training and continue to ask the following questions of them: "What is working and what isn't?"; "What do I plan to do next time?" In addition, parents and therapists worked together to determine strategies for ongoing monitoring (e.g., continuing journal, debriefing sessions) so that improvements could be maintained.

Here is an example of how a specific challenging situation was addressed by parents within the PFI training: if a problem situation was being described (e.g., child screaming at a store), in addition to discussing the possible reason for the difficulty (e.g., child wanting attention), the therapist would also help the parent identify self-talk (e.g., "My child is out of control") and problem-solve how this self-talk influenced the parent's behavior (e.g., "I yelled at my child and then spent a great deal of time lecturing on proper behavior"). In later sessions, parents were helped to create alternative strategies for both dealing with the child problem (e.g., attending to the child for good behavior) as well as their unproductive self-talk (e.g., using an alternative thought such as, "This is a situation I can handle"). Parents in the PBS-alone condition were provided with additional examples or extra time to discuss homework to equate the amount of therapist contact so that both groups received approximately 90 minutes for each of the eight sessions (see training procedures and fidelity).

Training procedures and fidelity

All sessions were conducted by therapists with Master's degrees or PhDs and background in PBS and/or clinical psychology. These sessions occurred individually with the parents (i.e., children were not in attendance) at the university or other professional sites. The sessions followed a consistent instructional process, in which the therapist introduced each concept by presenting a rationale and description of the features or steps, providing examples, offering an opportunity for the parent to apply the concept, and then assigning homework so that the parent could practice the concept with her child.

Several quality assurance methods were used to maximize the integrity of the interventions across therapists and participants, and over the course of the study. First, the clinical director provided initial training in the protocols by having the therapists review session tapes and discuss the strategies used, as well as assigning the therapists background reading as needed. The clinical director also facilitated periodic meetings among the therapists (via teleconferencing across sites) to problem-solve and achieve greater consistency among the therapists in implementation. Examples of cross-site and therapist brain-storming and problem-solving included addressing time constraints for particular sessions that required more lecture activities; how to conduct probe questions to help participants share or articulate thoughts and feelings; as well as how to redirect a conversation that has gone off on a tangent. All parent training sessions were videotaped and either delivered to the main research site or digitized and transferred via a virtual private network. Procedural fidelity assessments were then completed by research assistants by viewing approximately 90% of the sessions via videotapes. These assessments included 10 to 13 objectives to be covered in each session, scoring whether each objective was addressed. These data were then used to provide feedback to the therapists prior to the next scheduled session, so as to ensure that the protocols were followed and also that there was no coverage of optimism training elements in the PBS conditions. The fidelity data for the sessions (percentage of objectives included) are as follows: PBS = 98.4% and PFI = 94.6%. Interobserver agreement was assessed for more than 50% of the fidelity checklists by having a second recorder complete the fidelity checklists separately and by comparing scores on an item-by-item basis. Interobserver agreement for the procedural fidelity checklists 98.6% for PBS, 95.8% for PFI (calculated as the number of agreements/number of agreements +number of disagreements). There were no significant differences in session duration across groups.

Results

Pessimism ratings data

It was expected that families who completed the eight sessions of the PFI condition would demonstrate a decrease in pessimism (as measured by scores on the QRS-SF pessimism scale). A 2 (treatment condition: PFI vs. PBS) × 2 (measurement occasion: pre- vs. post-treatment) repeated-measure ANOVA with measurement occasion as a within-subject factor was used to test this hypothesis. This analysis yielded a significant main effect of measurement occasion on the scores of pessimism, $F (1, 33) = 16.41$, $p < 0.01$, partial $\eta 2 = 0.33$. For families who completed the eight sessions of either intervention, their post-treatment pessimism scores ($M = 5.77$, $SD = 2.83$) were significantly lower than their pre-treatment pessimism scores ($M = 7.71$, $SD = 1.23$). Neither the main effect of treatment condition, $F (1, 33) = 0.88$, $p > 0.10$, nor the interaction effect between treatment condition and measurement occasion, $F (1, 33) = 0.13$, $p > 0.10$, was significant on the pessimism scores.

GMI data

It was expected that the children of families who completed the eight sessions of the PFI condition would show significant behavioral improvements as measured by the GMI score of SIB-R. This hypothesis was also tested with a 2 (treatment condition: PFI vs. PBS) × 2 (measurement occasion: pre- vs. post-treatment) repeated-measure ANOVA. This analysis yielded a significant main effect of measurement occasion on the GMI scores, F (1, 33) = 102.46, p < 0.01, partial η2 = 0.76. Specifically, for children from families who completed the eight sessions of intervention, their post-treatment GMI scores (M = –21.51, SD = 10.81) were significantly improved over their pre-treatment GMI scores (M = –38.14, SD = 8.22). This main effect was further qualified by the significant interaction effect between treatment condition and measurement occasion on the GMI scores, F (1, 33) = 4.67, p < 0.01, partial η2 = 0.12. This significant interaction effect suggests that after completing the eight treatment sessions, children from the PFI group improved significantly more in their GMI scores as compared to the post-intervention scores of children from the PBS measurement occasion, F (1, 33) = 0.38, p > 0.10, The data showed a significant interaction effect, suggesting that while both groups reported improved child behavior after completing the eight treatment sessions, children from the PFI group improved significantly more in their GMI scores as compared to the post-intervention scores of children from the PBS measurement occasion.

Behavioral observation data

It was expected that the children of families who completed the eight sessions of PFI would show significant improvements in problem behaviors as measured by behavioral observations. This hypothesis was also tested with a 2 (treatment condition: PFI vs. PBS) × 2 (measurement occasion: pre- vs. post-treatment) repeated-measure ANOVA. This analysis yielded a significant main effect of measurement occasion on the observed problem behaviors, F (1, 33) = 122.91, p < 0.01, partial η2 = 0.79. Specifically, for children from families who completed the eight sessions of intervention, their post-treatment problem behaviors (M = 16.46, SD = 10.71) were significantly improved over their pre-treatment problem behaviors (M = 46.71, SD = 16.04). Furthermore, we calculated the reliable change index for each child (M = –1.64, SD = 0.87). For children from families who completed the eight sessions of either intervention, their post-treatment problem behaviors were significantly improved over their pre-treatment problem behaviors. Furthermore, 10 of the 17 children in the PFI condition showed reliable changes in their problem behaviors, whereas only 5 of the 18 children in the PBS condition showed reliable changes in their problem behaviors.

Attrition data

It was expected that the families in the PFI group would complete the eight sessions with a lower number of cancellations and rescheduling of sessions to completion and show less attrition (dropout) than the PBS group. First, to test whether the families in the PFI group would complete the eight sessions in a shorter time than the PBS group, survival analysis (i.e., Cox regression) was used. Specifically, the conditional probability, $h(t)$ (i.e., the "hazard probability" in survival analysis terms), for families to complete the treatment over time was predicted by the type of treatment they went through. The resulted Cox regression coefficient was not significant ($B = 0.10$, $SE = 0.35$, Wald Statistic [1] $= 0.09$, $p > 0.10$), indicating that there was no differences in the amount of time for PFI ($M = 79.39$ days, $SD = 26.89$) and PBS ($M = 82.00$ days, $SD = 22.08$) groups to complete the treatment sessions.

Second, to test whether families in the PFI group would show less attrition than in the PBS group, logistic regression was used. Specifically, the probability for families to drop out of the treatment was predicted by the type of treatment they went through. The resulted logistic regression coefficient was not significant ($B = 0.16$, $SE = 0.57$, Wald Statistic [1] $= 0.08$, $p > 0.10$), indicating that there were no differences in the attrition rates for PFI (33.33%) and PBS (37.04%). There were no differences in the amount of time for PFI and PBS groups to complete the treatment sessions. Second, there were no differences in the attrition rates for PFI and PBS families.

Parental satisfaction data

Parents in both groups rated the respective programs highly on a PSQ (for PBS condition: $M = 4.43$, $SD = 0.71$; for PFI condition: $M = 4.59$, $SD = 0.71$), indicating that they "slightly agreed" or "strongly agreed" with all questions related to their satisfaction with the skills taught through the project and their satisfaction with the outcomes. The two exceptions, "I am able to implement the strategies in my child's plan consistently" (for PBS condition: $M = 3.65$, $SD = 0.86$; for PFI condition: $M = 4.47$, $SD = 0.49$) and "My child's positive behavior has increased" (for PBS condition: $M = 3.71$, $SD = 0.77$; for PFI condition:

M = 4.50, SD = 0.51) indicated scores lower than "slightly agreed" for the PBS group. Independent sample t-tests indicated that the scores on these questions differed significantly between the two groups ($t = 3.47$, $p < 0.001$, Cohen's $d = 1.17$; and $t = 3.60$, $p < 0.001$, Cohen's $d = 1.21$, respectively), suggesting that the PFI group believed that they were better able to implement the strategies and that their child's positive behavior improved.

Discussion

This study evaluated the effectiveness of two forms of clinic-based behavioral parent training on the severe challenging behaviors of children with autism and other developmental disabilities. Children whose parents participated in either treatment group significantly improved their behavior problems as measured by both standardized scores (the GMI of the SIB-R) and behavioral observations during structured settings at home. Adding a cognitive-behavioral component to the PFI condition within the parent skill training resulted in even greater reductions in child problem behavior on the GMI when compared with the PBS alone group. These outcomes may suggest that parents might have been incorporated new cognitive tools for interpreting their child's behavior in a more positive light. The scores on a measure of pessimism were reduced for parents in both groups following intervention and there was no significant difference in the groups on measures of attrition. Although both groups were highly satisfied with the programs and the outcomes, parents in the PFI group reported that they were better able to implement the strategies for their child's behavior and thought that (in addition to reductions in challenging behavior) their child's positive behavior improved as well.

An important aspect of this study was delivering manualized parent training to families without direct feedback on the implementation of the procedures at home. At no time did the therapists or the observers give feedback to parents on how they were interacting with their child based on the home observations—which is common among other parent education programs (Shapiro, Kilburn, & Hardin, 2014). Feedback was delivered solely as a function of the discussion that took place during the eight sessions. In contrast, traditional PBS is almost exclusively delivered with training that includes role playing and direct feedback on parent responses to the child (e.g., Koegel, Bimbela, & Schreibman, 1996). The results of this study suggest that an 8-week clinic-based intervention could result in improvements not only on parental reports of child behavior but also on separate home observations of parent-identified problematic situations. Given the time-intensive nature of traditional PBS, it would be an important addition to our treatment armamentarium to be able to provide parents who face significant challenges at home with guidance that could be delivered in a more cost-effective manner. This finding will require replication and extension to demonstrate the effectiveness of this approach to parent training. One way of extending this model is to assess if it could be successful in a group format. Several research groups are currently exploring this approach.

It is important to reemphasize that the parents included in this study were selected based on their high scores on a measure of parental pessimism. More "optimistic" parents were explicitly excluded from participation in this program. Often, the families that were selected were referred to the project because they had dropped out of previous programs offered by their schools or because they resisted collaborative efforts with teachers. Therefore, the relative success of both intervention strategies (PBS and PFI) provides hope that our interventions can be disseminated to families with these types of personal challenges. Our ability to maintain participation by these families may have been the result of a number of factors.

We did not, for example, place a great deal of emphasis on the collection of large amounts of home data by the parents. When parents did not complete homework assignments (e.g., filling out a log of child problems or their thoughts about difficult situations), we had them reconstruct this information in the sessions. This population is particularly vulnerable to feelings of guilt (e.g., "I am not a good mother") and we therefore did not want to exacerbate these interfering thoughts. In addition, we emphasized in both groups the need for support teams (e.g., including grandparents, teachers, other caregivers) to assist them with their efforts, a strategy consistent with current PBS approaches (e.g., Hieneman *et al.*, 2006). This may have also contributed to the relatively low rate of attrition. It should be noted that small sample size may be the reason that there was nonsignificant findings in attrition. This is particularly the case for the logistic regression, as the attrition rate differed by almost 4% (i.e., less attrition for the PFI group).

Research on the serious challenging behaviors of children with developmental disorders almost exclusively relies on single-subject designs (Brookman-Frazee et al., 2006; Koegel, Bimbela, & Schreibman, 1996; Steiner et al., 2011). This study is one of the few randomized clinical trials (RCTs) designed to assess the effectiveness of PBS on the severe challenging behaviors observed among children with developmental disorders (for an exception, see Brookman-Frazee, Drahota, & Stadnick, 2012). Other RCTs focusing on helping parents with their children who display problem behavior typically limit the study population to those children with less severe challenging behaviors (e.g., Plant & Sanders, 2007; Quinn et al., 2007; Whittingham, Sofronoff, & Sheffield, 2006). The few studies that examined parent training interventions for serious behavior problems used medication alone or in combination with behavioral intervention (e.g., Aman et al., 2009). Our goal was to evaluate whether behavioral parent training alone could result in meaningful improvements in serious child behavior problems and the results support this hypothesis.

The next steps in this research involve identifying the mechanisms responsible for behavior change in the children. In particular, it will be important to understand the reasons behind the greater change in problem behavior in the PFI group. One clue to the differences may come from the reports by the parents in the PFI group that they were more confident in their ability to implement the behavior strategies (i.e., more likely to endorse the statement, "I am able to implement the strategies in my child's plan consistently"). Although we did observe improvements in the pessimism scores from pre- to post-intervention across groups, we did not observe differences in the measure of pessimism between the groups after intervention. This may reflect a limitation in using the pessimism scale of the QRS-SF to assess changes in parental perceptions. In general, this scale is designed to assess how parents perceive their child's future. Unfortunately, the scale does not directly assess self-efficacy (e.g., changes in how parents view their abilities or how they view the opinions of others), nor is it designed to measure changes in their attitudes about their child's potential for changing discrete behaviors in specific situations. In other words, the scale assesses their overall perceptions about their child's future, which, given the nature of the groups (e.g., autism spectrum disorder), may be more limited in the ability to affect change. Future research will need to use measures more sensitive to these aspects of optimism/pessimism.

An additional limitation of this first study was the absence of a control group that did not receive parent training (e.g., no treatment, waitlist, attention placebo). The purpose of such groups is to assess whether behavior changes as a function of factors such as maturation, the passage of time (e.g., spontaneous recovery), anticipation of change, and so on. However, this is less of a concern with the severe types of problem behavior exhibited by this group given their relative stability over time (e.g., Totsika *et al.*, 2008).

Conclusion

A unique aspect of this research is the explicit intervention on parental attitudes that may prove to be significant obstacles to successful child intervention. Although other studies report on the effects of parent training (i.e., the teaching of parent training skills) on concepts such as self-efficacy (e.g., Whittingham *et al.*, 2009), the PFI intervention is designed both to teach parenting skills and to directly assist parents with attitudes that may interfere with their ability to implement these skills. We need to address the obstacles to successful parent education (such as pessimistic attitudes towards the child or the parent's ability to implement programs) in order to assist all families to be more successful with behavioral interventions. Anyone who provides PBS to families may need to expand their repertoire to assist them with any personal difficulties that may be barriers to successful outcomes (Durand, 2011).

This research provides support for the success of PBS to improve the severe behavior problems of children with developmental disorders. The addition of a cognitive-behavioral intervention appears to have boosted the positive intervention effect for this population of pessimistic families. Fortunately, the protocols for PFI are published (Durand & Hieneman, 2008a, 2008b) and a training video is available to assist with replication (APA, 2014). Future efforts in this area will be needed to address the needs of this population of families who are in great need of psychological as well as educational support.

References

Aaron, K., Oliver, C., Moss, J., Berg, K., & Burbidge, C. (2011) "The prevalence and phenomenology of self-injurious and aggressive behaviour in genetic syndromes." *Journal of Intellectual Disability Research 55*, 109–120.

Abbeduto, L., Seltzer, M.M., Shattuck, P., Krauss, M.W., Osmond, G., & Murphy, M.M. (2004) "Psychological well-being and coping in mothers of youths with autism, Down syndrome, or fragile X syndrome." *American Journal on Mental Retardation 109*, 237–254.

Aman, M.G., McDougle, C.J., Scahill, L.M., Handen, B., *et al.* (2009) "Medication and parent training in children with Pervasive Developmental Disorders and serious behavior problems: Results from a Randomized Clinical Trial." *Journal of the American Academy of Child & Adolescent Psychiatry 48*, 12, 1143–1154.

American Psychological Association (Producer) (2014) APA Psychotherapy Video Series (DVD). *Parents of Children With Autism Spectrum Disorder with V. Mark Durand.* Washington, DC: APA.

Aspinwall, L.G. & Brunhart, S.M. (2000) "What I Do Know Won't Hurt Me: Optimism, Attention to Negative Information, Coping, and Health." In J.E. Gillham (ed.) *The Science of Optimism and Hope: Research Essays in Honor of Martin E. P. Seligman.* Philadelphia, PA: Templeton Foundation Press.

Brookman-Frazee, L.I., Drahota, A., & Stadnick, N. (2012) "Training community mental health therapists to deliver a package of evidence-based practice strategies for school-age children with autism spectrum disorders: A pilot study." *Journal of Autism and Developmental Disorders 42*, 8, 1651–1661.

Brookman-Frazee, L.I., Stahmer, A., Baker-Ericzén, M., & Tsai, K. (2006) "Parenting interventions for children with autism spectrum and disruptive behavior disorders: Opportunities for cross-fertilization." *Clinical Child and Family Psychology Review 9*, 3, 181–200.

Bruininks, R.H., Woodcock, R.W., Weatherman, R.F., & Hill, B.K. (1996) *Scales of Independent Behavior – Revised.* Chicago, IL: Riverside Publishing Company.

Byrd, R.S. & Weitzman, M.L. (1994) "Predictors of early grade retention among children in the United States." *Pediatrics 93*, 481–487.

Carver, C.S. & Scheier, M.F. (1990) "Origins and functions of positive and negative affect: A control-process view." *Psychological Review 97*, 1, 19.

Dangel, R.F., Yu, M., Slot, N.W., & Fashinger, G. (1994) "Behavioral Parent Training." In D. Granold (ed.) *Cognitive and Behavioral Treatment: Methods and Applications.* Belmont, CA: Thompson Brooks/Cole.

Drew, A., Baird, G., Baron-Cohen, S., Cox, A., Slonims, V., Wheelwright, S., and Charman, T. (2002) "A pilot randomised control trial of a parent training intervention for pre-school children with autism." *European Child & Adolescent Psychiatry 11*, 6, 266–272.

Dumas, J.E., Wolf, L.C., Fisman, S.N., & Culligan, A. (1991) "Parenting stress, child behavior problems, and dysphoria in parents of children with autism, Down's syndrome, behavior disorders, and normal development." *Exceptionality 2*, 2, 97–110.

Dunlap, G., Kern-Dunlap, L., Clarke, S., & Robbins, F.R. (1991) "Functional assessment, curricular revision, and severe behavior problems." *Journal of Applied Behavior Analysis 24*, 387–397.

Durand, V.M. (1990) *Severe Behavior Problems: A Functional Communication Training Approach.* New York: Guilford Press.

Durand, V.M. (2001) "Future directions for children and adolescents with mental retardation." *Behavior Therapy 32*, 633–650.

Durand, V.M. (2011) *Optimistic Parenting: Hope and Help for You and Your Challenging Child.* Baltimore, MD: Paul H. Brookes.

Durand, V.M. & Hieneman, M. (2008a) *Helping Parents with Challenging Children: Positive Family Intervention, Facilitator's Guide.* New York: Oxford University Press.

Durand, V.M. & Hieneman, M. (2008b) *Helping Parents with Challenging Children: Positive Family Intervention, Workbook.* New York: Oxford University Press.

Durand, V.M. & Moskowitz, L. (2015) "Functional communication training: 30 years of treating challenging behavior." *Topics in Early Childhood Special Education 35,* 2, 116–126.

Durand, V.M. & Wang, M. (2011) "Clinical Trials." In J.C. Thomas & M. Hersen (eds) *Understanding Research in Clinical and Counseling Psychology.* New York: Routledge.

Emerson, E. & Einfeld, S.L. (eds) (2011) *Challenging Behaviour* (3rd ed.). Cambridge: Cambridge University Press.

Emily, D., Andrew, J., & Fiona, K. (2006) "Mothers' attributions following their child's diagnosis of autistic spectrum disorder: Exploring links with maternal levels of stress, depression and expectations about their child's future." *Autism 10,* 5, 463–479.

Evans, I.M. & Meyer, L.H. (1985) *An Educative Approach to Behavior Problems.* Baltimore, MD: Paul H. Brookes.

Feldman, M., McDonald, L., Serbin, L., Stack, D., Secco, M.L., & Yu, C.T. (2007) "Predictors of depressive symptoms in primary caregivers of young children with or at risk for developmental delay." *Journal of Intellectual Disability Research 51,* 8, 606–619.

Floyd, F.J. & Gallagher, E.M. (1997) "Parental stress, care demands and use of support services for school age children with disabilities and behavior problems." *Family Relations 46,* 4, 359–371.

Fox, L., Hemmeter, M.L., Snyder, P., Binder, D., & Clarke, S. (2011) "Coaching early childhood educators to implement a comprehensive model for the promotion of young children's social competence." *Topics in Early Childhood Special Education 31,* 178–192.

Fox, L., Vaughn, B.J., Wyatte, M.L., & Dunlap, G. (2002) "'We can't expect other people to understand': Family perspectives on problem behavior." *Exceptional Children 68,* 4, 437.

Friedrich, W.M., Greenberg, M.T., & Crnic, K. (1983) "A short form of the questionnaire on resources and stress." *American Journal of Mental Deficiency 88,* 41–48.

Gilliam, W.S. & Shahar, G. (2006) "Preschool and child care expulsion and suspension: Rates and predictors in one state." *Infants & Young Children 19,* 3, 228–245.

Gimpel, G.A. & Collett, B.R. (2002) "Best Practices in Behavioral Parent Training." In A. Thomas & J. Grimes (eds) *Best Practices in School Psychology* (Vol. 1). Washington, DC: National Association for School Psychologists.

Hassiotis, A., Parkes, C., Jones, L., Fitzgerald, B., & Romeo, R. (2008) "Individual characteristics and service expenditure on challenging behaviour for adults with intellectual disabilities." *Journal of Applied Research in Intellectual Disabilities 21,* 5, 438–445.

Hassiotis, A., Robotham, D., Canagasabey, A., Marston, L., Thomas, B., & King, M. (2011) "Impact of applied behaviour analysis (ABA) on carer burden and community participation in challenging behaviour: Results from a randomised controlled trial." *Journal of Intellectual Disability Research 56,* 285–290.

Hastings, R.P. (2002) "Parental stress and behaviour problems of children with developmental disability." *Journal of Intellectual and Developmental Disability 27,* 3, 149–160.

Hastings, R.P. & Johnson, E. (2001) "Stress in UK families conducting intensive home-based behavioural intervention for their young child with autism." *Journal of Autism and Developmental Disorders 31*, 327–336.

Hayes, S.A. & Watson, S.L. (2013) "The impact of parenting stress: A meta-analysis of studies comparing the experience of parenting stress in parents of children with and without Autism Spectrum Disorder." *Journal of Autism and Developmental Disorders 43*, 3, 629–642.

Hieneman, M., Childs, K., & Sergay, J. (2006) *Parenting with Positive Behavior Support: A Practical Guide to Resolving Your Child's Difficult Behavior.* Baltimore, MD: Paul H. Brookes.

Hodapp, R.M., Fidler, D., & Smith, A. (1998) "Stress and coping in families of children with Smith-Magenis syndrome." *Journal of Intellectual Disability Research 42*, 5, 331–340.

Hoffman, C.D., Sweeney, D.P., Hodge, D., Lopez-Wagner, M.C., & Looney, L. (2009) "Parenting stress and closeness: Mothers of typically developing children and mothers of children with autism." *Focus on Autism and Other Developmental Disabilities 24*, 3, 178–187.

Horner, R.H., Dunlap, G., Koegel, R.L., Carr, E.G., *et al.* (1990) "Toward a technology of 'nonaversive' behavioral support." *Journal of the Association for Persons with Severe Handicaps 15*, 125–132.

Johnson, C.R., Handen, B.L., Butter, E., Wagner, A., *et al.* (2007) "Development of a parent training program for children with pervasive developmental disorders." *Behavioral Interventions 22*, 3, 201–221.

Kazdin, A.E. (2008) "Evidence-based treatment and practice: New opportunities to bridge clinical research and practice, enhance the knowledge base, and improve patient care." *American Psychologist 63*, 3, 146–159.

Koegel, R., Bimbela, A., & Schreibman, L. (1996) "Collateral effects of parent training on family interactions." *Journal of Autism and Developmental Disorders 26*, 3, 347–359.

Konstantareas, M.M., Homatidis, S., & Plowright, C.M.S. (1992) "Assessing resources and stress in parents of severely dysfunctional children through the Clarke Modification of Holroyd's Questionnaire on Resources and Stress." *Journal of Autism and Developmental Disorders 22*, 217–234.

Lecavalier, L., Leone, S., & Wiltz, J. (2006) "The impact of behaviour problems on caregiver stress in young people with autism spectrum disorders." *Journal of Intellectual Disability Research 50*, 3, 172–183.

Maughan, D.R., Christiansen, E., & Jensen, W.R. (2005) "Behavioral parent training as a treatment for externalizing behavior and disruptive behavior disorders: A meta-analysis." *School Psychology Review 34*, 267–286.

Meirsschaut, M., Roeyers, H., & Warreyn, P. (2010) "Parenting in families with a child with autism spectrum disorder and a typically developing child: Mothers' experiences and cognitions." *Research in Autism Spectrum Disorders 4*, 4, 661–669.

Meyer, L.H. & Evans, I.M. (1989) *Nonaversive Intervention for Behavior Problems: A Manual for Home and Community.* Baltimore, MD: Paul H. Brookes.

Morrissey-Kane, E. & Prinz, R.J. (1999) "Engagement in child and adolescent treatment: The role of parental cognitions and attributions." *Clinical Child and Family Psychology Review 2*, 3, 183–198.

Ozonoff, S. & Cathcart, K. (1998) "Effectiveness of a home program intervention for young children with autism." *Journal of Autism and Developmental Disorder 28*, 1, 25–32.

Plant, K.M. & Sanders, M.R. (2007) "Reducing problem behavior during care-giving in families of preschool-aged children with developmental disabilities." *Research in Developmental Disabilities 28*, 4, 362–385.

Quinn, M., Carr, A., Carroll, L., & O'Sullivan, D. (2007) "Parents Plus Programme 1: Evaluation of its effectiveness for pre-school children with developmental disabilities and behavioural problems." *Journal of Applied Research in Intellectual Disabilities 20*, 4, 345–359.

Rao, P.A. & Beidel, D.C. (2009) "The impact of children with high-functioning autism on parental stress, sibling adjustment, and family functioning." *Behavior Modification 33*, 4, 437–451.

Saloviita, T., Italinna, M., & Leinonen, E. (2003) "Explaining the parental stress of fathers and mothers caring for a child with intellectual disability: A double ABCX model." *Journal of Intellectual Disability Research 47*, 4/5, 300–312.

Scott, R.L., Sexton, D., Thompson, B., & Wood, T.A. (1989) "Measurement characteristics of a short form of the Questionnaire on Resources and Stress." *American Journal on Mental Retardation 94*, 331–339.

Seligman, M.E.P. (1998) *Learned Optimism: How to Change Your Mind and Your Life.* New York: Pocket Books.

Seltzer, M.M., Greenberg, J.S., Hong, J., Smith, L.E., Almeida, D.M., Coe, C., & Stawski, R.S. (2010) "Maternal cortisol levels and behavior problems in adolescents and adults with ASD." *Journal of Autism and Developmental Disorders 40*, 4, 457–469.

Serketich, W.J. & Dumas, J.E. (1996) "The effectiveness of behavioral parent training to modify antisocial behavior in children: A meta-analysis." *Behavior Therapy 27*, 171–186.

Shapiro, C.J., Kilburn, J., & Hardin, J.W. (2014) "Prevention of behavior problems in a selected population: Stepping Stones Triple P for parents of young children with disabilities." *Research in Developmental Disabilities 35*, 11, 2958–2975.

Shoham-Vardi, I., Davidson, P.W., Cain, N.N., Sloane-Reeves, J.E., Giesow, V.E., Quijano, L.E., & Houser, K.D. (1996) "Factors predicting re-referral following crisis intervention for community-based persons with developmental disabilities and behavioral and psychiatric disorders." *American Journal on Mental Retardation 101*, 109–117.

Smith, L., Hong, J., Seltzer, M., Greenberg, J., Almeida, D., & Bishop, S. (2010) "Daily experiences among mothers of adolescents and adults with autism spectrum disorder." *Journal of Autism and Developmental Disorders 40*, 2, 167–178.

Steiner, A.M., Koegel, L.K., Koegel, R.L., & Ence, W.A. (2011) "Issues and theoretical constructs regarding parent education for autism spectrum disorders." *Journal of Autism and Developmental Disorders 41*, 1, 1–10.

Totsika, V., Toogood, S., Hastings, R.P., & Lewis, S. (2008) "Persistence of challenging behaviours in adults with intellectual disability over a period of 11 years." *Journal of Intellectual Disability Research 52*, 5, 446–457.

US Department of Health and Human Services and US Department of Education (2014) *Policy Statement on Expulsion and Suspension Policies in Early Childhood Settings.* Retrieved on January 30, 2018 from www2.ed.gov/policy/gen/guid/school-discipline/policy-statement-ece-expulsions-suspensions.pdf

Whittingham, K., Sofronoff, K., & Sheffield, J.K. (2006) "Stepping Stones Triple P: A pilot study to evaluate the acceptability of the program by parents of a child diagnosed with an autism spectrum disorder." *Research in Developmental Disabilities 27*, 4, 364–380.

Whittingham, K., Sofronoff, K., Sheffield, J., & Sanders, M.R. (2009) "Do parental attributions affect treatment outcome in a parenting program? An exploration of the effects of parental attributions in an RCT of Stepping Stones Triple P for the ASD population." *Research in Autism Spectrum Disorders 3*, 1, 129–144.

Chapter 3

INCREDIBLE YEARS® PARENT TRAINING FOR FAMILIES WITH CHILDREN WITH DEVELOPMENTAL DISABILITIES

Laura Lee McIntyre and Mallory Brown

ABSTRACT

Webster-Stratton's Incredible Years® Parent Training (IYPT) program is a well-established prevention and treatment program for children with externalizing behavior problems. This chapter reviews the evidence for IYPT for children with intellectual and developmental disabilities, including autism spectrum disorder. We identified 11 published studies that used IYPT for these populations and report on the design features, outcomes, and limitations of the extant literature. Although there is a growing body of research using IYPT to treat child behavior problems, improve parenting practices, and reduce psychological distress in parents of children with disabilities, the current literature is lacking in rigorous evaluations of the intervention. Following a review of the published studies in this area, we describe an ongoing randomized controlled trial of IYPT that addresses some of the research limitations and offer our recommendations for practice and future research. These practice and research recommendations are aimed at improving services for children with intellectual and developmental disabilities and ultimately improving child and family well-being.

Keywords: Incredible Years® Parent Training; intellectual and developmental disabilities; autism spectrum disorder; challenging behavior; parenting; best practices

Introduction of the model
Overview of the Incredible Years®

In the 1980s, Carolyn Webster-Stratton developed a parent training program, the Incredible Years® Parent Training series (IYPT), which has been demonstrated to be more effective than control treatments in eight randomized trials and six independent replication studies in reducing children's maladaptive behavior and increasing parents' adaptive parenting skills (e.g., Webster-Stratton, 1984, 1994, 2000). Webster-Stratton's parent training series utilizes videotape modeling, using parent/child models, role playing, rehearsal, and weekly homework activities in small groups of 8–14 parents (see Webster-Stratton, 2000, for a review).

IYPT is an evidence-based parent training program based on principles of operant and social learning theories and is designed to be delivered in approximately 12 weekly sessions. Group leaders use discussion, video modeling, role playing, and didactics to cover topics in five main areas: play, praise, rewards, limit setting, and handling challenging behavior. Challenging behavior is reduced through altering negative and coercive parent–child interactions, which are implicated in the development and maintenance of aggressive and oppositional behavior in children and youth (Webster-Stratton, 2001).

In addition to targeting clinical samples of children with conduct problems, Webster-Stratton and her colleagues have used IYPT with families who have children at-risk for adverse academic-socio-behavioral outcomes, due in part to their poverty status (Gross, *et al.*, 2003; Webster-Stratton, Reid, & Hammond, 2001). Webster-Stratton has also added teacher and child skill-building components to the training series, which makes the model not only an efficacious treatment for children with conduct problems, but also a useful prevention technique for high-risk children and families. The Division 12 (clinical psychology) task force of the American Psychological Association deemed Webster-Stratton's Incredible Years® series as a well-established psychosocial treatment for childhood conduct problems (Brestan & Eyberg, 1998; Eyberg, Nelson, & Boggs, 2008), based on effect sizes, sampling, methodology, treatment integrity, and a host of other criteria (Lonigan, Elbert, & Johnson, 1998).

The IYPT series primarily focuses on caregivers of children aged 3–8 years with or at-risk for challenging behavior. The program has been used with preschool children at-risk for social, behavioral, and academic problems (e.g., Head Start samples, Webster-Stratton, Reid, & Stoolmiller, 2008), children with externalizing behavior disorders (Menting, Orobio de Castro, & Matthys, 2013), and children with developmental risk, including intellectual and developmental disabilities (IDD) (e.g., McIntyre, 2008a, 2008b), and autism spectrum disorder (e.g., Dababnah & Parish, 2014, 2016).

This chapter focuses on the IYPT delivery in samples of children with IDD and ASD. The IYPT model has been delivered with slight modifications for parents of children developmental disabilities (e.g., Dababnah & Parish, 2014; McIntyre, 2008a), as well as delivered in its standard format (e.g., Kleve *et al.*, 2011). Below, we review and summarize published studies that have used IYPT for children with or at-risk for IDD and ASD.

Evidence for the mModel
Sample
A total of 11 published studies (see Table 3.1) have investigated the effects of the IYPT in families with children with IDD and ASD (Barton & Lissman, 2015; Dababnah & Parish, 2014, 2016; George, Kidd, & Brack, 2011; Hutchings *et al.*, 2016; Kleve *et al.*, 2011; McIntyre, 2008a, 2008b; Phaneuf & McIntyre, 2007, 2011; Roberts & Pickering, 2010). Of the 11 studies, 8 focused exclusively on parents with preschool-aged children (Barton & Lissman, 2015; Dababnah & Parish, 2014, 2016; Hutchings *et al.*, 2016; McIntyre, 2008a, 2008b; Phaneuf & McIntyre, 2007, 2011). The other 3 studies focused on both early- and middle-childhood-aged children (George *et al.*, 2011; Kleve *et al.*, 2011; Roberts & Pickering, 2010). Of the 11 studies, 4 focused exclusively on children with ASD (Dababnah & Parish, 2014, 2016; Hutchings *et al.*, 2016; Roberts & Pickering, 2010), while the remaining 7 studies included a range of intellectual and developmental delay and disabilities, including ASD (Barton & Lissman, 2015; George *et al.*, 2011; Kleve *et al.*, 2011; McIntyre, 2008a, 2008b; Phaneuf & McIntyre, 2007, 2011). Taken together, the evidence is strongest for preschool-aged children with a range of intellectual and developmental disabilities. The support of IYPT for children with ASD is growing; however, the extant literature has focused on small-scale feasibility studies only with this population.

Table 3.1 Incredible Years® Parent Training (IYPT) intervention studies for child challenging behavior in children with DD (*n* = 10)

Study	Target group	Sample size	Intervention	Design/Approach	Dependent variables	Key outcomes
Barton & Lissman (2015)	Parents of 3–5-year-old children with DD	*n* = 2 No attrition reported	• Modified version of IYPT (as modified by EI agency, not researchers) with the addition of individualized coaching (provided by researchers) • Group-based plus individual coaching intervention	• Single case design; multiple baseline across behaviors • No procedural fidelity reported	• Observed parenting behaviors • Observed child behaviors • Child social emotional development (ASQ:SE) • Caregiver self-efficacy (adapted from PSOC)	• Increase in observed positive parenting practices • Increase in parenting self-efficacy • No changes in observed child behavior • Improvements in child social emotional development (reductions in challenging behaviors)
Dababnah & Parish (2014)	Parents of 3–6-year-old children with ASD	*n* = 17 Attrition 18%	• IYPT, with ASD Modifications • Group-based intervention	• Group design • No control group • No procedural fidelity reported	• Parent-reported treatment acceptability (weekly and post-intervention) • Parent-reported parent stress (PSI-IV) • Parent-reported child concerns (PSI-IV)	• Post-intervention, parents reported: • Decreased parent stress • Decreased child-related concerns, including distractibility/hyperactivity, adaptability, reinforces parent, mood, and acceptability • High treatment acceptability
Dababnah & Parish (2016)	Parents of 3–6-year-old children with ASD	*n* = 17 Attrition 18%	• IYPT, with ASD Modifications • Group-based intervention	• Group design • No control group • Procedural fidelity reported	• Treatment fidelity of program components	• Treatment fidelity data collected weekly show high fidelity and suggest feasibility of treatment implementation

Study	Participants	Intervention	Design	Measures	Outcomes
George, Kidd, & Brack (2011)	Parents of children with moderate to severe learning disabilities (M age = 6.25 years)	n = 5 (four children participants, as two carers attended for the same child); n = 2 for observational data study; Attrition 44%	• Incredible Years® Parent Training, with Modifications from Confident Parent Programme (HEADS, 2009) and Webster-Stratton's advanced program	• Small group/pilot design • No control group • No procedural fidelity reported	• Observed parent–child interactions • Parent-reported parent stress (QRS-F) • Parent-reported child behavior problems (DBC) • Consumer satisfaction (CSQ; Forehand & McMahon) and weekly feedback	• Decrease in observed negative parent–child interactions • Increase in observed positive parent–child interactions • Decrease in parent-reported stress
Hutchings et al. (2016)	Parents of preschool children with ASD	n = 9 Attrition 22%	• Incredible Years® Autism Spectrum and Language Delays Program	• Group design • No control group • No procedural fidelity reported	• Observed parent–child interactions (DPICS) • Parent-reported parenting behavior (AOPS) • Parent-reported well-being (WEMWBS) • Parent-reported child behavior (SDQ) • Parent-reported Autism Impact Measure (AIM) • Consumer satisfaction and weekly feedback	• Parents satisfied with program • No pre-post differences on parent-reported parenting behavior and well-being scales • Significant pre-post reductions on peer problems and improvements on pro-social skills on SDQ • No pre-post difference on the Autism Impact Measure • No pre-post difference on observed parent–child interactions
Kleve et al. (2011)	Parents of 2–11-year-old children with a range of neuro-developmental disorders and challenging behavior	n = 128 Attrition 31%	• IYPT • Group-based intervention	• Group design • No control group • No procedural fidelity reported	• Parent-reported behavior problems (ECBI) • Visual analogue scales	• Post-intervention, parents reported: • Decreased problem behavior

Study	Target group	Sample size	Intervention	Design/Approach	Dependent variables	Key outcomes
McIntyre (2008a)	Parents of 2–5-year-old children with IDD, including ASD	$n = 25$ Attrition 11%	• IYPT–DD Modifications • Group-based intervention	• Group design • No control group • Parent–child interaction observations scored by coders naive to study goals • Treatment integrity reported • RCI analysis • Analysis of correlates of change	• Parent-reported behavior problems (CBCL) • Observed parent–child interactions • Parent-reported impact of the child on family (FIQ) • Parent-reported depression (CES-D) • Consumer Satisfaction	Post-intervention: • Decreases in observed child problem behavior and negative parenting • Increase in parent-reported positive impact of the child • No significant changes in parent-reported behavior problems, child negative impact, or maternal depression
McIntyre (2008b)	Parents of 2–5-year-old children with IDD, including ASD	$n = 49$ $n = 24$ IYPT-DD $n = 25$ usual care control Attrition 10%	• IYPT–DD Modifications (IYPT-DD) • Group-based intervention	• Randomized control trial • Blinded evaluation • Procedural fidelity reported	• Parent-reported behavior problems (CBCL) • Observed parent–child interactions • Parent-reported impact of the child on family (FIQ)	• Post-intervention, children in IYPT-DD group showed: • Reductions in observed problem behavior and parent-reported problem behavior • Reductions in observed negative parenting • No treatment effect on parent-reported impact of the child on family
Phaneuf & McIntyre (2007)	Parents of 2–4-year-old children with DD	$n = 4$ No attrition reported	• Group-based program (IYPT-DD) • Individual sessions with video feedback	• Single case design; multiple baseline across mother–child dyads • Treatment integrity reported	• Observed parenting behavior	

Study	Sample / Attrition	Intervention	Design	Measures	Outcomes
Phaneuf & McIntyre (2011)	Parents of 2–4-year-old children with IDD, including ASD n = 8 Attrition 25% pre-follow-up	• Three-tier model of interventions based on the Incredible Years[a] • Self-administered • Group-based program (IYPT-DD) • Individual sessions with video feedback and modeling	• Single case design • Used parents' response to intervention to inform treatment • 3-month follow-up • Treatment integrity reported	• Parent-reported child behavior problems (CBCL) • Observed child problem behavior • Observed parenting behavior • Consumer satisfaction	• Decreased parent-reported child problem behavior • Decreased observed child problem behavior • Decreased observed negative parenting behavior
Roberts & Pickering (2010)	Parents of children with ASD, social communication and conduct problems (M age of 8) n = 8 Attrition not reported	• IYPT (with discussion of applying program content to children with ASD)	• Group design • No control group	• Parent-reported mental health (GHQ-30) • Parent-reported behavior problems (ECBI) • Parent-reported child's social anxiety (SWQ) • Parent-reported child's social communication difficulties (ASAS)	• Decreased parent-reported stress • Decreased parent-reported child behavior problems • No changes in parent-reported child social anxiety or social communication difficulties

Note. AIM = Autism Impact Measure (Kanne *et al.*, 2014); AOPS = Arnold O'Leary Parenting Scale (Arnold *et al.*, 1993); ASD = autism spectrum disorder; ASAS = Australian Scale for Asperger's Syndrome (Garnett & Attwood, 1988); ASQ-SE = Ages and Stages Questionnaire—Social-Emotional (Squires *et al.*, 2002); CBCL = Child Behavior Checklist (Achenbach, 2000); CES-D = Center for Epidemiology–Depression (Radloff, 1977); CSQ = Consumer Satisfaction Questionnaire (CSQ; Forehand & McMahon, 1981); DBC = Developmental Behaviour Checklist (Einfeld & Tonge, 1994); DPICS = Dyadic Parent–child Interaction Coding System (Eyberg & Robinson, 1981); ECBI = Eyberg Child Behavior Inventory (Eyberg & Pincus, 1999); EI = early intervention; FIQ = Family Impact Questionnaire (Donenberg & Baker, 1993); GHQ-30 = General Health Questionnaire-30 (Goldberg & Williams, 1988); IDD = intellectual and developmental disabilities; IYPT-DD = Incredible Years' Parent Training with Developmental Disabilities Modification (McIntyre, 2008a); PSI-IV = Parenting Stress Index, 4th Edition (Abidin, 2012); PSOC = Parenting Sense of Competence Scale (Johnston & Mash, 1989); QRS-F = Questionnaire on Resources and Stress—Family (Friedrich *et al.*, 1983); RCI = Reliable Change Index (Jacobson & Truax, 1991); SDQ = Strengths and Difficulties Questionnaire (Goodman, 1997); SWQ = Social Worries Questionnaire (Spence, 1995); WEMWS = Warwick Edinburgh Mental Well-being Scale (Tennant *et al.*, 2007).

Outcome variables

Although the majority of studies have included child problem behavior as a primary outcome, a number of studies also include parenting behavior, parent mental health, and treatment acceptability and fidelity as important outcomes. The evidence for IYPT on various outcome variables for children with IDD and their caregivers is described below.

Child problem behavior

Nine studies investigated the effects of Webster-Stratton's IYPT on behavior problems in children with IDD (Barton & Lissman, 2015; Dababnah & Parish, 2014; George *et al.*, 2011; Hutchings *et al.*, 2016; Kleve *et al.*, 2011; McIntyre, 2008a, 2008b; Phaneuf & McIntyre, 2011; Roberts & Pickering, 2010). McIntyre (2008a; 2008b; Phaneuf & McIntyre, 2011) used an adapted version of the Incredible Years® for use with parents of children with DD (IYPT-DD; McIntyre, 2008a). Phaneuf and McIntyre (2011) incorporated a three-tiered model of intervention (see McIntyre & Phaneuf, 2008) that increased the intensity of support depending on parents' responsiveness to intervention. The three tiers of intervention evaluated by Phaneuf and McIntyre included self-administered reading materials (based on the *Incredible Years®: A Trouble-Shooting Guide for Parents of Children Aged 2–8 Years*; Webster-Stratton, 2005), group-based parenting training based on the Incredible Years® with DD modifications (IYPT-DD), and individualized video feedback based on the behavioral skills training literature (e.g., Himle *et al.*, 2004) with content covering the IYPT-DD (see also Phaneuf & McIntyre, 2007).

Findings from McIntyre (2008b; Phaneuf & McIntyre, 2011) suggest a reduction in parent-reported behavior problems on the Child Behavior Checklist (Achenbach, 2000) in preschool-aged children with IDD following IYPT intervention. In addition to parent reports of problem behavior, McIntyre (2008a) and Phaneuf and McIntyre (2011) also included direct observations of child problem behavior during a home-based parent–child interaction task. Findings from McIntyre (2008a) and Phaneuf and McIntyre (2011) suggest a significant reduction in observed child problem behavior following IYPT intervention.

Kleve *et al.* (2011) and Roberts and Pickering (2010) used the standard IYPT group-based intervention and found significant reductions in parent-reported problem behavior on the Eyberg Child Behavior Inventory (ECBI; Eyberg & Pincus, 1999). Barton and Lissman (2015) used a modified version of IYPT involving the addition of individualized coaching sessions to the group-based parent training program. Barton and Lissman (2015) report reductions in parent-reported challenging behavior on the Ages and Stages Questionnaire: Social Emotional (ASQ:SE; Squires, Bricker, & Twombly, 2002); however, there were no changes in observed child behavior. George *et al.* (2011) used a modified version of IYPT, which included modifications from Confident Parent Programme (HEADS, 2009) and use of Webster-Stratton's advanced program (Webster-Stratton, 2002). The George *et al.* findings suggest no significant changes in parent-reported behavior problems on the Developmental Behavioral Checklist (Einfeld & Tonge, 1994). The results of Dababnah and Parish (2014) suggest that parents reported fewer child-related concerns on the Parenting Stress Index-IV (Abidin, 2012) following intervention. Hutchings *et al.* (2016) report significant pre-to-post-intervention improvements in parent-reported social skills and reductions of peer problems in children with ASD. Taken together, eight of the nine studies report reductions in child behavior problems through either parent-reported measures or observed child behavior.

Parenting behavior

Of the 11 studies that use IYPT with caregivers of children with IDD or ASD, 6 included parenting behavior as a target of intervention (Barton & Lissman, 2015; George *et al.*, 2011; Hutchings *et al.*, 2016; McIntyre, 2008a, 2008b; Phaneuf & McIntyre, 2011). Barton and Lissman (2015) report an increase in observed positive parenting practices following IYPT and individual coaching sessions. George *et al.* (2011) report decreases in observed negative parent–child interactions and increases in observed positive parent–child interactions following intervention. McIntyre (2008a, 2008b) and Phaneuf and McIntyre (2011) report reductions in observed negative parenting behavior following intervention. Hutchings *et al.* (2016) reported no changes in observed parenting behavior or reported parenting practices. Of note is that all 6 studies used direct observations of parenting behavior during parent–child interaction tasks. Taken together, these studies suggest a positive effect on improving parenting behavior during observed parent–child interaction tasks.

Parent mental health

Of the 11 studies that use IYPT with caregivers of children IDD or ASD, 7 of them included parent self-efficacy, parenting stress, depression, or other mental health outcome in parents. Barton and Lissman (2015) report an increase in parents' reported self-efficacy on the Parenting Sense of Competence Scale (Johnston & Mash, 1989) following intervention. Dababnah and Parish (2014) investigated the effects of the IYPT with ASD modifications on parent-reported stress using the Parenting Stress Index (PSI-IV; Abidin, 2012). Following intervention, Dababnah and Parish (2014) report reductions in parenting stress on the PSI-IV. Similarly, George et al. (2011) report reductions in parenting stress on the short form of the Questionnaire on Resources and Stress-Family (QRS-SF; Friedrich, Greenberg, & Crnic, 1983) following intervention. Hutchings et al. (2016) did not report significant improvements in parent well-being following the Incredible Years® Autism Spectrum and Language Delays Program intervention in caregivers of preschoolers with ASD. McIntyre (2008a) investigated the effects of IYPT-DD on child positive and negative impact on family and caregiver depression. McIntyre (2008a) found no significant changes in child negative impact on family and caregiver depression; however, there was a significant increase in parent-reported positive impact of the child on the family using the Family Impact Questionnaire (FIQ; Donenberg & Baker, 1993). In a follow-up study, McIntyre found no significant changes in positive or negative impact of the child on the family using the FIQ (McIntyre, 2008b). Roberts and Pickering (2010) investigated the extent to which intervention was associated with reductions in parent-reported stress. They reported that there was a significant decrease in parent-reported stress using the parent-reported General Health Questionnaire (GHQ-30; Goldberg & Williams, 1988). Taken together, the literature is mixed on whether IYPT results in reduction of parenting stress and mental health problems.

Social validity and treatment fidelity

Of the 11 studies using IYPT with parents of children with IDD or ASD, only 5 studies reported data on consumer satisfaction or intervention acceptability (Dababnah & Parish, 2014; George *et al.*, 2011; Hutchings *et al.*, 2016; McIntyre, 2008a; Phaneuf & McIntyre, 2011). Findings from these studies suggest high treatment acceptability. Of the 11 studies using IYPT with parents of children with IDD or ASD, 5 reported data on procedural fidelity/treatment integrity (Dababnah & Parish, 2016; McIntyre, 2008a, 2008b; Phaneuf & McIntyre, 2007, 2011). Results from studies reporting treatment integrity data suggest that IYPT can be implemented accurately in community contexts.

Study methodological features
Design and sample size

Three of the eleven studies used single-case research designs to evaluate the effects of IYPT on various child and parent outcomes (Barton & Lissman, 2015; Phaneuf & McIntyre, 2007; Phaneuf & McIntyre, 2011). Barton and Lissman (2015) and Phaneuf and McIntyre (2007) used multiple baseline designs and Phaneuf and McIntyre (2011) used a changing conditions design. The remaining 8 studies used group designs to investigate the effects of IYPT on child and parent outcomes (Dababnah & Parish, 2014, 2016; George *et al.*, 2011; Hutchings *et al.*, 2016; Kleve *et al.*, 2011; McIntyre, 2008a, 2008b; Roberts & Pickering, 2010). The sample size for the group designs varied substantially. For example, Kleve *et al.* (2011) included a sample size of 128 parents and George *et al.* (2011) reported a sample size of 5. Although eight studies used group designs to investigate the effects of IYPT on child and parent outcomes, only one study (McIntyre, 2008b) used a control group and random assignment to intervention or control condition. Single-group pre-post designs have methodological problems that threaten internal validity (Campbell & Stanley, 1963). Taken as a whole, the literature on the use of IYPT with children with IDD or ASD is limited by the design flaws inherent in group designs that do not include control or comparison groups and do not randomize to condition.

Attrition

Sample attrition was reported in 8 of the 11 studies using IYPT with parents of children with IDD or ASD (Dababnah & Parish, 2014, 2016; George *et al.*, 2011; Hutchings *et al.*, 2016; Kleve *et al.*, 2011; McIntyre, 2008a, 2008b; Phaneuf & McIntyre, 2011). Attrition rates were variable, with a low of 10% (McIntyre, 2008b) and a high of 44% (George *et al.*, 2011). High rates of attrition can limit the extent to which findings can generalize to other samples and settings but may also be a reality when working with high-risk community samples of families.

Generalization/maintenance

None of the 11 studies reported intervention effects that generalized to other behaviors, settings, or informants. For example, teacher (or other caregiver) reports of child challenging behavior were not included, nor were generalization effects across important domains (e.g., setting). Only one study (Phaneuf & McIntyre, 2007) included a three-month follow-up data collection. Barton and Lissman (2015) included two follow-up data points immediately after the parent coaching phase of their multiple baseline design. Taken together, evidence is lacking in support of generalization or long-term treatment effects of IYPT on child or parent outcomes in families with children with IDD or ASD.

Interobserver agreement

Of the 11 studies, 6 included direct observations of parent–child interactions (Barton & Lissman, 2015; George *et al.*, 2011; Hutchings *et al.*, 2016; McIntyre, 2008a, 2008b; Phaneuf & McIntyre, 2011). Parenting behaviors were observed and coded using three frameworks (i.e., a framework developed by Phaneuf & McIntyre, 2007, a framework developed by Barton & Lissman, 2015, and the Dyadic Parent–Child Interaction Coding System developed by Eyberg & Robinson, 1981). Of these 6 studies, 4 (Barton & Lissman, 2015; McIntyre, 2008a, 2008b; Phaneuf & McIntyre, 2011) included evidence of reliability of observations, by reporting adequate levels of interobserver agreement on parent–child interactions and discrete parent and child behavior. Taken together, these studies demonstrate the reliability of direct observation strategies for capturing parenting behavior and parent–child interactions taken during naturalistic play tasks.

Below, we provide additional detail and description of IYPT with modifications made to support parents of children with IDD and ASD. The IYPT-DD modifications (McIntyre, 2008a) are described, followed by an overview and description of an ongoing, large-scale randomized controlled trial evaluating the efficacy of IYPT-DD.

Full description of the Model
Modifications

Before modifying the IYPT for use with parents of preschool children with developmental delays, McIntyre received training from certified *Incredible Years®* trainers on the implementation of the program and conducted a pilot intervention group. The purpose of the pilot was to become more familiar with the procedures and seek input from caregivers of children with DD regarding which aspects of the program were most acceptable to them. Furthermore, input from community stakeholders (e.g., preschool teachers, early childhood specialists, therapists, and parents attending support groups for ID) was solicited regarding the most applicable components of the program for families with children with DD. Behavioral theory, specifically the contributions of applied behavior analysis, guided the modifications. Throughout the sessions and content covered, developmentally appropriate practices were emphasized. Parents were encouraged to think about how the general topics applied to their specific children.

Based on pilot work and input from stakeholders, a slightly modified IYPT for children with developmental delays (IYPT-DD) was developed (McIntyre, 2008a). Table 3.2 provides the session topics and a brief description of modifications and Table 3.3 lists key elements and procedural considerations. Webster-Stratton's main content areas of play, praise, rewards, limit setting, and handling challenging behaviors were retained; however, the toddler program modifications (see Webster-Stratton, 2001) were followed due to the chronological and developmental age of the children. In addition to the scripted discussion questions used for each vignette (see Webster-Stratton, 2001), all parents were encouraged to identify the key points that could be generalized to their children with developmental delay and were asked to identify which aspects of the vignettes did not relate. Additional modifications included: having parents identify blessings and challenges of raising a child with a delay, in addition to articulating their goals for the series (session 1); excluding the content on timeout, due to the age and developmental level of the children, and focusing on predicting and avoiding problem behavior by collecting information on antecedents and consequences to their child's problem behaviors (sessions 6–7); and, providing informational handouts to parents on disability-related support groups and advocacy organizations in the community (session 10). Each group session had approximately 12–14 parent participants and two group leaders/facilitators (Master's-level therapists).

The size of the groups was kept small, according to recommended practices by Webster-Stratton (2001), and caregivers were encouraged to bring a partner/friend. Further, parents played a collaborative role with the group facilitator (Webster-Stratton, 1994; Webster-Stratton & Herbert, 1993). The parent training groups were structured around videotape vignettes and utilized discussion, role playing, modeling, and feedback techniques to foster mastery of the presented materials (see Webster-Stratton, 2001). Parents had an opportunity to practice their skills each week through homework assignments.

Table 3.2 Session topics and modifications for parents of preschool children with IDD

Session	Topic	Modifications
1	Introduction & goals	Blessings and challenges of raising a child with special needs.
2	Developmentally appropriate play—I	Consider child's developmental level, interests, and support needs. When viewing vignettes, consider which aspects apply to children with DD and which do not.
3	Developmentally appropriate play—II	Consider child's developmental level, interests, and support needs. When viewing vignettes, consider which aspects apply to children with DD and which do not.
4	Positive strategies—Praise	Consider child's developmental level, interests, and support needs. When viewing vignettes, consider which aspects apply to children with DD and which do not.

5	Positive strategies— Rewards	Discuss altering traditional token economy systems and sticker charts to children's developmental levels. Discuss conducting preference assessments to identify possible reinforcers.
6	Handling challenging behaviors	Discuss conducting functional assessment (using antecedents, behaviors, and consequences). Complete ABC chart.
7	Handling challenging behaviors	Developing behavioral intervention plans based on results of FBAs. Discuss functionally equivalent replacement behaviors.
8	Effective limit setting—Part I (Commands)	Consider child's developmental level, interests, and support needs. When viewing vignettes, consider which aspects apply to children with DD and which do not.
9	Effective limit setting—Part II (Ignoring and redirecting)	Consider child's developmental level, interests, and support needs. When viewing vignettes, consider which aspects apply to children with DD and which do not.
10	Advocacy, working with professionals, and transition to kindergarten	Discuss services provided through local agencies. Discuss strategies for engaging in meaningful parent–professional partnerships. Discuss special education law and issues pertaining to transition from preschool to elementary school.
11	Review: Challenging behavior and limit setting	Review material discussed to date, emphasizing content from sessions 6–9.
12	Putting it all together/ celebration	No modifications made.

Note: The toddler program modifications were followed (see Webster-Stratton, 2001), in addition to the DD modifications.
Source: McIntyre (2008a, p.1184)

Table 3.3 Key procedural elements for IYPT-DD

Key elements	Description
Rapport building	A collaborative style is taken whereby the group leaders acknowledge their expertise and the expertise that the caregivers bring. Kindness, empathy, and perspective-taking all help establish rapport and trust with participants. The group leaders ensure that all caregivers have opportunities to share and that no single person dominates the discussion. Rapport is built throughout the weekly sessions.

Key elements	Description
Introductions and goal setting	During the first session, the group leaders ask each parent to provide a brief introduction and state a few goals related to participating in IYPT-DD. Notes are written on the board. Following this exercise, blessings and challenges of raising a child with a disability are discussed as a group. Responses are written on the board.
Ground rules	Ground rules are established during the first session. The group facilitator leads the discussion and ensures that the ground rules reflect shared values, privacy, and dignity of group members. Example rules include begin and end on time, one person talks at a time, everybody has the right to pass, and we keep other peoples' information private. Ground rules are posted weekly and referred to as needed to redirect discussion.
Benefits and barriers activity	This activity is used each week when a new topic is being introduced. The group facilitator leads a discussion with caregivers to brainstorm the barriers and benefits of engaging in particular parenting behaviors (such as playing, setting limits, etc.) Notes are taken on the board.
Vignettes and discussion	Each week, the group facilitator leads a discussion of videotaped clips of parent–child interactions. Scripted questions that correspond to each video-clip are designed to facilitate discussion and the identification of key content points for the session.
Role playing	Role plays are intended to provide practice to caregivers learning to implement particular strategies. Group leaders provide supportive feedback to caregivers and group leaders ask pointed questions to increase caregivers' understanding and reflection. Example questions include, "What did that feel like when you followed your child's lead in play?" or "What changes did you notice in your child's behavior when you used specific praise?"
Homework	At the end of each session, the group leaders describe the home activities for the week and address caregiver questions. The group leaders instruct caregivers to identify a goal for completing homework and tracking the goal in the individual self-monitoring checklist. Homework is briefly reviewed at the beginning of the following week.
Weekly evaluation	At the conclusion of each session, caregivers are asked to complete a four-question evaluation, covering content, video examples, group leader's teaching, and discussion, using a 4-point scale. There is also a space for open-ended comments. The weekly evaluation data serves as a means for facilitators to hear from caregivers regarding what is more and less helpful each week. It is also a way to hear from caregivers directly if they are experiencing difficulties.
Meal/snack break	A 15–20-minute food break midway through allows participants to eat, use the restroom, and, if needed, check on their children in the childcare facilities. Facilitators may resume the class while caregivers are finishing up their meal.

Weekly check-ins	Facilitators should plan to call, email, or text caregivers at least once per week. These brief check-ins serve as a reminder for the upcoming class, but, beyond that, allow the facilitator to hear how the caregiver's week has been going, how the homework completion is coming along, and generally build rapport outside of the group sessions.
Buddy calls	Beginning session 4, caregivers are assigned to serve as buddies for their peers. Buddies are assigned by the facilitator, not selected by the participating caregiver. Time in group is set aside to exchange contact information and develop a plan for connecting each week. Some caregivers prefer text messaging, while others prefer a phone call after their children are in bed. Buddy calls do not replace the group leader weekly check-in.
Final celebration and follow-up	The final celebration occurs during the last group meeting and is designed to serve as a review of all content and a graduation ceremony for participants. Certificates of completion are given and awards for perfect attendance can be given. A special meal can be provided instead of the usual snack/meal. Often, caregivers wish to exchange contact information and continue to meet informally for social support. The group leader can pass around a contact information list so that caregivers can provide their contact details.

Source: Adapted from Webster-Stratton (2001)

Setting

IYPT-DD, like the original IYPT, is intended to be delivered in community settings, such as schools, churches, or community centers. Settings that have meeting space for the parent group as well as childcare space (e.g., gymnasium, classroom, playground area) are ideal. Given that intervention sessions are traditionally offered in the evening with food provided to participants, access to a kitchen is helpful. Thus, a church or school with classroom space, a cafeteria or kitchen, and parent meeting room is ideal. Intervention sessions involve watching and discussing videotaped vignettes pre-recorded on DVD. Thus, access to a DVD player and television monitor is essential.

Dosage

IYPT-DD sessions are intended to occur weekly for 12 consecutive weeks. Session duration is approximately two-and-a-half hours (inclusive of a short break for a meal or snack). The break is an important opportunity for group facilitators to informally check in with participants and have one-on-one conversations with them about topics relevant to the program. Intervention dosage is approximately 25 hours, spread over three months.

Training paradigm

The primary training paradigm used in IYPT-DD is therapist-facilitated discussion based on session topics, goals, and objectives. Each session has an agenda that includes topics, activities (review of previous content and home activities, introduction to the session topics, benefits and barriers discussion activity, vignette viewing, discussion question, active practice/role-playing), review of key points, and discussion of the week's home activities. Group facilitators are trained to be empathetic, collaborative, and supportive, while keeping discussion meaningful and on-task.

Measures

An adaptation of the Consumer Satisfaction Questionnaire (CSQ; Forehand & McMahon, 1981) is commonly used with IYPT-DD to assess parents' perceptions of the group leader's effectiveness, the group dynamics, the videotape vignettes, the usefulness of content covered, and the effectiveness of the program's methods. This adaptation of the CSQ has been used extensively for evaluating parents' satisfaction with the IYPT series (Reid, Webster-Stratton, & Beauchaine, 2001; Webster-Stratton, 1994, 1998; Webster-Stratton, Hollinsworth, & Kolpacoff, 1989), and has been used with caregivers of children with IDD (McIntyre, 2008a, 2008b; Phaneuf & McIntyre, 2007, 2011). In addition to the consumer satisfaction questionnaire administered at the conclusion of the 12-week intervention, parent feedback during weekly sessions is typically obtained regarding the session content, videotape vignettes, teaching, and group discussion. This weekly evaluation feedback has been used successfully in McIntyre's work (e.g., McIntyre, 2008a, 2008b; Phaneuf & McIntyre, 2007, 2011).

Fidelity

Given the manualized nature of IYPT and the adaptations developed by McIntyre (IYPT-DD; McIntyre, 2008a), procedural fidelity is relatively simple to track. McIntyre (2008a, 2008b; Phaneuf & McIntyre, 2007, 2011) created checklists for each session and had group facilitators self-monitor using the checklists indicating the number of activities and content areas that they covered during each session. The number of activities and content areas were tallied and divided by the total and multiplied by 100 to convert to a treatment fidelity percentage. In addition to the self-monitoring checklists, all intervention sessions were videotaped and 25–33% were coded by an independent observer to calculate percentage of treatment fidelity.

Group format

IYPT was originally developed to be delivered in a small group format, with typically between 8 and 14 participants (see Webster-Stratton, 2001). IYPT-DD uses this same small group format (McIntyre, 2008a). The small group format allows families to receive more therapist attention in comparison to a self-administered format. Although group-based programs require more resources to implement, they are still more cost-efficient than individually delivered intervention. A collateral benefit of group programs is the support and kinship available from other participants, possibly increasing parental engagement with the intervention and their child's early education program. Greater parental engagement is an important benefit of group formats, especially for those who may be socially isolated (e.g., low-income single mothers) with little support and few friendships (Dumas & Wahler, 1983). Although group-based parent training programs have many advantages, not every family benefits from this approach (Webster-Stratton & Hammond, 1997). Further, if parents miss a group session, there is no way in which to make up the content unless sessions are delivered individually. Individually administered parent training, in contrast to group formats, allow participants to receive the most intensive, flexible, and individualized support.

Individually administered programs

There are many advantages to providing parents with individually administered programs, over self-administered or group-based programs. In individually administered programs, there is increased flexibility in scheduling sessions and individualizing the content. Therapists who provide individualized sessions can give parents feedback specific to their situation and address parents' questions and concerns in a more individualized, tailored fashion. The primary disadvantage of individually administered programs is the cost. Webster-Stratton (1984) suggested that group-based programs were more efficient and effective for many families. As previously discussed, individually administered programs also lack the provision of social support provided by group members. On the other hand, parents may be more likely to accept and participate in individually based intervention than group intervention (Chadwick *et al.*, 2001). In a meta-analysis examining the variability of treatment effects in terms of participant and treatment characteristics, Lundahl, Nimer, and Parsons (2006) found individually delivered intervention to be superior to group delivered intervention for financially disadvantaged groups. That is, families with low socio-economic status who participated in individually delivered parent programs had larger treatment effects than those who participated in group delivered programs, which suggests a greater need for more individualized support for these individuals.

Phaneuf and McIntyre (2007, 2011) described procedures for adding individualized supports to caregivers who may need additional assistance beyond what a group-based intervention could offer. IYPT offers videotaped vignettes of parent–child interactions, but these vignettes do not include recordings of the participating group members. Phaneuf and McIntyre (2007) investigated the effects of adding an individualized video feedback (IVF) component to standard group treatment. IVF sessions consisted of parents viewing a previously videotaped clip of themselves interacting with their child and receiving therapist facilitated positive and corrective feedback regarding their interactions with their child. Results of a single-case research design study across four mother–child dyads suggested that IYPT-DD + IVF reduced maternal inappropriate behavior during parent–child interactions to levels below IYPT-DD alone.

Although the combination of individualized and group-based treatment was more effective than group-based (IYPT-DD) treatment alone, this combination of interventions is laborious and costly and may not be feasible to implement with a larger sample of participants. This study led McIntyre and Phaneuf (2008) to consider the use of an increasing intensity design to examine the feasibility of adding more intensive interventions for participants who required additional intervention to produce a clinically significant change in their parent–child interactions. Phaneuf and McIntyre (2011) investigated a multi-tiered intervention framework such that parents' responsiveness to increasingly intense levels of intervention dictated intervention dosage and intensity. This work suggests that self-guided reading materials (tier 1—least intensive intervention), when combined with early childhood usual care, may be as effective for reducing negative parent–child interactions as more intensive IYPT-DD in approximately 22% of the small sample. Another 44% responded to IYPT-DD (tier 2—group treatment), and the remaining participants (34%) required more intensive, individualized video feedback treatment (tier 3) to respond to intervention (see Phaneuf & McIntyre, 2011).

Overview of an ongoing randomized controlled trial of IYPT-DD

In an effort to address many of the gaps identified in the literature (e.g., small sample size, single-group pre-post design, sole reliance on parent-reported data, no follow-up data collection), McIntyre is currently investigating the efficacy of IYPT-DD in a larger scale randomized controlled trial (McIntyre, 2011).

Study aims

The study aims of the randomized controlled trial include the following (McIntyre, 2011; see Figure 3.1):

1. Test the efficacy of the IYPT-DD in comparison with treatment as usual for reducing child maladaptive behavior and increasing child adaptive behavior immediately post-treatment and at 6-month, 12-month, and 18-month follow-up assessments.

2. Test the efficacy of the IYPT-DD in comparison with treatment as usual for reducing inappropriate/negative parent–child interactions, increasing positive parenting practices, and increasing parental competence and self-efficacy immediately post-treatment and at 6-month, 12-month, and 18-month follow-up assessments.

3. Test the efficacy of IYPT-DD in comparison with treatment as usual for increasing adaptation to school as measured by teacher assessments of children's early sociobehavioral adjustment.

4. Determine if changes in child maladaptive and adaptive behavior are a function of changes in parenting behavior.

5. Determine if contextual influences, such as parenting stress, maternal depression, and partner support/relationship quality, moderate child outcomes.

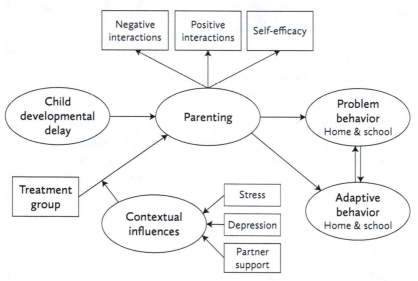

Figure 3.1 Study model of relationships among child, family, and contextual variables

Sample

The sample for the current RCT includes 181 families with three-year-old children with developmental delay recruited through early intervention and early childhood special education programs in the Pacific Northwest region of the United States (McIntyre, 2011). Child inclusionary criteria included the following: (1) age between 30 and 42 months; (2) documented developmental delay or disability; (3) services received through an Individualized Family Service Plan (IFSP); (4) ambulatory; and (5) living with the parent/primary caregiver for at least one year. Children were excluded if they were deaf or blind.

A simple randomization strategy was used, whereby every second family who met eligibility criteria was assigned to the IYPT-DD intervention condition ($n = 90$). Alternating families were assigned to the usual care control group ($n = 91$). Table 3.4 provides demographic information for the RCT sample. Children and family demographic variables did not statistically differ by IYPT-DD intervention or control condition. Children were approximately 3 years old. The majority were white/Caucasian and receiving early intervention services for a speech delay or other developmental delay. The majority of primary caregivers were mothers who were married or living with a partner and eligible for the state Medicaid plan (see Table 3.4).

Table 3.4 Child and family demographics by intervention or control condition ($n = 181$)

Demographic	Intervention ($n = 90$)	Control ($n = 91$)	t or X2
Child			
Age in months—M (SD)	36.50 (4.84)	37.42 (4.48)	$t = 1.32$
Male n (%)	67 (74)	70 (77)	$X2 = 0.51$
White/Caucasian n (%)	83 (92)	83 (91)	$X2 = 0.00$
Diagnosis n (%)			$X2 = 0.55$
Speech Delay	46 (51)	46 (50)	
Global Delay	12 (13)	13 (14)	
Autism Spectrum Disorder	10 (11)	12 (13)	
Other	15 (17)	15 (16)	
Unknown	2 (2)	1 (1)	
Vineland Adaptive Behavior—M (SD)	82.37 (10.97)	81.01 (12.75)	$t = -0.76$

Demographic	Intervention (n = 90)	Control (n = 91)	t or X2
Primary Caregiver (PC)/Family			
PC Age in Years—M (SD)	31.81 (7.41)	33.21 (7.43)	t = 1.23
PC Status—n (%) Mother	67 (74)	70 (77)	X2 = 0.51
Married/Partner in Home—n (%)	74 (81)	64 (71)	X2 = 2.60
BA/BS Degree	19 (21)	24 (26)	X2 = 0.69
Employed—n (%)	36 (39)	44 (48)	X2 = 1.28
State Medicaid Plan Recipient—n (%)	57 (63)	54 (59)	X2 = 0.58

Note: * $p < 0.05$ *** $p < 0.001$.

Design and assessment plan

The design involves random assignment to one of two treatment conditions (IYPT-DD group treatment or treatment as usual) and involves initial screening for eligibility, pre-treatment, post-treatment, 6-month, 12-month, 18-month follow-up assessments of child and family functioning, and a kindergarten transition school assessment focused on sociobehavioral adjustment. The data collection involves home-based observations, parent-reported checklists and question-naires, and teacher-reported measures of adaptation to kindergarten. Collection procedures represent multiple informants and methods, including parent self-report, direct observations of behavior in naturalistic (home) environments, and teacher reports of child adjustment at school. Families assigned to the IYPT-DD treatment arm receive a booster session following the 12-month follow-up assessment. These are offered elements of intervention are recom-mended as a part of regular follow-up and monitoring of child and family progress (Eyberg et al., 1998). The booster session consists of a review of the key elements of the IYPT-DD treatment, followed by IVF based on the videotaped parent–child interaction observation collected at the 12-month follow-up assessment. Thus, the IYPT-DD intervention draws on the strengths of both a group format and individualized booster sessions.

Preliminary findings

McIntyre and DeGarmo (in preparation) tested the intent-to-treat efficacy hypothesis that children in the IYPT-DD condition would exhibit a decrease in child behavior problems (observed noncompliance during parent–child interactions) over time relative to the control group. Results supported the key hypothesis. Controlling for initial noncompliance status, child age, gender, and caregiver depression, assignment to IYPT-DD was associated with a greater rate of decrease in child noncompliance over 9 months relative to the control condition ($\beta = -0.20$, $p < 0.05$). Among the control variables, girls decreased at a marginally greater rate than boys ($\beta = -0.17$, $p < 0.10$), and higher levels of caregiver depression were associated with increases in child noncompliance over time ($\beta = -0.28$, $p < 0.01$). These results are promising in that they demonstrate longitudinal effects of IYPT-DD on child behavior problems (observed noncompliance) in young children with developmental delay (McIntyre & DeGarmo, in preparation). The direct effects of caregiver depression are important to consider in that caregiver depression, regardless of intervention condition, had an impact on caregivers with more depression relative to children with more behavior problems over time. At the conclusion of this randomized controlled trial, McIntyre will be reporting findings that address all the specific aims of the study.

Implementation and dissemination efforts of IYPT
Implications for practice

IYPT is used widely in practice as an intervention to promote positive parenting, reduce challenging behavior, and enhance family well-being among caregivers with children with IDD and ASD. Because IYPT intervention materials are commercially available for purchase from the Incredible Years® website[1] and marketed for community practitioner and researcher use, dissemination of IYPT as an evidence-based intervention has become easy. Group leader trainings are routinely scheduled for researchers and practitioners who wish to be

---

1   www.incredibleyears.com

trained on leading the interventions. The comprehensive website also provides a number of the measures used in evaluations of IYPT and a relatively comprehensive bibliography of published and unpublished studies using IYPT. The website, training materials, measures, and other resources available on the Incredible Years® website make dissemination and uptake of IYPT easy for community providers and researchers. The training materials can be purchased through the website and monthly email newsletter can be accessed.

Limitations

Although the Incredible Years® programs have been evaluated in numerous rigorous randomized controlled trials for the prevention and treatment of externalizing problems in children, the evidence base for the IYPT for caregivers with children with IDD and ASD is just being established. Our search for published studies using IYPT with parents of children with IDD and ASD yielded 11 published studies. The most notable limitation to the evidence base is that, with the exception of 1 published study (McIntyre, 2008b) and 1 study underway (McIntyre & DeGarmo, in preparation), the group design studies do not include a control condition to allow for a more rigorous evaluation of intervention efficacy. Single-group pre-post evaluations of intervention effects are a weak test of efficacy due to the numerous threats to internal validity (Campbell & Stanley, 1963).

Other methodological limitations to our current literature on IYPT for families with children with IDD and ASD include variable attrition rates, lack of longitudinal evaluations to determine maintenance effects of intervention, and a lack of monitoring and reporting fidelity of implementation in over half of the published studies using IYPT with parents of children with IDD and ASD. Inherent with the design flaws is our small sample sizes, consistent with feasibility or pilot studies, and the lack of power to detect significant changes as a function of intervention. Further, at this time, we do not have evidence of underlying mechanisms of change or moderators of treatment outcomes. These limitations could be addressed in future studies. Indeed, in McIntyre's NIH-funded randomized controlled trial (McIntyre, 2011), she is addressing all of these methodological limitations.

Future directions

Beyond addressing the design flaws articulated above, future research could evaluate the use of IYPT in an integrated model of family health promotion in families with children with IDD and ASD. McIntyre and Phaneuf (2008) proposed a three-tiered system of parent training and education for use in early childhood settings, but this model could be expanded to incorporate tailored interventions based on child and family assessments of strengths, asset, and areas in need of attention. Such a model has been evaluated in the prevention science literature (e.g., Family Check-Up; Dishion & Stormshak, 2007), but has not been adopted in the health and mental health promotion fields within IDD and ASD. Such a tailored approach could add in further intervention supports to specifically address individual family needs and barriers, such as significant stress or mental health problems in caregivers, support needs of siblings, and inclusion and involvement of fathers, to name a few.

Although we argue for an evaluation of comprehensive programs to support and promote child and family health in families with children with IDD and ASD, an equally important need is to conduct systematic dismantling studies (Papa & Follette, 2015) to determine the important ingredients necessary to impart the most meaningful changes for families. With a better understanding of key ingredients associated with important treatment outcomes, we can better quantify the cost-effectiveness of prevention and treatment (Yates, 1994). A final recommendation for future research involves making evidence-based programs to support families with children with IDD and ASD accessible. IYPT interventions have been delivered traditionally in face-to-face group settings. Although these settings have a number of benefits, families who are isolated and socially disadvantaged may be less likely to participate (Breitenstein & Gross, 2013). Thus, providing flexible alternatives, such as web-delivered programs, telehealth coaching, or web-based learning communities may help with overcoming access issues.

Conclusion

There is a growing body of evidence supporting the use of IYPT with families who have children with IDD and ASD. The use of IYPT with this population is undoubtedly a by-product of the strong research support for IYPT with populations who do not have IDD or ASD. Nevertheless, we argue that additional research is needed to determine the efficacy of IYPT, the important clinical components of treatment, and the mechanisms responsible for change. Furthermore, IYPT has the potential to be embedded within other public health or public education models of prevention, early intervention, and treatment. We are optimistic that there is wide uptake of IYPT but suggest caution when making claims about the evidence base for use with families with children with IDD or ASD, as the evidence is still under development. For practitioners who are looking for an easy-to-use and access manualized curriculum, we suggest that IYPT has strong utility and is based on solid empirical underpinnings.

Author note

This research was funded in part by a grant from the Eunice Kennedy Shriver National Institute of Child Health and Human Development (R01 HD059838) awarded to the first author. We thank Angela Relling and project staff at the University of Oregon Prevention Science Institute for assistance with data collection and Leslie Finlay and Nancy Weisel for assistance with intervention implementation. We especially appreciate the participation of the children and families in this study.

Correspondence concerning this article should be addressed to Laura Lee McIntyre, Department of Special Education and Clinical Sciences, 5208 University of Oregon, Eugene, OR 97403-5208 USA. Email: llmcinty@uoregon.edu.

References

Abidin, R.R. (2012) *The Parenting Stress Index Manual* (4th ed.). Lutz, FL: Psychological Assessment Resources, Incorporated.

Achenbach, T.M. (2000) *Manual for the Child Behavior Checklist 1½–5*. Burlington, VT: Department of Psychiatry, University of Vermont.

Arnold, P.S., O'Leary, S.G., Wolff, L.S., & Acker, M.M. (1993) "The Parenting Scale: A measure of dysfunctional parenting in discipline situations." *Psychological Assessment 5*, 137–144.

Barton, E.E. & Lissman, D.C. (2015) "Group parent training combined with follow-up coaching for parents of children with developmental delays." *Infants & Young Children 28*, 220–236.

Breitenstein, S.M. & Gross, D. (2013) "Web-based delivery of a preventive parent training intervention: A feasibility study." *Journal of Child and Adolescent Psychiatric Nursing 26*, 149–157.

Brestan, E.V. & Eyberg, S.M. (1998) "Effective psychosocial treatments of conduct-disordered children and adolescents: 29 years, 82 studies, and 5,272 kids." *Journal of Clinical Child Psychology 27*, 2, 180–189.

Campbell, D.T. & Stanley, J. (1963) *Experimental and Quasi-Experimental Design for Research.* Boston, MA: Houghton Mifflin Company.

Chadwick, O., Momcilovic, N., Rossiter, R., Stumbles, E., & Taylor, E.A. (2001) "Randomized trial of brief individual versus group parent training for behaviour problems in children with severe learning disabilities." *Behavioural and Cognitive Psychotherapy 29*, 151–167.

Dababnah, S. & Parish, S.L. (2014) "Incredible Years program tailored to parents of preschoolers with autism: Pilot results." *Research on Social Work Practice*, 1–14.

Dababnah, S. & Parish, S.L. (2016) "Feasibility of an empirically based program for parents of preschoolers with autism spectrum disorder." *Autism 20*, 85–95.

Dishion, T.J. & Stormshak, E.A. (2007) *Intervening in Children's Lives: An Ecological, Family-Centered Approach to Mental Health Care.* Washington, DC: American Psychological Association.

Donenberg, G. & Baker, B.L. (1993) "The impact of young children with externalizing behaviors on their families." *Journal of Abnormal Child Psychology 21*, 179–198.

Dumas, J.E. & Wahler, R.G. (1983) "Predictors of treatment outcome in parent training: Mother insularity and socioeconomic disadvantage." *Behavioral Assessment 5*, 301–313.

Einfeld, S. & Tonge, B. (1994) *Manual for the Developmental Behavior Checklist (Primary Carer Version).* Monash University Centre for Developmental Psychiatry, Melbourne, Australia.

Eyberg, S.M., Edwards, D., Boggs, S.R., & Foote, R. (1998) "Maintaining the treatment effects of parental training: The role of booster sessions and other maintenance strategies." *Clinical Psychology-Science & Practice 5*, 544–554.

Eyberg, S.M., Nelson, M.M., & Boggs, S.R. (2008) "Evidence-based psychosocial treatments for children and adolescents with disruptive behavior." *Journal of Clinical Child and Adolescent Psychology 37*, 1, 215–237.

Eyberg, S. & Pincus, D. (1999) *Eyberg Child Behavior Inventory & Sutter-Eyberg Student Behavior Inventory-Revised: Professional Manual.* Odessa, FL: Psychological Assessment Resources.

Eyberg, S.M. & Robinson, E.A. (1981) *Dyadic Parent–Child Interaction Coding System.* Seattle, WA: Parenting Clinic, University of Washington.

Forehand, R.L. & McMahon, R.J. (1981) *Helping the Noncompliant Child: A Clinician's Guide to Parent Training.* New York: Guilford Press.

Friedrich, W., Greenberg, M., & Crnic, K. (1983) "A short form of the Questionnaire on Resources and Stress." *American Journal on Mental Deficiency 88*, 41–48.

Garnett, M.S. & Attwood, A.J. (1988) *The Australian Scale for Asperger's Syndrome.* Retrieved on March 31, 2017 from www.aspennj.org/pdf/information/articles/australian-scale-for-asperger-syndrome.pdf.

George, C., Kidd, G., & Brack, M. (2011) "Effectiveness of a parent training programme adapted for children with a learning disability." *Learning Disability Practice 14*, 18–24.

Goldberg, D.P. & Williams, P. (1988) *A User's Guide to the General Health Questionnaire.* Windsor: NFER-Nelson.

Goodman, R. (1997) "The Strengths and Difficulties Questionnaire: A research note." *Journal of Child Psychology and Psychiatry 38*, 581–586.

Gross, D., Fogg, L., Webster-Stratton, C., Garvey, C., Julion, W., & Grady, J. (2003) "Parent training of toddlers in day care in low-income urban communities." *Journal of Consulting and Clinical Psychology 71*, 261–278.

HEADS (2009) *Confident Parenting* (DVD). HEADS, Newcastle. Retrieved on March 31, 2017 from www.headstraining.co.uk.

Himle, M.B., Miltenberger, R.G., Flessner, C., & Gatheridge, B. (2004) "Teaching safety skills to children to prevent gun play." *Journal of Applied Behavior Analysis 37*, 1–9.

Hutchings, J., Pearson-Blunt, R., Pasteur, M., Healy, H., & Williams, M. (2016) "A pilot trial of the Incredible Years® Autism Spectrum and Language Delays Programme." *Good Autism Practice 17*, 1, 15–22.

Incredible Years® Parents, Teachers, and Children's Training Series (2013) Retrieved on March 31, 2017 from www.incredibleyears.com.

Jacobson, N.S. & Truax, P. (1991) "Clinical significance: A statistical approach to defining meaningful change in psychotherapy research." *Journal of Consulting and Clinical Psychology 59*, 12–19.

Johnston, C. & Mash, E.J. (1989) "A measure of parenting satisfaction and efficacy." *Journal of Clinical Child Psychology 18*, 167–175.

Kanne, S.M., Mazurek, M.O., Sikora, D., Bellando, J., *et al.* (2014) "The Autism Impact Measure (AIM): Initial development of a new tool for treatment outcome measurement." *Journal of Autism and Developmental Disorders 44*, 168–179.

Kleve, L., Crimlisk, S., Shoebridge, Ph., Greenwood, R., Baker, B., & Mead, B. (2011) "Is the Incredible Years® programme effective for children with neurodevelopmental disorders and for families with social services involvement in the 'real world' of community CAMHS?" *Clinical Child Psychology and Psychiatry 16*, 253–264.

Lonigan, C.J., Elbert, J.C., & Johnson, S.B. (1998) "Empirically supported psychosocial interventions for children: An overview." *Journal of Clinical Child Psychology 27*, 138–145.

Lundahl, B.W., Nimer, J., & Parsons, B. (2006) "Preventing child abuse: A meta-analysis of parent training programs." *Research on Social Work Practice 16*, 251–262.

McIntyre, L.L. (2008a) "Adapting Webster-Stratton's Incredible Years® Parent Training for children with developmental delay: Findings from a treatment group only study." *Journal of Intellectual Disability Research 52*, 1176–1192.

McIntyre, L.L. (2008b) "Parent training in young children with developmental disabilities: A randomized controlled trial." *American Journal on Mental Retardation 113*, 356–368.

McIntyre, L.L. (2011) "An RCT of Parent Training for Preschoolers with Delays." NICHD Grant, Five-Year Award (R01 HD059838), Laura Lee McIntyre, P.I.

McIntyre, L.L. & DeGarmo, D.S. (in preparation) "Longitudinal Outcomes of Incredible Years® Intervention on Noncompliance in Children with Developmental Delays: Understanding the Role of Caregiver Depression." Manuscript in preparation.

McIntyre, L.L. & Phaneuf, L. (2008) "A three-tier model of parent education in early childhood: Applying a problem-solving model." *Topics in Early Childhood Special Education 27*, 4, 214–222.

Menting, A.T.A., Orobio de Castro, B., and Matthys, W. (2013) "Effectiveness of the Incredible Years® parent training to modify disruptive and prosocial child behavior: A meta-analytic review." *Clinical Psychology Review 33*, 901–913.

Papa, A. & Follette, W.C. (2015) "Dismantling studies of psychotherapy." *Encyclopedia of Clinical Psychology*, 1–6.

Phaneuf, L. & McIntyre, L.L. (2007) "Effects of individualized video feedback combined with group parent training on maternal inappropriate behavior." *Journal of Applied Behavior Analysis 40*, 737–741.

Phaneuf, L. & McIntyre, L.L. (2011) "The application of a three-tier model of intervention to parent training." *Journal of Positive Behavior Interventions 13*, 198–207.

Radloff, L.S. (1977) "The CES-D Scale: A self-report depression scale for research in the general population." *Applied Psychological Measurement 1*, 3, 385-401.

Reid, M.J., Webster-Stratton, C., & Beauchaine, T.P. (2009) "Parent training in Head Start: A comparison of program response among African American, Asian American, Caucasian, and Hispanic mothers." *Prevention Science 2*, 209–227.

Roberts, D. & Pickering, N. (2010) "Parent training programme for autism spectrum disorders: An evaluation." *Community Practitioner 83*, 27–30.

Spence, S.H. (1995) *Social Skills Training: Enhancing Social Competence with Children and Adolescents.* Windsor: NFER-Nelson.

Squires, J., Bricker, D., & Twombly, L. (2002) *Ages and Stage Questionnaires: Social Emotional.* Baltimore, MD: Brookes.

Tennant, R., Hiller, L., Fishwick, R., Platt, S., *et al.* (2007) "The Warwick-Edinburgh Mental Well-Being Scale (WEMWBS): Development and UK validation." *Health and Quality of Life Outcomes 5*, 63–75.

Webster-Stratton, C. (1984) "A randomized trial of two parent training programs for families with conduct-disordered children." *Journal of Consulting and Clinical Psychology 52*, 4, 666–678.

Webster-Stratton, C. (1994) "Advancing videotape parent training: A comparison study." *Journal of Consulting and Clinical Psychology 62*, 3, 583–593.

Webster-Stratton, C. (1998) "Preventing conduct problems in Head Start children: Strengthening parent competencies." *Journal of Consulting and Clinical Psychology 66*, 715–730.

Webster-Stratton, C. (2000) "The Incredible Years® Training Series." *Office of Juvenile Justice and Delinquency Prevention Bulletin Review*, June, 1–24.

Webster-Stratton, C. (2001) *The Incredible Years®: Parents, Teachers and Children Training Series. Leader's Guide.* Seattle, WA: Author.

Webster-Stratton, C. (2002) *The Incredible Years®: Parents and Children Videotape Series: A Parenting Course (ADVANCE).* Divided into three programs. Seattle, WA: Author.

Webster-Stratton, C. (2005) *The Incredible Years: A Troubleshooting Guide for Parents of Children Aged 2-8 Years.* Seattle, WA: Author.

Webster-Stratton, C. & Hammond, M. (1997) "Treating children with early-onset conduct problems: A comparison of child and parent training interventions." *Journal of Consulting and Clinical Psychology 65*, 93–109.

Webster-Stratton, C. & Herbert, M. (1993) "What really happens in parent training?" *Behavior Modification 17*, 407–456.

Webster-Stratton, C., Hollinsworth, T., & Kolpacoff, M. (1989) "The long-term effectiveness and clinical significance of three cost-effective training programs for families with conduct-problem children." *Journal of Consulting and Clinical Psychology 57*, 4, 550–553.

Webster-Stratton, C., Reid, M.J., & Hammond, M. (2001) "Social skills and problem solving training for children with early-onset conduct problems: Who benefits?" *Journal of Child Psychology and Psychiatry 42*, 943–952.

Webster-Stratton, C., Reid, M.J., & Stoolmiller, M. (2008) "Preventing conduct problems and improving school readiness: Evaluation of the Incredible Years® teacher and child training programs in high-risk schools." *Journal of Child Psychology and Psychiatry 49*, 5, 471–488.

Yates, B.T. (1994) "Toward the incorporation of costs, cost-effectiveness analysis, and cost–benefit analysis into clinical research." *Journal of Consulting and Clinical Psychology 62*, 729–736.

Chapter 4

THE EARLY START DENVER MODEL

Parent Adaptation

Melissa A. Mello, Meagan R. Talbott, and Sally J. Rogers

ABSTRACT

In this chapter, we provide an overview of the Early Start Denver Model (ESDM), an empirically supported, behavior-developmental, and relationship-based treatment for young children with ASD. The emphasis of this chapter is on the methods, practice, and evidence for parent-mediated ESDM, or P-ESDM, and includes information that will help students, practitioners, and parents understand the goals, structure, and evidence for the efficacy of this approach to coaching parents of young children with ASD to incorporate ESDM techniques into their daily routines and everyday lives.

Keywords: autism; Early Start Denver Model; ESDM; parent coaching

The Early Start Denver Model (ESDM) is a comprehensive, developmental-behavioral, relationship-based treatment for young children aged 12–60 months with autism spectrum disorder (ASD). It is both manualized and empirically validated.

The ESDM is based on an integrated developmental-behavioral approach constructed from empirical findings from multiple sources of studies, particularly studies of early typical and atypical development, communication development, infant learning styles, learning science, studies of parent–child relationships and effects on development, and studies of effective intervention approaches for young children with developmental difficulties of various types, including those with ASD.

The integration of these bodies of knowledge shapes all aspects of treatment delivery in the ESDM.

Because young children with ASD are more similar to than different from young children with typical development, ESDM intervention approaches build on variables that facilitate learning in all young children. Only in areas where it is known that early development in ASD differs from that of typical development does the intervention take a specialized approach. This perspective also applies at the level of the individual. We begin intervention using the general ESDM approach and then alter and individualize our approaches via a systematic decision tree based on the feedback attained from an individual child's trajectory of progress and clinical experiences with the child.

Working from the developmental principle that the same environmental and interactional variables that facilitate learning in all other young children will also likely facilitate learning in young children with ASD leads to several core ESDM features. The first is that the optimal learning environment is located within the typical activities and interactions that a child experiences in their nurturing daily environment. In ESDM, adults embed learning opportunities throughout all of the routines that fill children's daily lives, including caregiving, meal time, park outings, family play, object play, and other family routines. ESDM focuses on increasing the pleasure (both social pleasure and personal enjoyment) and interest that these experiences provide for an individual child. This core feature also targets provision of responsive, warm and socially rewarding interactions with the caregiving adults within daily activities.

As stated above, both behavioral and developmental intervention approaches are integrated in ESDM. The naturalistic use of applied behavior analysis (ABA) in ESDM was influenced by Pivotal Response Treatment (PRT), which was developed in the 1980s and thoroughly tested in numerous single-subject designs (Koegel, O'Dell, & Koegel, 1987). The foundational developmental intervention is the Denver Model, which was developed in the 1980s and was tested and published using group designs which featured baseline performance as the comparison condition (Rogers & DiLalla, 1991; Rogers et al., 1986). What do PRT and the Denver Model each contribute to the ESDM? Teaching strategies are built from the science of learning articulated by applied behavioral analysis: prompting (a support offered to help the child respond correctly), chaining (linking behaviors together), fading (reducing prompts) and delivering clear antecedent–behavior–consequence contingencies (the instruction delivered to the child, their response, and how the adult responds to their behavior). The use of daily data for feedback about success of learning strategies is also part and parcel of ABA practice. Contributions of PRT to ESDM include articulated strategies and practices for supporting child initiation (for shared control between child and adult in the activity, for enhancing child motivation to practice skills, for varying trials between mastery and maintenance, and for working from children's own goals as the source of reinforcement). These strategies fit well into a developmental framework.

The original Denver Model strategies were first described in 1986 by Rogers *et al.*, and involved a naturalistic style of interaction and teaching (a characteristic that PRT and Denver Model each independently developed), in which control of the activity choice, theme, and length is shared by adult and child. Other Denver Model strategies included following the child's lead, becoming a play partner, balanced interactions in terms of directing and responding to the partner, and using language appropriate for the child's age and language level. From the Denver Model came components involving use of typical developmental trajectories for treatment objectives, the use of developmental curriculum, the importance of a sensitive, responsive quality of adult interaction with the child for promoting learning and social communicative growth. Other continuities from the Denver Model to ESDM include the focus on play and other activities from daily life, the four-step structure of joint activity routines, the building-up of speech and language from a starting point in intentional gesture and joint attention, and the practice of addressing treatment objectives involving multiple areas of a child's development during a specific activity, including communication objectives in every activity. The contributions of PRT and all its foundations in behavior science, and the Denver Model and all its foundations in developmental science, came together to create ESDM practices: the use of natural, positive interactions between child and adult to facilitate multimodal learning, embedded within the joint activity routines of a child's daily life.

Joint activity routines

In ESDM, joint activity routines (JARs; Bruner, 1975, 1981) involve dyadic interaction involving multiple rounds between partners focused on the same activity. The joint activity structure has four parts: set up, theme, variations, and closure/transition. The *set up* involves a transition that starts an activity. It occurs when an adult offers the child an activity or choice, or when a child spontaneously shows interest in or begins an activity appropriate to the context. The child "lands" on something and the adult immediately joins in and some action occurs that the two will trade back and forth, or share—this is the *theme*: the first purposeful activity that emerges from the child's interest, such as playing with blocks and starting to build a block tower, or playing peekaboo with a blanket. Once the child has interest and motivation for the activity, the adult begins to embed learning opportunities from the child's list of learning goals into the ongoing play *theme*. For instance, in the case of a block tower, for a child who has an objective of color learning the adult may hold up two blocks of different colors and ask which one the child wants next. For the child who has an objective about noun learning, the therapist might hold up a block and a cotton ball and ask which one the child wants next, cotton or block? This would be repeated several times throughout the natural play, but not drilled, and the therapist will also be taking turns consistently, labeling what the therapist is doing vis-à-vis child objectives, and will also let the child just take some blocks without demands. This is also an example of the principle of alternating maintenance and target skills, a PRT practice that supports child motivation.

Next, the adult or the child begins to *vary* the activity, adding different ideas. This fosters flexibility and use of objects in multiple ways. It also ensures that the activity doesn't become too repetitive, and it adds the opportunity to practice other objectives. So, using the examples of the stacking block theme, the adult might start to make a train with the blocks and start to work on imitation of actions and sounds, as well as symbolic play. Once the activity has come to a natural end, or is feeling repetitive, or the therapist is ready to move, the adult and child start to close the activity down. The *closing and transition* is a very important teaching phase of the activity, in which more objectives can be worked in (following instructions: "Give me the red block, please"; sorting or classifying: "Let's put the squares here and the rectangles here"; carrying out sequences of activities: "Get the

cleanup box, then materials in the box and then box to the shelf";
increasing independence and personal responsibility: "First, we put
away, then we get something else"; commenting on the past: "We are
all done with blocks"; and planning for the future: "What shall we
do next?" so that these mental/representational processes begin to
be developed, and the capacities for reflection and for planning are
stimulated).

Types of joint activities

The ESDM focuses on two types of joint activity routines: object-based
activity routines and sensory social routines. Object-based routines
occur inside play with objects and inside daily life routines that involve
objects (meals, dressing, chores, bath, outdoor play, grocery store).
The idea is to target as many different goals from as many different
domains as can be fitted inside these object-based routines, and to
have the learning tasks be related to daily life activities. For example,
inside an object routine with crayons and paper, you might work on
the child's fine motor goals of coloring, choosing the correct color
crayon, imitating various shapes, and sharing materials and turns.
Inside a chore such as tooth-brushing, one can practice skills such
as receptive language for choosing the named materials, sequencing
various activities, imitating actions in a mirror with a partner, learning
how to spit out things, learning to unscrew and screw a cap on, wiping
the mouth, and the motor sequence involved in the whole routine.

Sensory social routines (SSRs) are the second type of joint activity
routine in which teaching occurs in ESDM. In SSRs, learning activities
that focus on social communication and social interactions between
partners and do not involve child object manipulation, are the focus of
learning. SSRs include physical games, songs and chants with actions,
and peek-a-boo. They also include interactions with interesting objects
such as bubbles, lotion, balloons, water—that the adults manipulate
and that the children control through communications. The dyadic
interactions that occur inside SSRs are particularly helpful in creating
moments of strong positive shared affect (emotional contagion), eye
contact, communicative gestures, and facial/vocal imitation because
they focus so much attention on faces and eyes. In an ESDM treatment
hour, the therapist works between object-based routines and SSRs both
in order to keep therapy interesting and to create a balance for the child.

Some children have an easier time engaging in object routines than social ones, and others show the reverse pattern. Spending time in both assures that children are well prepared for the kinds of activities that typically occur between adults and small children.

The ESDM can be delivered by a therapist who has completed the ESDM certification process[1] and those directly supervised by an ESDM therapist in a variety of formats. ESDM can be delivered in a variety of formats, including intensive 1:1 direct delivery, in a group setting such as a preschool or daycare (see Vivanti *et al.*, 2014, 2016; Eapen, Črnčec, & Walter, 2013), or through parent-implemented practice. Training and certification in ESDM delivery (all formats) involves a combination of didactic workshops, hands-on training and feedback, individual work with families, and the demonstration of reliability in administering assessments, running sessions and use of techniques. All of these delivery formats use the same interaction techniques, fidelity rating systems, curriculum assessments, generation of treatment objectives, and routines and settings from daily life. They differ in: (1) the training methods and background experiences of the person delivering the treatment to the child (e.g., therapist, teacher, or parent); (2) treatment intensity in terms of ratios of children to adults and hours per week of delivery; (3) type of data collected; and (4) location of treatment delivery. The details of the ESDM and all of the training and practices for each of these delivery systems are outlined in published manuals (Rogers & Dawson, 2010; Rogers, Dawson, & Vismara, 2012; Vivanti *et al.*, 2016). While this chapter focuses on parent-implemented ESDM, readers interested in the intensive and group-based formats should refer to the published manuals for more detailed information. In the following sections, we provide an overview of the methods, training, and evidence for parent implemented ESDM or P-ESDM.

Parent implemented ESDM

Parent implemented ESDM (P-EDSM) takes place through the support of a highly skilled therapist, called a "parent coach." ESDM parent coaches in the US are Master's level clinicians with extensive experience in the field of autism, certified ESDM therapists, and trained in P-ESDM by one of the ESDM trainers.

---

1   www.ucdmc.ucdavis.edu/mindinstitute/research/esdm/workshops.html

In P-ESDM, coach and parents work together in every stage of the intervention. Coaches are not instructors and parents are not learners. Instead, they are partners and each is valued for the specific expertise brought to the collaboration. While coaches have expertise in ASD and in ESDM, parents are the experts on their child, family, and childrearing culture. Examples of the specific roles that parents play in collaborating in P-ESDM intervention are described in Table 4.1.

Table 4.1 Description of parental involvement/ roles in various stages of P-ESDM coaching

Stage	Examples/parent involvement
Identifying need and initiating treatment	Parents typically initiate treatment, deciding (to the extent they have a choice) what format of treatment is right for their child and family
Assessing child's initial strengths and needs	Coach: Administer curriculum checklist Parent: Join in assessment activities, contribute information about child's abilities in skills and/or contexts that the coach is unable to observe
Setting 12-week goals	Parents identify their priorities for their child learning the 12-week period; these domains are incorporated into the broader set of objectives/goals that the coach writes, built from assessment data, sense of the child's pace/learning rate, family goals, family setting and needs. Parents review and approve objectives before treatment begins
Identifying routines/ settings to use techniques	Parents know the child's everyday activities, activities that the child enjoys, and routines/interactions that are naturally rewarding for the child, and the coach and parent work together to identify ways in which ESDM techniques can be incorporated into these existing routines to support learning, etc.
Session planning	Parents reflect on past week's success and problems, and help to set the plan for the session
Problem solving	When problems are identified, coach and parents reflect and generate ideas for addressing them
Parent learning/ coaching	Parents and coach carry out ESDM teaching procedures inside the child's daily activities, with coach providing parent with support and opportunities to reflect on parent learning and practice. Parent identifies preferred learning modalities, own goals, pace, and priorities

Upon the first meeting between the coach and family, the coach and family assess the child using the ESDM curriculum checklist. The results of this checklist will give both the family and coach ideas about the child's strengths and needs. The results of the checklist, along with an interview with the parents about what their needs and desires are for their child, become the foundation for the teaching that will take place in the coaching sessions and lead to a set of treatment goals for the child. The coach uses the information to construct a set of approximately 12–15 quarterly treatment objectives that will guide the coach and family in their interactions with the child during both coaching sessions and, more importantly, during every activity at home with the child. Each objective is then broken down into four to six small teaching steps that will guide the focus on child learning on a weekly basis. The objectives are written using parent-friendly language, which means using everyday language and concepts while avoiding professional jargon. See Table 4.2 for examples.

Table 4.2 ESDM goal examples

ESDM Professional objective and steps	Family-friendly version
Objective: During a treatment session, when offered preferred materials or foods, the child will verbalize the object name to gain access to the item 8–10 times in a treatment hour across 3 treatment sessions with both parents and therapists, at home and at the clinic for at least 10 different preferred items or foods	When you offer foods or objects that your child wants, she will say a word to request it
Step 1: Vocalizes to request with a verbal prompt	Step 1: Makes a sound after you model it
Step 2: Vocalizes to request with pause and expectant look	Step 2: Makes a sound when you pause and wait
Step 3: Spontaneously produces a sound	Step 3: Makes a sound independently
Step 4: Spontaneously produces object name approximation	Step 4: Says a version of the object name
Step 5: Requests 3 items spontaneously	Step 5: Asks for 3 different things by name
Step 6: Requests spontaneously 8/10 times in a treatment hour across 3 treatment sessions with both parents and therapists, at home and at the clinic for at least 10 different preferred items or foods	Step 6: Consistently names things once every 5 minutes throughout the day

The coach and parent use these objectives to identify ways to embed these into the child's everyday routines, to identify toys and household objects to use, and to track weekly child progress.

Parents indicate their preferred learning media and coaches tailor learning tools to parent preferences and strengths. Parents are given the ESDM parent manual (Rogers *et al.*, 2012), which outlines all the ESDM techniques in a parent-friendly way. If reading the manual is too difficult for a family or reading is not their preferred learning method, each chapter in the manual is summarized in a "refrigerator sheet," a one-page list that families can easily place on their refrigerator that captures the key strategies of the chapter. Coaches bring this list to coaching sessions as well, for both coach and parent to reference. Coaches may create videos of sessions for the family, focus on verbal information, use photos and cue cards, create schedules or lists, or provide anything else the parent identifies to help facilitate success. Parents receive a copy of the goal sheet created for their child and coaches provide a personalized data sheet, designed specifically to meet the needs of the child and parent. Coaches collect data during sessions with parents as a way to help parents learn to use the data sheets and to experience the value of data. For example, some parents are motivated to collect data throughout the day and others find that they can only focus on data once daily, so a system will be designed to meet those needs.

After the initial curriculum and goal-setting session, a parent coaching schedule is determined. Depending upon the needs of the family and child, parent coaching may be conducted alongside of an intensive, in-home ESDM intervention program. In this situation, parents meet with the lead ESDM supervisor weekly or biweekly. Parent coaching can also be carried out prior to initiating an intensive treatment program, to start intervention while on a waiting list, for example. In this case, coaching sessions may be held up to twice per week. And, finally, when infants of 12–18 months of age are identified as showing early signs of ASD, parent coaching sessions implemented twice a week for 12 weeks is a developmentally appropriate approach to delivering individualized intervention (Rogers *et al.*, 2014).

The parent manual describes 10 intervention topics essential to P-ESDM: (1) social attention and motivation for learning; (2) sensory social routines; (3) dyadic engagement; (4) non-verbal communication; (5) imitation; (6) antecedent–behavior–consequence relationship (ABCs of learning); (7) joint attention; (8) functional play; (9) symbolic play; and (10) speech development. These are described in Table 4.3.

Primary caregivers are supported to learn the practices outlined under each topic and then to embed child objectives into the appropriate activities in daily play and caretaking routines at home. Over the course of intervention, parents are taught the interactive principles associated with P-ESDM and gain mastery in applying these principles with their children. Daily data on child progress are gathered by the coaches during coaching sessions with parents and child. Typically, one parent will self-identify as the primary caretaker and that parent will attend all parent coaching sessions. However, ESDM parent coaching can be used with additional caretakers and family members, including parents, grandparents, siblings, and childcare providers.

Table 4.3 The 10 topics of ESDM/techniques/skill domains

Theme	Description	Example
1. Social attention and motivation for learning	Attending to social cues and having an interest in learning the material. This sometimes has to be added by the adult to assist with child motivation for learning.	If the child is highly interested in trains, then trains might be used as the initial tools for teaching so as to capture the child's attention and motivation.
2. Sensory social routines	A routine based around activities without objects, where social interaction is the focus of the activity and face-to-face learning is encouraged.	Song and games such as: tickles, peek-a-boo, happy and you know it, itsy bitsy spider, etc.
3. Dyadic engagement	Reciprocal engagement with turn taking and partners sharing interest in the activity with one another.	Putting together pieces into a puzzle, each partner taking a turn, and looking to share interest in the other's turn.
4. Non-verbal communication	Communication involving the use of gestures and eye contact, not vocal language.	Pointing to an item, waving hello, shaking head yes or no, eye contact.
5. Imitation	Performing an action following someone's model of the action.	Adult waves hello, then the child waves hello.
6. Antecedent–behavior–consequence relationship (ABCs of learning)	An instruction provided by an adult, the performance of the instruction by the child (with or without help), and a consequence provided to the child for performing the instruction.	Adult says, "Give me the bubbles" (Antecedent). The child hands the bubbles to the adult (Behavior, could include a prompt). The adult blows the bubbles for the child (Consequence).

7. Joint attention	Two partners sharing interest in the same material, evidenced by both partners looking at the material and at each other.	When a train goes by on a track, child looks to the train and points at it, then looks at the parent to share the interest in the train. Parent also looks at the train and back to the child to share enjoyment.
8. Functional play	The use of play items as intended.	Child puts shapes into a shape sorter.
9. Symbolic play	The use of play items for imaginative play.	Child uses blocks to create a train track and a train, and run the "train" along the "track."
10. Speech development	The process of developing new ways of communicating, leading up to vocal speech. May begin with gestures, then sounds, then vocal approximations, single words, two words, and into sentences.	Child begins to babble, then says "ba" for ball and, finally, "ball." Eventually, the child can request "more ball" or "red ball," followed by "Let's roll the ball!"

Parent coaching sessions typically follow a consistent structure. Treatment sessions of 1–1½ hours are broken into eight-minute periods, each with a different activity:

1. Greetings and getting settled

2. Summary of week's progress and focus

3. Warm-up activity and reflection

4. Topic of the session

5. Practice activity with coaching and reflection

6. Practice different activity with coaching and reflection

7. Discussion period

8. Plan for week and closing.

In the greeting and summary, parents share their progress, practicing the previous week's theme at home with discussion of successes and unsuccessful experiences. In the warm-up, parents and their child engage in a preferred play activity (e.g., toy play, books, bubbles) so as to demonstrate the main focus of the past week. (Coaches often collect parent fidelity of treatment implementation data during the warm-up in order to examine progress and needs). Every activity is followed by a reflective time, in which parents and coaches share their experiences and observations about the interactions that just occurred. In block 4, the coach explains the next P-ESDM theme verbally, while providing written materials. The coach often grounds the topic in a behavior seen during the session or reported by the parent. Then comes a practice block, in which parents practice the new concepts, while the coach coaches them as needed, followed by reflection and planning. During the next practice block, the parent practices with coaching, using a different type of activity to support parent generalization at home. Reflection time assures that parents have a solid grasp of the techniques just practiced and have a plan for incorporating them into everyday routines at home with the child. A general discussion time allows parent and coach to address any remaining parent interest or questions and ends with an action plan of daily times and activities, when parents feel that they can embed the targeted topics and facilitate child learning within home routines. Then, a goodbye is offered to the child and the parent, thus bringing closure to the session.

The parent coaching process parent-focused interactive strategies used by the therapist throughout the session are based on the work of Hanft, Rush, and Shelden (2004), who have provided early childhood professionals with an important model for coaching as a partnership, in which the strengths, existing knowledge, values, and goals of the parent are incorporated into the entire process of intervention, in contrast to a traditional parent training model, in which the therapist takes the role of authority to set goals and teach the parent.

Parent mastery of the ESDM strategies is monitored via the ESDM Teaching Fidelity Rating System. This fidelity rating system is the same as the one used to monitor therapist fidelity. Through parent coaching, parents learn the 13 teaching skills that comprise the ESDM Teaching Fidelity Rating system: (1) management of child attention; (2) quality of the A–B–C teaching episode; (3) quality of instructional techniques; (4) modulation of child affect and arousal; (5) management of unwanted behavior; (6) dyadic engagement; (7) child motivation; (8) adult affect; (9) adult sensitivity and responsivity; (10) communicative opportunities and functions; (11) appropriateness of adult's language; (12) elaboration of activities;

and (13) transitions between activities. Parent and/or therapist skills across each of these 13 domains are rated using a Likert-based rating system, where 1 reflects non-competent teaching and 5 reflects optimal use of the strategies within a domain.

During a P-ESDM treatment session, the coach typically gathers fidelity data for parents during the warm-up activity. In addition to monitoring parent technique fidelity, coaches also score themselves on their use of P-ESDM coaching techniques. Furthermore, sessions are often filmed and colleagues monitor the coach's fidelity as well. P-ESDM coaching fidelity is also rated (Rogers & Vismara, 2012) using a Likert-scale rating, ranging from 1 (low fidelity) to 4 (high fidelity). The coaching fidelity rating covers 13 domains: (1) greeting and check-in; (2) warm up activity; (3) introduction of the topic; (4) coaching on the topic: activity 1; (5) coaching on the topic: activity 2; (6) closing; (7) collaborative; (8) reflective; (9) nonjudgmental; (10) conversational and reciprocal; (11) ethical conduct; (12) organization and management; and (13) managing conflict and implementation difficulties. Fidelity items and descriptions are available from the authors.

Parent use of ESDM strategies during everyday activities at home is an essential component of the ESDM as a comprehensive model. Through parent coaching, parents can become highly skilled ESDM deliverers, who understand and use the principles and approaches of ESDM. Parents' ability to complement therapists' delivery of ESDM allows for children to be in very supportive learning environments throughout their waking hours.

What is the best use of parent coaching? For preschoolers with ASD, parent coaching is a complement to educational/treatment services delivered by professionally trained, multidisciplinary teams. Close coordination of learning objectives across the child's various interventions and activities, including home, allows for maximal intensity of learning opportunities and support for generalization of learning across multiple environments, activities, and people. Data is taken every session to monitor this learning. For toddlers, parent coaching is the heart of Part C services, and coordination of a consistent approach to coaching content across the various providers of Part C services provides parents with a unified comprehensive plan for addressing a toddler's needs across everyday activities at home.[2] For children waiting for a diagnostic workup or specialized services, parent coaching fills a very important gap and allows parents to move into action while waiting for additional help. Adjunctive parent-delivered intervention can supplement community services and provide high-quality learning opportunities at home during early childhood when learning and developmental change is occurring at a rapid pace. Parent involvement in delivery of a child's plan is consistent with best practices in early childhood intervention and Part C services. Parent involvement in setting treatment objectives is critical for delivering culturally sensitive treatment, individualized to each family's unique needs, and applying ESDM in diverse communities. The skills and approaches that parents learn as partners with ESDM providers set the course for positive parent–child interaction and effective parent advocacy across the lifespan.

Evidence

Several research studies have been conducted to evaluate the efficacy of ESDM delivered by professionals as well as by parents. These studies have consisted both of single-case research designs and randomized controlled trials, and have demonstrated positive effects of parent coaching on child learning, specifically in regards to child progress in play, language, and imitation.

Data gathered from professionally delivered ESDM forms the foundation of the evidence supporting the ESDM. Dawson and colleagues (2010) published the results of the first randomized controlled trial comparing ESDM to a community treatment control group in 48 toddlers with ASD. They found that after two years, children receiving 15 hours per week of ESDM, delivered in the home 1:1 by paraprofessionals and parents who had received coaching and reported using ESDM techniques themselves, made significantly

---

2   The Program for Infants and Toddlers with Disabilities (Part C of IDEA) is a federal grant program that assists states in operating a comprehensive statewide program of early intervention services for infants and toddlers with disabilities, ages birth through age 2 years, and their families. Part C services include screening, interdisciplinary evaluation, and, for children who qualify, family-centered intervention in natural environments focused on child and family support needs.

more developmental progress than children receiving community treatment. Children in the ESDM group gained an average of 17.6 standard score points on the MSEL, while the community group gained an average of 7.0 points. The ESDM group also had better receptive and expressive language and adaptive functioning outcomes. While the community group declined in adaptive skills, the ESDM group maintained their standard scores, indicating that although still delayed overall, they gained adaptive skills at the same rate as the normative sample.

Dawson *et al.* (2012) analyzed children's social behavior outcomes, based on the Pervasive Developmental Disorder–Behavior Inventory (PDD-BI; (Cohen & Sudhalter, 1999), as well as their neurophysiological responses (event-related brain potentials and EEG spectral power) in response to face and non-face stimuli at the conclusion of treatment in the same cohort. Children who had received community treatment demonstrated an electrophysiological pattern of responses indicating greater attentional and cognitive processing for objects than for faces. Children in the ESDM group displayed the opposite pattern of responses, responding both more quickly and with decreased α power and decreased θ power (indicative of increased attention and active cognitive processing) when viewing faces than objects. The pattern observed in the ESDM group was also observed in a typically developing control group (Dawson *et al.*, 2012). Furthermore, children who received ESDM showed improved social behavior on the PDD-BI. Children's level of improvement in social behavior was correlated with their pattern of brain responses to social stimuli, with greater improvement associated with greater levels of brain activity while viewing social stimuli. This sample had follow-up to age 6, two years after the cessation of active intensive early treatment. In this follow-up sample, a large majority of children in the ESDM group (86%) showed maintained or improved IQ scores (Estes *et al.*, 2015).

Assessments were conducted across multiple domains of functioning by clinicians who were naïve to previous intervention group status. The ESDM group, on average, maintained or increased improvements during the follow-up period in overall intellectual ability, adaptive behavior, symptom severity, and challenging behavior. No group differences in core autism symptoms were found immediately post-treatment; however, two years later, the ESDM group demonstrated improved core autism symptoms, as well as adaptive behavior and peer relations, as compared with the community-intervention-as-usual group. The two groups received equivalent intervention hours during the original study, but the ESDM group received fewer hours during the follow-up period. These results indicate sustained and, in some domains, enhanced long-term effects of early ASD intervention.

Parent coaching

Both group and individual intensive ESDM delivery formats include simultaneous parent coaching in ESDM techniques. The inclusion of parents in children's treatment not only supports children's progress by increasing the number of learning opportunities throughout the day, but is also consistent with the recommendations of the National Research Council (National Research Council, 2001). Seven studies, including the modified infant version described earlier in this review, have evaluated the effectiveness of P-ESDM in terms of fidelity of implementation, acceptability, and effects on parental mental health, in addition to analyzing concurrent changes in children's behavior (Estes *et al.*, 2014; Rogers *et al.*, 2012, 2014; Vismara *et al.*, 2009; Vismara, McCormick *et al.*, 2013; Vismara & Rogers, 2008; Vismara *et al.*, 2012). These investigations have demonstrated that parents are able to successfully learn and apply ESDM techniques when interacting with their children. The majority of parents reach high levels of fidelity (e.g., 80%) over the course of a short, low-intensity, coaching process.

Two studies have evaluated these features in a distance-learning program, with coaching sessions occurring via telehealth services, including web-based video conferencing and a self-guided website (Vismara, McCormick, *et al.*, 2013; Vismara *et al.*, 2012). These investigations reported similarly high levels of parent fidelity by the end of the active treatment period, with average group scores increasing significantly from baseline to ratings of 4.15 and 4.29 (of a possible 5) at post-treatment follow-up. Both live and distance parent coaching programs report that the majority of parents reach fidelity in fewer than 12 weeks, often after 6–7 weeks of training (Vismara *et al.*, 2009; Vismara, McCormick *et al.*, 2013; Vismara & Rogers, 2008; Vismara *et al.*, 2012).

In terms of acceptability, parents receiving P-ESDM training report both high satisfaction with the coaching procedure as well as strong working alliances with their therapist (Rogers *et al.*, 2012, 2014; Vismara, McCormick, *et al.*, 2013; Vismara *et al.*, 2012). Compared to parents receiving treatment in the community, parents receiving P-ESDM coaching report significantly less parenting-related stress in the first three months after their child's diagnosis (Estes *et al.*, 2014). This group difference in parental stress is driven by a significant increase in stress reported by the community treatment group; parents in the P-ESDM group reported no such changes during the same three-month period.

The effectiveness of P-ESDM in promoting children's development has been described in earlier sections, and has consistently documented significant changes in children's language, social communication, and developmental level using both fine-grained behavioral coding analyses and scores on standardized measures. Both live and telehealth single-case research designs have reported increases in children's frequency of vocalizations, imitations, social initiations, and social engagement (Vismara *et al.*, 2009; Vismara, McCormick, *et al.*, 2013; Vismara & Rogers, 2008; Vismara *et al.*, 2012). A randomized controlled trial comparing P-ESDM to community treatment found that both groups of children made significant gains on standardized measures of language and significant decreases in autism symptoms. While these results might seem to suggest a limited benefit of P-ESDM, results are actually quite impressive, considering that children in the control group received nearly twice as many treatment hours as children in the P-ESDM group (Rogers *et al.*, 2012).

Clearly, more work is needed to understand the effectiveness of P-ESDM, particularly when implemented in community practice and when compared to more intensive intervention formats. A follow-up P-ESDM randomized controlled trial is currently underway through the University of Washington and University of California (UC) Davis MIND Institute sites, the results of which will help to answer questions about how best to coach parents in this model, mechanisms of change within both parents and children, and families for whom P-ESDM may be particularly effective. A fuller discussion of future research needs is included below.

ESDM dissemination science
Therapist training

While the ESDM materials (Manual and Curriculum Checklist) are publicly available, it is important to remember that the studies demonstrating the most significant child change at the group level have been conducted in an intensive format (15 or more hours per week) by certified therapists. The procedure for becoming a certified ESDM therapist is described earlier in this chapter, but generally involves a combination of reading, didactic instruction, hands-on training, self-evaluation, and feedback on treatment implementation and use of ESDM techniques. The dissemination process, feasibility, and implementation of ESDM have been evaluated in several studies that have generally supported the use of didactic workshops and ongoing supervision and feedback in reaching and maintaining high levels of therapist and program fidelity (Vismara, Young, & Rogers, 2013; Vismara, Young, *et al.*, 2009; Vivanti *et al.*, 2014). Vismara *et al.* (2009) evaluated the contribution of several features in training therapists to fidelity. These features included live vs. distance (telehealth) learning, and the use of self-instruction, didactic, and team-supervision teaching techniques for both direct ESDM delivery and parent coaching. Learning occurred equally well for both live and distance learners and that fidelity of implementation significantly improved once therapists received didactic training and team supervision, features incorporated into the current certification procedure.

The workshop-based procedure now used to provide initial therapist training has also been evaluated. Vismara, Young, and Rogers (2013) analyzed therapists' fidelity in ESDM delivery directly following a training workshop, as well as their understanding of the treatment techniques and overall satisfaction with the procedure. Significant increases in therapist fidelity in ESDM technique use were observed both during the workshop itself and at the four-month follow-up. Notably, the majority of professionals rated the procedure as highly satisfactory and all 24 attained full fidelity (80%) by the conclusion of training. Despite their success in reaching fidelity by the end of the workshop, only half of the participants submitted post-workshop follow-up materials, although there are several possible explanations for this attrition rate, including lack of resources or support in their community organizations, or deciding not to adopt ESDM as the primary intervention approach.

More detailed information regarding the community and organization support necessary to provide group-based ESDM comes from programs recently implemented in Australia. Both the Sydney and Melbourne sites were established as part of the government-funded day-long childcare centers for children with autism (Autism Specific Early Learning and Care Centre, ASELCC). The ESDM Manual (Rogers & Dawson, 2010) provides specific guidelines for conducting ESDM treatment in a group-based delivery program. These will not be detailed here, but include recommendations for structuring the physical space, daily flow, and overall schedule for the classroom, organizing staff time and roles, strategies for addressing individual children's objectives into group activities, taking and maintaining accurate data on child learning, and other key features. Results from these two investigations demonstrate that children in these ESDM group-based programs make significant gains in cognitive, social, and adaptive skills and, thus, are effective programs for treating young children with ASD (Eapen et al., 2013; Vivanti et al., 2014).

In terms of feasibility, Vivanti et al. (2014) evaluated several specific features: acceptability, demand, implementation, practicality, and adaptation and integration into the existing center system. The use of ESDM was supported on each of these dimensions. More than 90% of parents indicated that they found the program both suitable and satisfactory for their children, and more than 250 families requested placement in the program, far more than capacity. The program was also rated highly by government-led evaluations in terms of providing service consistent with government regulations, collaboration with families and communities, and ease of integration into the public childcare system provided in that region of Australia. The most significant drawbacks identified by both the authors and the government evaluation is that demand far exceeded capacity, and thus, quality of educational childcare for young children with ASD needed to be increased throughout the country (Vivanti et al., 2014).

Recommendations for future research

The existing body of ESDM research demonstrates that it is an effective treatment approach for young children with ASD, leading to significant developmental growth in children's cognition, language, social abilities, and adaptive functioning. These changes are observed both on an individual level and in group comparisons. There is also support for the training procedures for both therapist and parent models, demonstrating that both groups are able to learn the ESDM techniques and implement them with high fidelity. Despite these impressive results, there are several areas where additional research is likely to be particularly fruitful.

The first area of research need is in comparing the outcomes of children in low-intensity ESDM (generally parent-implemented) models to the strong results observed in therapist-delivered formats (Dawson *et al.*, 2010, 2012; Vivanti *et al.*, 2014). While the results of several parent-implemented ESDM trials demonstrate significant gains in children's language, social communication, and developmental functioning, whether these gains are as strong as those obtained in intensive therapist-delivered ESDM formats is an open research question. There is initial evidence that P-ESDM is at least as effective as some higher-intensity non-ESDM community treatment models (Rogers *et al.*, 2012). However, whether it is appropriate to expect parents to be the main provider of early intensive services is an important question for public policy. Public policy concerning funding for early intervention for ASD needs to flow from: (1) real-world discussions about the cost–benefit analysis of quality early education for all young children; (2) dissemination to voters and policy makers about findings from evidence-based practices and studies; and (3) findings from community-based effectiveness studies that can help communities learn how to implement evidence-based practice in real-life settings. It needs to be made much more evident to voters and their representatives that dollars not spent for quality early childhood education for all children will be spent in much, much greater amounts later on in the lives of those children who did not receive it, and this is particularly true of children with ASD and other DDs and impoverished children. A major focus of ESDM research going forward will be in conducting community-based effectiveness studies and in evaluating wider dissemination of this efficacious treatment.

Finally, the results from the pilot study of infant intervention are quite exciting, and suggest that intervening as soon as symptoms begin to appear may have particularly strong effects in reducing symptom severity and diagnostic rates and improving functional outcomes. This possibility has significant implications for public policy in terms of screening, resource allocation, and the potential to significantly reduce the long-term costs associated with autism-related impairments (Ganz, 2015; Peters-Scheffer *et al.*, 2012).

Considerations for practitioners and families interested in the ESDM

In terms of specific benefits to families over other treatment approaches, ESDM offers several positive features. First, the generalist model employed in the ESDM means that parents see only one primary therapist, who delivers a comprehensive treatment plan that addresses children's learning needs across all domains. This approach limits the parents' need to integrate and reconcile potentially conflicting advice and plans from multiple professionals, which may contribute to the lower levels of parenting-related stress reported by parents receiving ESDM training (Estes *et al.*, 2014). Second, the rigorous certification process for professionals ensures that treatment delivered by these therapists is of high quality and adheres to the manualized protocols. A list of certified trainers and certified therapists is maintained through the UC Davis MIND Institute website,[3] where families can search for certified therapists in their area. Third, the parent training provided in the ESDM, whether in combination with therapist delivery or in the parent implemented model, is consistent with the recommendations from the national research council to include parents in their child's treatment plan (National Research Council, 2001). Parents who receive training in ESDM techniques report stronger working alliances with their therapists than parents whose children receive treatment in the community, suggesting that the ESDM supports parents in playing an active role in their child's intervention (Rogers *et al.*, 2012). Finally, there is strong support for the efficacy of the ESDM in improving children's outcomes. This has now been demonstrated in both single-subjects designs and randomized controlled trials, across therapist, parent, and group-based treatment delivery, as reviewed above. These results suggest that the ESDM not only improves children's language and cognition, but results in deep,

---

3   www.ucdmc.ucdavis.edu/mindinstitute/research/esdm

long-lasting changes in the children's ability to both participate in and learn from social interactions.

Conclusion

ESDM is one of the empirically validated early intervention approaches to demonstrate significant developmental change in very young children affected by ASD. We have shown that parents can learn to implement the ESDM at home with their children to treatment fidelity. Parents are often in the best position to do this as they are the ones with their child during most or all waking hours of the child's life. Therapists tend to come and go, but parents usually remain a constant. Empowering parents with the tools to deliver intervention during every routine in the child's life will not only accelerate the child's progress, but will also strengthen the bond between the parent and child. Furthermore, it creates a family system that is not solely dependent on therapist intervention and can fill in gaps in treatment due to delay in starting services, changing vendors, absences, etc. So, while P-ESDM can meet this need for low-intensity, high-quality, empirically validated treatment for very young children with autism, and fit nicely within a 0–3 framework requiring parent involvement, we do not yet have evidence that it is as effective as high-intensity services, and there are complications to having parents being "responsible" for their child's treatment. On the one hand, it empowers parents to feel effective in supporting their child's development, being proactive and supporting parents in advocating for their child's needs, but, on the other hand, delivering the intervention can add pressure on parents to be both parent and therapist (although ESDM data shows that it does not increase stress). These issues also vary by socio-economic status (SES), community, culture, etc., since families in very low-resource areas may not have any ASD-specific services available at all, whereas families in service-rich areas may have access to higher-intensity services like 1:1 ESDM for many hours/week. However, for young children, parents expect to be involved in the child's treatment. One of their first questions upon receiving a diagnosis is: "What can we do to help him at home?" Giving parents the tools to help, and giving them the opportunity to experience firsthand the developmental growth that good treatment stimulates in young children with ASD, helps parents move into a position of personal action and personal efficacy. Knowing what good treatment entails and knowing how to deliver it not only enhances feelings of competence in parents *of young children* whose initial reactions to a diagnosis may be a powerful dose of feeling incompetent, but it also enhances the parents' abilities to be knowledgeable consumers of treatment for their children. Professional partnership and support of parental expertise at the start of treatment provides young parents with a strong base for stepping into the role of advocates for their children in the world of professional services. It also supports maximizing child involvement in ongoing learning from parents across their waking hours. Thus, parent coaching provides a powerful first experience for young families and young children as they enter the world of autism spectrum disorder.

References

Bruner, J. (1975) "The ontogenesis of speech acts." *Journal of Child Language 2*, 1–19.

Bruner, J. (1981) "The social context of language acquisition." *Language and Communication 1*, 155–178.

Cohen, I. & Sudhalter, V. (1999) *Pervasive Developmental Disorder Behavior Inventory (PDDBI-C)*. New York: NYS Institute for Basic Research in Developmental Disabilities.

Dawson, G., Jones, E.J.H., Merkle, K., Venema, K., *et al.* (2012) "Early behavioral intervention is associated with normalized brain activity in young children with autism." *Journal of the American Academy of Child and Adolescsent Psychiatry 51*, 11, 1150–1159. http://doi.org/S0890-8567(12)00643-0 [pii]\r10.1016/j.jaac.2012.08.018

Dawson, G., Rogers, S., Munson, J., Smith, M., *et al.* (2010) "Randomized, controlled trial of an intervention for toddlers with autism: the Early Start Denver Model." *Pediatrics 125*, 1, e17–23.

Eapen, V., Črnčec, R., & Walter, A. (2013) "Clinical outcomes of an early intervention program for preschool children with Autism Spectrum Disorder in a community group setting." *BMC Pediatrics 13*, 1, 3.

Estes, A., Munson, J., Rogers, S.J., Greenson, J., Winter, J., & Dawson, G. (2015) "Long-term outcomes of early intervention in 6-year-old children with autism." *Journal of the American Academy of Child and Adolescent Psychiatry*, (advance online publication).

Estes, A., Vismara, L.A., Mercado, C., Fitzpatrick, A., *et al.* (2014) "The impact of parent-delivered intervention on parents of very young children with autism." *Journal of Autism and Developmental Disorders 44*, 2, 353–365.

Ganz, M.L. (2015) "The lifetime distribution of the incremental societal costs of autism." *Archives of Pediatrics & Adolescent Medicine 161*, 343–349.

Hanft, B.E., Rush, D.D., & Shelden, M.L. (2004) *Coaching Families and Colleagues in Early Childhood*. Baltimore, MD: Brookes Publishing.

Koegel, R.L., O'Dell, M., & Koegel, L.K. (1987) "A natural language teaching paradigm for nonverbal autistic children." *Journal of Autism and Developmental Disorders 17*, 187–199.

National Research Council (2001) *Educating Children with Autism*. Washington, DC: National Academy Press.

Peters-Scheffer, N., Didden, R., Korzilius, H., & Matson, J. (2012) "Cost comparison of early intensive behavioral intervention and treatment as usual for children with autism spectrum disorder in The Netherlands." *Research in Developmental Disabilities 33*, 6, 1763–1772.

Rogers, S.J. & Dawson, G. (2010) *Early Start Denver Model for Young Children with Autism: Promoting Language, Learning and Engagement.* New York: The Guilford Press.

Rogers, S.J., Dawson, G., & Vismara, L. (2012) *An Early Start for Your Child with Autism: Using Everyday Activities to Help Kids Connect, Communicate, and Learn.* New York: The Guilford Press.

Rogers, S.J. & DiLalla, D. (1991) "A comparative study of the effects of a developmentally based instructional model on young children with autism and young children with other disorders of behavior and development." *Topics in Early Childhood Special Education 11*, 29–48.

Rogers, S.J., Estes, A., Lord, C., Vismara, L.A., *et al.* (2012) "Effects of a brief Early Start Denver model (ESDM)-based parent intervention on toddlers at risk for autism spectrum disorders: A randomized controlled trial." *Journal of the American Academy of Child and Adolescent Psychiatry 51*, 10, 1052–1065.

Rogers, S.J., Herbison, J., Lewis, H., Pantone, J., & Reis, K. (1986) "An approach for enhancing the symbolic, communicative, and interpersonal functioning of young children with autism and severe emotional handicaps." *Journal of the Division of Early Childhood 10*, 135–148.

Rogers, S.J. & Vismara, L.A. (2012) ESDM Parent Coaching Fidelity Rating System (available from authors).

Rogers, S.J., Vismara, L.A., Wagner, A.L., McCormick, C., Young, G., & Ozonoff, S. (2014) "Autism treatment in the first year of life: A pilot study of Infant Start, a parent-implemented intervention for symptomatic infants." *Journal of Autism and Developmental Disorders 44*, 12, 2981–2995.

Vismara, L.A., Colombi, C., & Rogers, S.J. (2009) "Can one hour per week of therapy lead to lasting changes in young children with autism?" *Autism: The International Journal of Research and Practice 13*, 1, 93–115.

Vismara, L.A., McCormick, C., Young, G.S., Nadhan, A., & Monlux, K. (2013) "Preliminary findings of a telehealth approach to parent training in autism." *Journal of Autism and Developmental Disorders 43*, 12, 2953–2969.

Vismara, L.A. & Rogers, S.J. (2008) "The Early Start Denver Model: A case study of an innovative practice." *Journal of Early Intervention 31*, 1, 91–108.

Vismara, L.A., Young, G.S., & Rogers, S.J. (2012) "Telehealth for expanding the reach of early autism training to parents." *Autism Research and Treatment, 2012*, 121878.

Vismara, L.A., Young, G.S., & Rogers, S.J. (2013) "Community dissemination of the Early Start Denver Model: Implications for science and practice." *Topics in Early Childhood Special Education 32*, 4, 223–233.

Vismara, L.A., Young, G.S., Stahmer, A.C., Griffith, E.M., & Rogers, S.J. (2009) "Dissemination of evidence-based practice: Can we train therapists from a distance?" *Journal of Autism and Developmental Disorders 39*, 12, 1636–1651.

Vivanti, G., Dissanayake, C., and the Victorian ASELCC Team (2016) "Outcome for chidlren receiving the Early Start Denver Model before and after 48 months." *Journal of Autism and Developmental Disorders 46*, 2441–2449.

Vivanti, G., Paynter, J., Duncan, E., Fothergill, H., Dissanayake, C., & Rogers, S.J. (2014) "Effectiveness and feasibility of the Early Start Denver Model implemented in a group-based community childcare setting." *Journal of Autism and Developmental Disorders 44*, 12, 3140–3153.

Chapter 5

PADRES EN ACCIÓN

A Parent Education Program for Latino
Parents of Children with ASD

Sandy Magaña, Wendy Machalicek, Kristina Lopez, and Emily Iland

ABSTRACT

As the incidence of autism spectrum disorder (ASD) continues to rise and the Latino population continues to grow in the US, greater numbers of Latino families are impacted by ASD. Latino families, particularly immigrant families, may be disadvantaged by socio-economic, cultural, and political factors in seeking a diagnosis and care for their children. Having multiple unmet needs for information and support, and experiencing barriers to services, can place tremendous stress on these families and negatively impact their vulnerable children.

Presented here is preliminary evidence about the effectiveness of Padres en Acción (PTA) as an ecologically valid parent education program specially designed to help Latino families access information, advocate for their children, and to cope with the complex demands of caring for their children with ASD on a daily basis. By educating and empowering families, PTA provides a promising, feasible tool in the collective effort to help reduce documented inequities in the health, education, and service systems and to improve the lives of Latino children with autism and their families. We describe development of the PTA intervention using a cultural adaptation framework, our experimental evaluation, preliminary effectiveness, and feasibility of a parent education curriculum for Latina mothers of young children with suspected or diagnosis of autism spectrum disorder (ASD). We discuss the intervention components, implementation of the program, preliminary outcomes, and dissemination efforts. The chapter concludes with suggestions for practice and future research.

Keywords: inequity; Latino; autism; parent education program; Ecological Validity Framework

Autism in Latino families and the need for evidence-based intervention

Latinos are the largest and one of the fastest growing ethnic minority groups in the US (Colby & Ortman, 2015). Moreover, autism prevalence increased by 110% between 2002 and 2008 among Latino children, as compared to a 70% increase for white children (Centers for Disease Control and Prevention, 2012). Unfortunately, Latino children with ASD and other developmental disorders remain under-diagnosed and underserved (Centers for Disease Control and Prevention, 2014; Magaña et al., 2013). Latino children are more likely to be diagnosed later and are less likely than white children to receive autism specific intervention, including interventions based on the principles of behavior analysis (Magaña et al., 2013; Ratto, Reznick, & Turner-Brown, 2016). Indeed, even when Latino children with ASD have severe adaptive behavior limitations, they receive fewer autism specific specialty services than white children with similar conditions (Magaña, Parish, & Son, 2016). Furthermore, more than 63% of Latino children live in immigrant households (Fry & Passel, 2009), and these children are under-diagnosed with autism when compared to children of US-born parents (Schieve et al., 2012).

Disparity in diagnosis and the provision of services to Latino children with ASD can be linked to a combination of psychosocial, economic, political, and healthcare factors affecting their mothers, resulting in increased needs and decreased access (Iland, Weiner, & Murawski, 2012; Magaña & Smith, 2006). Latino parents may have less understanding about child development and the typical development of skills (Schulze et al., 2002) and may also be less concerned about the delays associated with ASD (Schulze et al., 2002). Additionally, language barriers may be present for foreign-born Latinos with limited English as there are shortages of bilingual specialists. A recent qualitative study reporting the perceptions of 33 parents of Latino children diagnosed with an ASD suggested that a number of individual parent characteristics contributed to barriers to obtaining a diagnosis of ASD. These included low levels of information about ASD, limited proficiency in English and a lack of social capital to navigate services, community-level variables such as mental health and disability stigma, poverty, and pediatricians' dismissal of parent concerns (Zuckerman *et al.*, 2014).

Delayed diagnosis and provision of services and supports likely exacerbates the stress and depression that parents of children with ASD report in higher levels than parents of typically developing children or children with other developmental disorders (Hauser-Cram *et al.*, 2013; Bonis, 2016). In heteronormative Latino families, the mother often bears the majority of this burden as she is more likely than her husband to be responsible for obtaining a diagnosis, becoming informed about the child's disability, and accessing therapies and other support services (e.g., Clifford & Minnes, 2013). Some of the greatest reported needs for Latina mothers of children with ASD are for information about their child's disability and how to manage it, information about services to support their child's development, and ways to navigate educational and other service systems be better consumers of service systems (Iland *et al.*, 2012).

In recent years, researchers have shown renewed interest in developing interventions that positively impact parent outcomes as much as they do child outcomes (Wainer, Hepburn, & McMahon Griffith, 2017). Recent systematic reviews of parent training programs suggest that parent implementation of interventions improves outcomes for young children with ASD, while also potentially reducing parental stress and improving family quality of life (Oono, Honey, & McConachie, 2013; Nevill, Lecavalier, & Stratis, 2016; Postorino *et al.*, 2017; Strauss *et al.*, 2013). Specifically, a strong literature base exists on the use of behavioral parent training (BPT) programs to effectively teach parents targeted skill use to reinforce and teach child adaptive behavior and prevent and decrease challenging behavior (Machalicek, Lang, & Raulston, 2015; McIntyre, 2013); and recent BPT interventions have demonstrated their effectiveness with underrepresented racial and ethnic minority groups and low-resourced families (Bagner *et al.*, 2013; McCabe *et al.*, 2012).

While these findings have important practice and policy implications, with few exceptions, families from culturally and linguistically diverse (CLD) and economically diverse backgrounds have largely been absent from the intervention literature (West *et al.*, 2016), thereby limiting the generalizability of the goals, procedures, and outcomes of the extent literature for families from CLD backgrounds. For Latino mothers, initially targeting their knowledge of interventions and treatments may also help to prepare them to be better consumers of service systems and professionals that often offer an array of both evidence-based practices and unestablished interventions unlikely to improve child behavior (Schreck et al., 2016). In particular, psychoeducational parenting interventions may assist in addressing these unmet needs for Latino families and may be especially beneficial in improving parent self-efficacy in instances where the duration and intensity of BPT is a barrier.

Cultural adaptation of evidence-based interventions

In addition to the contextual variables contributing to worsened outcomes around access to screening and diagnostic services as well as early intervention for ASD for Latino families, beliefs at both the family and cultural level affect parent perceptions of ASD and can influence a myriad of variables related to improved outcomes for children with ASD (Ravindran & Myers, 2012). For instance, parent beliefs can impact available social and educational resources for their children, can affect the parents' regard and valuation of the professional–parent relationship, and can influence treatment decisions and expectations of treatment outcome (Dyches et al., 2004; Ravindran & Myers, 2012).

Although researchers have long recognized the influence of culture on ASD and encouraged a multicultural perspective on education and intervention for children with ASD (Dieker, Voltz, & Epanchin, 2001; Wilder et al., 2004), parent education programs have rarely considered the cultural context of families of children with ASD or other developmental disorders from racial/ethnic minority cultures (Robertson et al., 2017). Importantly for this population, culturally adapted programs may improve access to essential information and service utilization for minority populations, while decreasing reliance on emergency mental health services (Snowden, Hu, & Jerrel, 1999). However, few studies have described the cultural adaptation of evidence-based parent education programs with this population (Cardona et al., 2012; Matos, Bauermeister, & Bernal, 2009).

Studies that carefully apply a cultural adaptation process have shown promise in parent and child outcomes such as the adaption of Parent–Child Interaction Therapy (PCIT) for Puerto Rican preschool children with Attention Deficit Hyperactivity Disorder (ADHD) and behavior problems (Matos *et al.*, 2009). Parent education interventions need to be developed in order that the intervention goals, procedures, and outcomes are socioculturally aligned with Latino understanding of ASDs and that linguistically and culturally match the needs, preferences, and cultural learning styles of this underserved and growing population.

The development and adaptation of interventions for use with diverse families has been categorized by Bernal (2006) into several possible pathways: translation or cultural adaptation of an existing empirically supported intervention, or development of a culturally informed new intervention. The first approach assumes that evidence-based interventions for non-minorities will work as well for ethnic minorities. Unfortunately, past research evaluating the use of evidence-based interventions with Latino families of individuals with mental health concerns demonstrates a failure to achieve similarly positive outcomes for Latinos (e.g., Huey & Polo, 2008). The development of a new intervention based on our understanding of sociocultural contexts and values for Latino families may improve outcomes (Miranda *et al.*, 2005). In the case of Padres en Acción, we created a new culturally informed intervention, inclusive of existing evidence-based information that we adapted to be fitting for Latina mothers of children with ASD.

Description of the program

Padres en Acción (PTA) is a parent education program originally designed for Latino immigrant families to address disparities in information, services, and knowledge about evidenced-based treatments for their children with ASD (Magaña, Lopez, & Machalicek, 2017). PTA uses a *promotores de salud,* or health-promoter, delivery model. Promotores are typically lay people who come from the target communities, speak the same language, and engage in health promotion activities. The model has been used successfully with Latino populations to educate and support positive health behavior

(Balcázar *et al.*, 2005; Elder *et al.*, 2005; Reinschmidt *et al.*, 2006; WestRasmus *et al.*, 2012). Many elements of PTA are also relevant for low-resource families from other communities.

PTA uses a unique parent-to-parent training model, in which a parent of a child with ASD is trained and supported by researchers with expertise in early intervention for ASD and parent education to deliver the intervention to participating parents. The health-promoters in our research to date have all been mothers of older children (e.g., adolescents) with autism, engaged in volunteer or paid leadership activities through their community-based organization (e.g., parent-to-parent support and training to assist families in understanding their rights in special education service provision); thus, the term "promotora" will be used throughout this chapter. None of the promotoras participated in Padres en Acción prior to serving as promotoras and no criterion was set for the highest education achieved or past experience in special education. The promotora delivers content knowledge, models target behavior, and supports opportunities for the participant parent to use the targeted skills. Through this personalized, relationship-based intervention, the promotora may effectively address motivation and participation in the education program, to the benefit of the participant parent, child, and entire family.

Theoretical frameworks

We believe that use of a culturally informed intervention may be an active ingredient in effective approaches for reducing access and treatment disparities for children with ASD from underserved populations. When developing the program, we took into account three guiding frameworks: (1) a community-based approach; (2) the Ecological Validity Framework (EVF) used for culturally developing the intervention; and (3) self-efficacy theory.

Using a community-based approach, we partnered with Wisconsin Facets, a community organization in Milwaukee that provides parent education for parents of children with developmental disabilities including ASD. We then formed an advisory committee (AC) that consisted of Spanish-speaking Latino parents of children with ASD, bilingual medical, allied health, and mental health clinicians who worked with a local clinic serving Latino children with ASD, staff from the community-based organization, and research team members. Aside from the research team and staff from Wisconsin Facets, AC stakeholders were invited through existing agency relationships with community professionals. The AC provided feedback on the content and structure of the intervention using the EVF as guidance (Bernal, Bonilla, & Bellido, 1995) in order to ensure that the intervention was developed in a culturally relevant way. The EVF consists of seven dimensions to consider in creating or adapting an intervention for particular populations including language, persons, metaphors, content, goals, methods, and context (see Table 5.1). Using EVF as a guide, and feedback from the AC, the intervention includes the following elements that have been emphasized by Bernal and colleagues so as to ensure its feasibility and acceptability to Latino immigrant parents: (1) it is delivered through home visits that overcome transportation and child care barriers; (2) the written materials were developed at an eighth-grade reading level and included videos to enhance written content; (3) some concepts were given more contextual explanation because of unfamiliarity with these concepts among target parents; (4) metaphors, stories, and case studies were used to highlight important concepts; and (5) the intervention and materials were delivered in the language of preference.

Table 5.1 Ecological Validity Framework and PTA

Dimension	Incorporation into intervention and materials
Language	Materials created in Spanish and English, promotoras are native Spanish speakers
Persons	Promotoras come from the same culture and geographic community
Metaphors	Common Spanish sayings or "dichos" as well as storytelling were incorporated into the materials
Content	Incorporated cultural values into content, explanations of information and strategies provided in user friendly and interactive ways
Goals	Goals are set with parents that take into account socio-cultural context
Methods	Home visits provide scheduling flexibility, using peer promotoras fosters relationship building
Context	Home visit model overcomes barriers to participation such as transportation and childcare

An important ecologically valid aspect of PTA is *persons*, the peer mentoring and leadership offered through the Promotores de Salud Model. To enhance the peer aspect of our intervention, we ensure that the promotoras are also mothers of children with ASD. This provides a rich aspect to the learning process, that of shared experiences raising children with ASD. Following a pilot of the intervention, we held focus groups with promotoras to assess their perceptions about the goals, procedures, and outcomes of the intervention. We found that shared experiences, or *convivencia*, were considered to be highly valued, critical aspects of behavioral change and parent support (Magaña *et al.*, 2017).

The promotora model fits well with self-efficacy theory, the theoretical framework on which PTA is based. Self-efficacy theory is based on the belief that if people are confident in their ability to carry out a positive behavior, they are then able to engage in behavior change (Bandura, 2007). To develop self-efficacy or confidence, Bandura (1977) outlined five mechanisms: performance, accomplishment, vicarious experience, verbal persuasion, and positive emotional states. Promotoras, who are also parents of children with ASD can promote these mechanisms by modeling advocacy behavior, such as describing a child's unique learning needs to a teacher or other professional and advocating for needed services by continuing to state the child's needs, the rationale for meeting those needs, and describing the specific actions they would like to see happen. Promotoras support parent use of targeted strategies and practices through verbal persuasion in the form of positive descriptive praise of actions that the parent is already taking or initiates during the intervention, and offering opportunities for performance accomplishment through provision of homework activities to practice specific skills targeted by the curriculum. For example, parents were asked to set aside parent–child play time, where they could practice being responsive to their child's communication attempts. Homework activities were reviewed at the beginning of the next intervention session and parents were asked to reflect on how the activity or reflection went. During this reflection, promotoras reinforced parent attempts and engagement with encouragement and praise. They can also promote positive emotional states through sessions on reducing maternal stress and obtaining social support from family and friends. As a result, the PTA program may support motivational variables related to participant engagement (Reinschmidt *et al.*, 2006) and improve participant outcomes through increased self-efficacy when implementing intervention (Bandura, 1986; Lorig, Ritter, & Gonzalez, 2003).

Program content

In the PTA program, promotoras delivered 14 weekly home visits to primary biological mothers of children with ASD between the ages of 2 and 8 years. The age range reflects the range of diagnosis commonly seen with autism with consideration of the later age of diagnosis often seen in Latinos (Mandell *et al.*, 2009). During each two-hour-long home visit, a single session was presented from the intervention curriculum. Other family members were allowed to be present during the sessions. However, our experience is that the primary parents are most often mothers, who frequently choose to schedule appointments while their child is at school. This may not be conducive to the schedules of other family members and does not allow for incorporation of parent coaching of strategy use with their child, which we anticipate is integral to strategy use by parents. Nevertheless, the PTA program focuses on improving knowledge of parents about autism and evidence-based practices to address the symptoms of autism, improving parent knowledge and navigation of service systems, including schools, decreased stress, and depression for parents, and increased access to services and supports rather than increasing the frequency of targeted parent skill use. Sessions focused on child intervention (i.e., communication, play, social skills, challenging behavior) were largely conceptualized as improving parent knowledge of strategies that were likely already in use by early intervention professionals and teachers working with the family and offering some discrete steps that parents could take to support their child's development in these areas. The training and supervision of promotoras to obtain sufficient levels of fidelity in child assessment and treatment planning, intervention delivery, data collection and data analysis, ongoing adaptation of research-based practices, and behavioral parent training would be sizable and beyond the cost-effective model that we implemented. We believe that a professional such as promotora, in place of or in addition to the parent promotora model, would be better aligned with an intervention aiming to improve parent skill use and improve child symptoms.

The content of the curriculum is focused on helping parents better understand their child with ASD, learn about the importance of evidenced-based treatments and services, and develop advocacy skills to access these treatments and services. The content also focuses on teaching parents evidenced-based naturalistic behavioral strategies that they can use with their children at home in order to support their child's development of social-emotional, communication and play skills, and function-based behavioral strategies so as to prevent and address challenging behavior. Sessions focused on teaching parents strategies for reducing parent stress and expanding social support are also essential components of the program. See Table 5.2 for a list of the topics and goals that are included in the curriculum.

Table 5.2 Program sessions and goals

Session	Goals
Session 1: Introduction to the program	Meet the promotora and receive an overview of the program
Session 2: Understanding child development	Discuss developmental milestones and recognizing signs
Session 3: Understanding the autism spectrum and your child's needs	Learn about how autism is diagnosed and what autism symptoms relate to your child
Session 4: What works to address symptoms of autism	Learn about evidenced-based practices and how to tell if a practice works for your child
Session 5: How to be an effective advocate	Learn about the importance of being an advocate for your child and advocacy strategies
Session 6: Advocacy in the school system	Learn about the individualized education plan (IEP) process and advocacy strategies to use in your child's school
Session 7: Play together, learn together	Learn about the importance of play and ways to engage your child in play
Session 8: Creating everyday opportunities to encourage communication	Learn strategies for enhancing communication through daily routines
Session 9: Helping your child make friends and interact with others	Explore activities parents can do to help their child interact with peers
Session 10: Challenging behavior is communication	Learn why children engage in challenging behavior

Session 11: How to reduce challenging behaviors and respond appropriately when they occur	Explore strategies for preventing and reducing challenging behavior
Session 12: Reducing stress and recognizing signs of depression	Learn about risks to parental health and well-being and how to reduce stress
Session 13: Talking about autism to others and social support	Discuss how to share information with others about your child and the importance of social support
Session 14: Looking ahead	Set future goals and explore how to sustain growth. Celebrate completion!

Another aspect of the program is a home activity that is assigned at the end of each session. This activity may involve the parent setting goals, having a family discussion, or carrying out a behavioral strategy with the child. The promotora may call the parent midweek to offer support towards completing the assignment. Each new session begins with a check-in on the previous week's home activity and a discussion about any barriers to completion and potential solutions for completion of the next week's home activity.

Program implementation

The format of each session includes a check-in and review of objectives and interactive delivery of the content that includes discussion between the promotora and parent about the main points and how they relate to their children. To highlight important points, the promotora often shares personal experiences about her own child and family and encourages the parent to connect with relevant examples from her own family and context. Materials for the program included a promotora manual and a participant manual. The promotora manual included the curricular content and instructions and scripts on how to deliver it. The parent received the printed, ring-bound participant manual, which included all of the content but not the promotora instructions. Each session was comprised of the following instructional or navigational components: (1) key terms, including professional jargon; (2) a check-in, where the promotora reinforced the mother's continued engagement in the intervention and an introduction to the content of that week's session;

(3) learning objectives (e.g., practice the stages of child development with a picture dictionary); (4) an anchoring activity, which was a dicho read by the promotora or delivered via video shown on a DVD, followed by discussion; and (5) didactic content with embedded activities to ensure active engagement with the material. The majority of sessions included opportunities for the mother to role play discussions or strategy use with the promotora. For example, session 2 asks the mother to role play asking a doctor to administer the Modified Checklist for Autism and Toddlers (M-CHAT). Finally, there would be an explanation of a homework activity (e.g., share information about the M-CHAT with another parent of a young child) that the mother was asked to complete prior to the next visit.

Repeated picture icons (e.g., a line drawing of a light bulb represented an idea for discussion called a "check-in") were used for each of the aforementioned components in each session to ease navigation for the promotoras and mothers. The intended use and meaning of each of the icons was described at the beginning of the manual. In addition to the printed manuals, promotoras were equipped with a portable DVD player and a DVD with video-clips related to the manual content. Video-clips were used to anchor each session and promote parent engagement and discussion. Video-clips of a bilingual mother using intervention strategies with her children served as an important source of modeling during sessions targeting intervention. In addition, video-clips were used to show researchers narrating case studies or information in a conversational manner to increase parent engagement and to ensure procedural fidelity in implementation of the intervention. Parents were given a copy of the DVD for their own use and to serve as a resource for future reference. In addition, parents also received a folder with local community service resources, which was referred to during the sessions to help parents navigate the service system based on their child's needs.

There are several aspects that organizations should consider when offering the program. These include: (1) recruitment and hiring of promotoras; (2) promotora training and compensation; (3) coordination and supervision of the program; and (4) maintaining fidelity. A "train-the-trainer" model is used to assist in this training and outline the aforementioned points.

We have found that a successful way to identify potential promotoras is by working with organizations that serve Latino families who have children with ASD (e.g., through support groups or family resource centers). Organizational staff can often identify parents of children with ASD who have emerged as leaders by volunteering and helping other families. These parents can be invited to an informational session on the program and the role of promotoras. In our program, the promotoras were parents of an older child with autism and had not been a prior participant of the curriculum.

Those who are interested in fulfilling this role can be asked to complete an application. The organization will need to decide how promotoras will be compensated. In our experience, promotoras have been compensated in different ways, depending on organizational preferences and infrastructure. For example, they have been hired as part-time staff, given a stipend for each family they serve, or hired as independent contractors. Compensation to promotoras has averaged above the state minimum wage. The organization should also take into account mileage and travel expenses of promotoras. Training of promotoras is conducted using a group format. Because there are 14 sessions, training requires 28 to 30 hours. Promotoras are compensated for their training time.

In addition, it is important to have a staff member or consultant who supervises the work of the promotoras. This person is responsible for checking in with each promotora after each weekly visit; they should be available to answer questions and resolve any difficulties, and collect all of the paperwork for the case, including the fidelity checklists and notes made by the promotoras. These staff have held concurrent employment in the organization as program director and regularly supervised staff in the course of their daily work. Our criteria for supervisors were agreement on the goals of the intervention, access to the community we were seeking, and a community-based organization with a solid infrastructure. In each of the sites that we have conducted PTA, this person has been a parent of a child with ASD; however, this is not a requirement of the protocol. In addition, research personnel have provided ongoing feedback and support to this supervisor to ensure treatment fidelity.

In order to ensure fidelity in implementing the intervention, a fidelity checklist was created that consists of 16 items and included items such as: I provided parent with positive feedback and helped them problem-solve any issues with homework; I reviewed objectives of the session; I presented information (from the manual or DVD) to explain the key points of the intervention/practice; I encouraged discussion, comments, questions, and concerns by using questions, examples and dialogue; and I did not attempt to provide counseling, but offered professional resources for parent when needed. Promotoras complete the self-report version after each home visit session. It is recommended that the organization also does periodic observations using the observation checklist and discusses the results with the promotora. The promotoras should have at least 80% reliability using the fidelity checklist, which should be confirmed by observation. We have typically conducted an observation visit with the promotora and parent at the onset of the 14-week program and at one additional time. However, if a curriculum asks a promotora to deliver more complex content or to implement behavioral parent training, we suggest additional observation visits at the onset of the intervention so as to ensure acquisition of coaching behaviors following didactic promotora education.

We believe that this program can be adapted for other low-resource and racial and ethnic communities. Program elements that make it feasible for other low-resource groups include the home visit model, having a peer mentor who comes from the community of the target population, providing materials at an appropriate reading level, and providing videos and other interactive approaches. As previously mentioned, the videos used in our intervention are left with the parent in the form of a DVD for future review. Some considerations for adaptation include changing the family stories in order to be more relevant for the target population, and making sure that the resource folder reflects the local community resources of the geographic area.

Evidence for the model

The development of the content for the PTA program was dependent on an interdisciplinary body of practices, derived from social work (e.g., content on advocacy, self-care to reduce stress and depression, and strategies for building social support networks), developmental psychology (e.g., content on typical and atypical child development), early childhood special education (e.g., incidental teaching strategies, routine and activity-based intervention), and, importantly, autism research. The evidence-based strategies from autism research that parents are informed about were based on the principles of applied behavior analysis and emphasized naturalistic, play-based strategies and positive behavior support.

In this section, we present evidence on the use of the promotora model with parents of children with learning challenges, results from a pilot study of PTA that provides evidence for the feasibility and acceptability of the program with Latina mothers of children with ASD, and preliminary findings from the ongoing multi-site randomized control trial of the PTA program.

Evidence of promotora effectiveness

Home visits by promotoras are effective at retaining Latino parents' interventions designed to improve child health (Hoeft *et al.*, 2015; Rashid *et al.*, 2014) and in enhancing adult Latinas physical and mental health (Tran *et al.*, 2014). For example, in a parent education intervention designed to improve children's oral health care, Latina mothers preferred lay health educators (promotoras) to deliver the program content rather than dental or oral health professionals (Hoeft *et al.*, 2015). Williamson and colleagues (2014) trained promotoras to deliver a home visitation program aimed at improving parents' understanding of their child's development, positive parent–child interactions, behavior management, and ability to navigate community resources. The use of promotoras in the home visit model was shown to be successful with the 196 Latina mothers included in the study. Following intervention, the mothers reported increases in their positive parenting skills and family functioning as well as decreases in their children's externalizing behavior problems.

Evidence of parenting program for parents of children with ASD

Although promotoras have not been traditionally used in interventions for parents of young children with ASD, parent-to-parent support has been found to be an effective mechanism to develop connections to similar others to enhance knowledge of their children's special needs (Ainbinder *et al.*, 1998). A culturally informed parent education program delivered by promotoras to Latina mothers of children with intellectual or developmental disabilities was developed to improve self-efficacy as well as maternal physical and mental health (Magaña *et al.*, 2015). A randomized trial that included 100 Latina mothers found that compared to the control group, those receiving the intervention had higher levels of self-efficacy and positive health behaviors such as nutrition, exercise, and self-care habits between pre- and post-tests. The evidence from this study suggested that a culturally informed psychoeducation program for Latina mothers of children with ASD could be a successful and cost-effective method of intervention.

PTA pilot study

Drawing from this literature, the PTA program used a similar model by training mothers of Latino children with ASD to deliver the intervention in the homes of other Latinas raising young children with ASD. The pilot study was conducted in the Midwest, with 19 Latina Spanish-speaking mothers (Magaña *et al.*, 2015). The pilot study examined the feasibility, acceptability, and preliminary outcomes of a culturally derived intervention. A mixed-methods design including one group pre- and post-test design and focus groups were used to evaluate the outcomes.

As mentioned previously, this program was developed using a community-based approach. While the current program consists of 14 sessions, the original pilot study consisted of two 8-session modules. Parents and promotoras who participated in the pilot study indicated that a shorter intervention would be ideal and, from an economic perspective, a shorter intervention was favorable. In the first module, the focus was on basic information about autism, advocacy, and navigating the service system. The second module included information about evidence-based interventions as well as instruction on intervention strategies to prevent and manage challenging behaviors and improve children's communication and social and play skills. More details about this study can be found in Magaña *et al.* (2017); however, we will summarize the findings here.

Pilot study participants

In the pilot study, eligible participants were native Spanish speakers, of Latin American descent, and mothers of a child between the ages of 2 and 8 years who had a medical diagnosis of ASD. Families were recruited primarily by the community-based organization, Wisconsin Facets. Of the 22 eligible Latina mothers who were enrolled in the pilot study, 19 had completed the eight sessions included in Module I (retention rate of 86.4%). Of the 3 mothers who left the pilot study: 1 mother stopped participating after session five for undisclosed reasons and the other 2 mothers left the study after their second session due to competing responsibilities and time constraints.

Mothers who participated in the study were on average about 33 years of age, primarily foreign born and of Mexican descent, and had about 11 years of education. The children with ASD were between 5 and 6 years of age on average, primarily male (90%), and US born (100%). Module II was offered only to those mothers who completed Module I; 16 mothers were enrolled in Module II (84% retention rate). The eight sessions in Module II were completed by 14 mothers (87.5% retention rate). The 2 participants who did not choose to complete Module II stated time constraints as the reason for their dropout. Sessions for both modules were held in the home of participating mothers.

Pilot study measures

The first session of each module included a pre-test and the final session included the post-test. Measures used in the pre- and post-tests included: the Maternal Autism Knowledge Questionnaire (Kuhn & Carter, 2006); Family Outcome Survey Revised (FOS; Bailey *et al.*, 2008); Center for Epidemiologic Studies Depression Scale (CESD; Radloff, 1977); and measures of parent burden, satisfaction, and efficacy (Heller, Miller, & Hseih, 1999). Because the main focus of our intervention was on facilitating the use of evidenced-based strategies among the mothers, we created measures specific to the intervention called, "Caregiver Efficacy in Use of Strategies" and "Use of Strategies." The Use of Strategies measure was comprised of 14 items and asked parents to report on their use of strategies on a 4-point Likert scale. Sample items included: I immediately reward my child for positive behaviors; I provide my child with choices to prevent problem behavior. These were used to assess the degree to which mothers reported having used the targeted strategies. The Caregiver Efficacy in Use of Strategies measure included 11 items and asked mothers to report on the confidence they had in their ability to use strategies using a 4-point Likert scale. Sample items included: I feel confident setting the stage for learning for my child; and I feel confident modeling for my child. We also included the following child measures: the Autism Behavior Checklist (ABC; Krug, Arick, & Almond, 1993) and the Scales of Independent Behavior Revised (SIB-R; Bruininks *et al.*, 1996).

Pilot study results and implications

For Module I, paired sample *t*-tests were used to compare pre- and post-test measure scores. We found that mothers reported significant increases between pre- and post-test on the empowerment-oriented measures such as greater knowledge about autism, increases in their understanding of their child's needs and strengths, enhanced knowledge of their rights and how to advocate for their child, greater information about how to help their child develop and learn, increased knowledge of support systems, and greater access to the community. Effect sizes for these outcomes were all in the large range, suggesting positive clinical significance. We did not find a decrease in parent burden, or depressive symptoms, or greater parent satisfaction; however, these were secondary outcomes (Magaña *et al.*, 2017).

For Module II, the primary outcomes were efficacy in use of strategies and actual use of strategies. We found a significant increase in efficacy in use of strategies. There was an increase in the use of strategies; however, it was not significant, possibly due to the small sample size. Keeping in mind that our primary outcomes for this study were parent outcomes, we did find a significant increase in language use among the children in the study based on the ABC, suggesting potential for impacting child outcomes as well.

Focus group data from the pilot study indicated that post-intervention mothers ($n = 14$) felt empowered to speak out about their child's rights to services in the systems they encountered, had an improved capacity to speak to their family members about autism, and were more familiar with strategies to help their children communicate and manage behaviors. Importantly, the mothers expressed optimistic statements about their entire program experience and about the ability of the promotoras to support them through the program (Magaña *et al.*, 2017). The mothers discussed the importance of the promotora's experience as a parent of a child with autism and the empathetic, nonjudgmental conversations that took place during home visits. Readers interested in the responses of parents during the focus groups are referred to Magaña *et al.* (2017).

We also conducted focus groups with the promotoras and found that they benefited from their role as promotoras (Magaña *et al.*, 2014). The promotoras reported that they learned important information that they found useful for their own families as they were teaching the information to other mothers. They discussed how they received satisfaction with teaching and supporting other mothers who were similar to them.

Despite the small sample in the pilot, the quantitative and qualitative results of the modules indicated evidence of the feasibility of the PTA program and its acceptability to families. We found preliminary evidence that the intervention impacted Latina mothers' understanding of autism, their capacity to advocate for their children, and their ability to manage behaviors and enhance their children's social communication.

Padres en Acción randomized control trial

Following the promising results from the pilot trial, a three-year, two-site randomized control trial (RCT) of the PTA program, funded by the National Institute of Disability, Independent Living, and Rehabilitation Research (NIDILRR), is currently underway. At the time of writing this chapter, we are in the third year of this RCT, which is being conducted in Chicago, Illinois, and Los Angeles, California.

Given changes to the DSM-IV criteria of ASD, the location of the studies, as well as the results and feedback from participants in the pilot study, several modifications were made to the original format of the project for use in the randomized control study. First, the study eligibility was open to Latino children formally diagnosed or suspected of having ASD or a speech language disorder. Second, the intervention materials were offered in either English or Spanish, depending on the participant's preference. Thus, some of the community members who were recruited and trained to be promotoras were bilingual in English and Spanish (whereas in the pilot study, they were Spanish-speaking only). Third, the intervention program was condensed from two 8-session modules to a single 14-session program based on participant feedback regarding the length of the program. The revised program can be seen in Table 5.2.

Participants were recruited through community organizations and schools that served Latino families of children with ASD and other developmental disabilities, and through word of mouth. Families interested in the project contacted study staff to determine eligibility. If families were eligible, they were consented in person and had their baseline assessment (Time 1; T1). The T1 assessment consisted of similar measures used in the pilot study (e.g., Caregiver Efficacy in Use of Strategies, Use of Strategies, ABC, SIB-R), a ten-minute video recorded parent–child interaction, and the Childhood Autism Rating Scale (CARS; Schopler *et al.*, 1980) was added to provide a better understanding of the severity levels of autism among the children in the study.

Following completion of the baseline assessment, parents were provided with a sealed envelope, indicating whether they had been randomized to the "intervention now" or "intervention later" group. Those randomized to intervention now were immediately connected to a promotora to begin the 14-session Padres en Acción program.

Parents who were assigned to intervention later completed a Time 2 assessment (T2; four months post-enrollment) and a Time 3 assessment (T3; eight months post-enrollment). Following the final assessment, mothers in the intervention later group were offered the 14-session PTA program. For parents in the intervention now group, T2 assessments were conducted after they completed the 14 sessions with a promotora. The T3 assessment occurred four months after their second assessment, followed by a focus group. For intervention group participants, the time between T2 and T3 represents maintenance of any intervention effects.

Randomized control trial participants

To date, we have enrolled 88 parent–child dyads across the two sites, with a goal of ultimately recruiting 120 dyads; 68 (77%) of them have completed all three assessments. Here, we report preliminary results from the 68 families on our primary outcomes, *efficacy in use of strategies* and *frequency in use of strategies*. The findings from the RCT should be considered preliminary, as this is an ongoing study and the final results will be published when the study is complete.

Of the 68 parent–child dyads, 29 were randomized to intervention now and 39 were randomized to intervention later. Table 5.3 illustrates the parent and child demographics. The mothers' average age was 37 years and children were on average 6 years of age at T1. The majority of the children were male in the intervention and control group, 87% and 88%, respectively. Table 5.3 presents full demographic characteristics of the sample, including information related to ASD severity, family income, and mother's education level and English proficiency.

Table 5.3 Demographic characteristics for PTA participants in the randomized control trial

	Intervention		Control	
	M	*SD*	*M*	*SD*
Parent characteristics	*n* = 29		*n* = 39	
Age	38.2	5.3	36.8	7.1
	n	*%*	*n*	*%*
Education				
Less than HS	7	24	17	44
HS	10	35	14	36
Post-HS education	12	41	8	21
Income ≥ $20K[n]	16	57	25	66
Any employment	8	28	12	31
Married or living with partner	21	72	27	69
English proficiency				
Speaks English well or excellent	7	24	6	15
Reads English well or excellent	11	38	9	23
Writes English well or excellent	9	31	6	15

	Intervention		Control	
	M	*SD*	*M*	*SD*
Child characteristics	$n = 30$		$n = 41$	
Age	6.4	1.8	5.8	1.7
	n	%	*n*	%
Gender, Male	26	87	36	88
CARS severity[n]				
Minimal	15	52	15	37
Mild to moderate	5	17	10	24
Severe	9	31	16	39

Notes: The data represent those families who have completed three assessments; Income ≥ $20k: Intervention group $n = 23$ due to missing data. CARS severity: Control group $n = 31$ due to missing data. Unless otherwise indicated, all categorical variables are dichotomous.

Efficacy in use of strategies

Figures 5.1 and 5.2 illustrate the trends for efficacy in use of strategies across the three time points of assessment. Higher scores suggest higher levels of self-efficacy. The highest possible score was 44. Figure 5.1 indicates that while the intervention and control groups began the study with similar levels of efficacy in use of strategies, the groups are distinctly different by T2. Specifically, the intervention group at T1 had an average level of 34.1 ($SD = 5.4$), increasing to 38.6 ($SD = 4.1$) at T2 and 37.1 ($SD = 5.5$) at T3. The control group had an average level of 34.4 ($SD = 5.2$) at T1, 34.8 ($SD = 4.9$) at T2, and 35.5 ($SD = 5.1$) at T3. The changes over time indicate that the intervention group was impacted more positively in their efficacy as compared to the control group, after controlling for the number of services that children were receiving at baseline ($p < 0.01$). From T2 to T3 (maintenance), the intervention group decreased slightly in efficacy, yet remains at a higher average than that found among the control group.

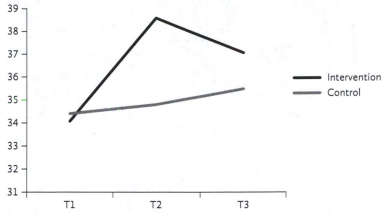

Figure 5.1 Efficacy in use of strategies among the intervention and control groups from Time 1 (T1) to Time 3 (T3) after controlling for the number of services children were receiving at T1

Frequency of using the intervention strategies

Figure 5.2 illustrates the trends for frequency of using the intervention strategies across the three time points of assessment. A similar pattern of change was found for the frequency of using intervention strategies after controlling for the number of services that children were receiving at their baseline assessment. Higher scores suggest higher levels of use of strategies. The highest possible score was 56. Specifically, the intervention group at T1 had an average level of 40.6 ($SD = 7.3$), increasing to 45.8 ($SD = 6.9$) at T2, and to 44.9 ($SD = 6.0$) at T3. The control group had an average level of 40.3 ($SD = 7.6$) at T1, 42.9 ($SD = 8.3$) at T2, and 41.6 ($SD = 6.7$) at T3. No significant difference existed between the two groups at T1 for frequency in using the intervention strategies. However, the intervention group increased in frequency compared to the control group from T1 to T2, suggesting an intervention effect. From T2 to T3 (maintenance), the intervention group decreased slightly in frequency, yet remained at a higher average of using strategies than the control group.

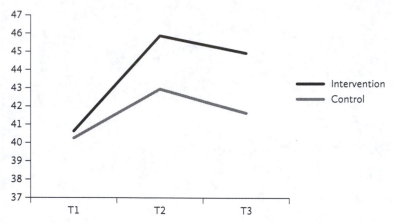

Figure 5.2 Frequency in use of intervention strategies among the intervention and control groups from Time 1 (T1) to Time 3 (T3) after controlling for the number of services children were receiving at the T1 assessment

Prescriptive implications and recommendations

The effects of autism are pervasive for the child and family. Whether the child with ASD is affected mildly, moderately, or severely, families face numerous challenges. Having multiple unmet needs for information, support, and services, and experiencing barriers to care can place considerable stress on Latino immigrant families and negatively impact the child with ASD. The findings from the ongoing RCT suggest that the PTA program may be efficacious in our primary parent outcomes. These findings are promising as these two outcomes are strongly linked to evidence-based practice.

PTA may benefit families in multiple ways, by improving parent knowledge of autism and evidence-based practices and improving family quality of life. The information shared through the program may improve understanding of their children and their disorder and create consensus within families by providing mothers with the tools to discuss issues concerning their child and their experience of parenting with other caregivers. Mothers may experience positive emotional states and greater social support, countering feelings of isolation and depression. Together, these outcomes may contribute to the mother's well being, benefiting both the child and the family.

PTA may also benefit participants in the areas of self-efficacy. Participants learn and practice practical strategies to improve their child's communication, socialization, and behavior, which may improve functioning on a daily basis. This outcome is evidenced by our findings that study participants used the strategies more frequently than the control group. Preliminary results also showed that children of mothers in PTA received more services post-intervention compared to the control group. Moreover, mothers may feel empowered to advocate for their children and secure needed services for the benefit both of the child and of the family.

Participants also learned about the M-CHAT (Modified Checklist for Autism in Toddlers; Robins, Fein, & Barton, 1999), one example of a screening tool that can help parents understand child development and start the referral process when delays are suspected. Participants were asked to share this information with friends and neighbors, which they did consistently. While this may be a minor task, this kind of grassroots awareness effort can help reverse the trend of late diagnosis and give more Latino children access to early intervention services.

Strengths and limitations of the study

This is one of very few randomized controlled studies with an adequate sample size focusing on Latinos and autism. There are few, if any, studies that examine the effectiveness of a parent education program specially designed to overcome multiple barriers faced by Latino immigrant families. A strength of this research is that many participants were not yet part of parent support organizations and not all of the children had a confirmed diagnosis. This suggests that the information baseline of such participants was quite low and reported improved outcomes were more likely related to the intervention than to other factors.

Limitations of the study include that the research sample was limited geographically to two large, urban areas, and did not include participants in small towns or rural areas. It is culturally appropriate to primarily focus the PTA intervention on Latina mothers as they are typically the primary parents. However, fathers and other members could also benefit from such a program. Thus, an intervention that targets fathers by perhaps using male promotoros may be warranted. Given the underrepresentation of fathers in early intervention research for children with autism (Flippin & Crais, 2011), increasing involvement of fathers in parenting interventions like PTA is essential. Although research on the engagement of Latino fathers of children with developmental disabilities in parenting interventions is lacking, we suspect that the engagement of Latino fathers might be supported by adaptations known to improve engagement for minority mothers of children with autism (Carr & Lord, 2016; Kasari *et al.*, 2014). For example, allowing for flexible scheduling and liberal cancellation and rescheduling of home visits, incentives for completion of assessment measures, and decreased length of intervention may be particularly attractive to working fathers. Nevertheless, Latino fathers may respond differentially to interventions when compared to mothers in the same family, necessitating comparative study of different components of cultural adaptation (Parra-Cardona *et al.*, 2017). Because the PTA RCT is ongoing, we have not yet analyzed child outcomes. However, because PTA focuses on parent education and not directly on coaching the parent in using strategies with the child, it is expected that child outcomes may be weaker. Families could also benefit from coaching that involves the parent and child, which would be more likely to lead to positive child outcomes.

Future research and dissemination

Conducting a larger study that includes a more geographically diverse sample would be helpful to measure the ecological validity and effectiveness of our program in different parts of the country, where challenges faced by Latino families and the resources available to them may differ dramatically from the two urban settings where the present study was implemented. Another potential application is to study the effectiveness of the program in different low- and middle-income countries. Such research would help determine whether PTA is an acceptable and feasible education tool for Latinos living in different parts of the world, and for different Latino or Hispanic subgroups. For example, we are currently working with a partner in Colombia to adapt and implement PTA. Adaptation will follow a similar cultural adaptation framework as was used in the development of PTA, but, thus far, adaptations have included the addition of animated video-clips in place of videoed researchers delivering essential content and the use of professionals as promotoras rather than parents. Dissemination will require the identification of the core components of the intervention as well as those components that can be delivered flexibly and the development of feasible measures of treatment fidelity that can be used by community-based providers to ensure that the intervention is delivered as intended.

Future plans for ongoing research could include the use of PTA with Latino parents of children with disabilities other than ASD (e.g., other developmental delay and emotional behavior disorder) and with non-Latino parents to determine its utility for other populations. The cultural adaptation of interventions is generally undertaken to meet the unique learning, cultural, and contextual needs of a specific minority population, but the resultant interventions may, in turn, be well suited to other minority or non-minority populations. For example, the use of flexibly scheduled home visits delivered by a parent of a child with autism, the consideration of literacy level in presentation of materials, and the use of a multi-media curriculum may also be ideal for all low-resourced families. Lastly, an intervention that integrates the parent education elements of PTA with a BPT approach that uses performance feedback and coaching while the parent practices strategies with their child with ASD could be beneficial in increasing parent use of targeted evidence-based practices and ultimately improve adaptive behavior and decrease challenging behavior for children. Combining parent education with parent training may be especially warranted if the child engages in comorbid challenging behavior such as aggression, noncompliance, self-injury, or high rates of rigid and repetitive behaviors. A recent RCT comparing the effectiveness of parent training and parent education for children with autism suggests that parent training may be more beneficial in reducing overall autism symptoms as well as disruptive and noncompliant behavior (Bearss, Johnson, & Smith, 2015). Alternatively, BPT programs have not typically emphasized advocacy, self-care, and service navigation, but these education components, which are present in PTA, may be helpful in improving Latino parent engagement in available services and supports for their child with ASD.

Conclusion

As the incidence of autism continues to rise and the Latino population continues to grow, greater numbers of Latino families will be impacted by ASD. Latino families, particularly immigrant families, may be disadvantaged by socio-economic, cultural, and political factors in seeking care for their children. This study provides preliminary evidence about the effectiveness of Padres en Acción as an ecologically valid parent education program specially designed to help this population access information, advocate for their children, and cope with the complex demands of caring for their children on a daily basis. By educating and empowering families, PTA offers a promising tool in the collective effort to help reduce the documented inequities in the health, education, and service systems and improve the lives of Latino children with autism and of their families.

References

Ainbinder, J.G., Blanchard, L.W., Singer, G.H.S., Sullivan, M.E., Powers, L.K., Marquis, J.G., & Santelli, B. (1998) "A qualitative study of parent to parent support for parents of children with special needs." *Journal of Pediatric Psychology 23*, 2, 99–109.

Bagner, D.M., Rodríguez, G.M., Blake, C.A., & Rosa-Olivares, J. (2013) "Home-based preventive parenting intervention for at-risk infants and their families: An open trial." *Cognitive and Behavioral Practice 20*, 334–348.

Bailey, D.B., Hebbeler, K., Olmsted, M.G., Raspa, M., & Bruder, M.B. (2008) "Measuring family outcomes: Considerations for large-scale data collection in early intervention." *Infants and Young Children 21*, 194–206.

Balcázar, H., Alvarado, M., Hollen, M., Gonzalez-Cruz, Y., & Pedregón, V. (2005) "Evaluation of salud para su coraz\n (Health for your heart): National Council of la Raza Promotora Outreach Program." *Preventing Chronic Disease 2*, 1–9.

Bandura, A., (1977) "Self-efficacy: Towards a unifying theory of behavioral change." *Psychological Review 84*, 191–215.

Bandura, A. (1986) *Social Foundations of Thought and Action: A Social Cognitive Theory.* Englewood Cliffs, NJ: Prentice-Hall.

Bandura, A. (2007) "Much ado over a faulty conception of perceived self-efficacy grounded in faulty experimentation." *Journal of Social and Clinical Psychology 26*, 641–658.

Bearss, K., Johnson, C., & Smith, T. (2015) "Effect of parent training vs parent education on behavioral problems in children with autism spectrum disorder: A randomized clinical trial." *Journal of American Medical Association 313*, 15, 1524–1533.

Bernal, G. (2006) "Intervention development and cultural adaptation research with diverse families." *Family Process 45*, 2, 143–151.

Bernal, G., Bonilla, J., & Bellido, C. (1995) "Ecological validity and cultural sensitivity for outcome research: Issues for the cultural adaptation and development of psychosocial treatments with Hispanics." *Journal of Abnormal Child Psychology* *23*, 1, 67–82.

Bonis, S. (2016) "Stress and parents of children with autism: A review of literature." *Issues in Mental Health Nursing 37*, 3, 153–163.

Bruininks, R.H., Woodcock, R.W., Weatherman, R.F., & Hill, B.K. (1996) *Scales of Independent Behavior – Revised Comprehensive Manual*. Itasca, IL: Riverside Publishing.

Cardona, J.R.P., Domenech-Rodriguez, M., Forgatch, M., Sullivan, C., *et al.* (2012) "Culturally adapting an evidence-based parenting intervention for Latino immigrants: The need to integrate fidelity and cultural relevance." *Family Process 51*, 1, 56–72.

Carr, T. & Lord, C. (2016) "A pilot study promoting participation of families with limited resources in early autism intervention." *Research in Autism Spectrum Disorders 2*, 87–96.

Centers for Disease Control and Prevention (2012) "Prevalence of autism spectrum disorders—Autism and Developmental Disabilities Monitoring Network, 14 sites, United States, 2008." *Morbidity and Mortality Weekly Report (MMWR) 61*, 1–19.

Centers for Disease Control and Prevention (2014) "Prevalence of autism spectrum disorders among children aged 8 years – Autism and Developmental Disabilities Monitoring Network, 11 sites, United States, 2010." *Morbidity and Mortality Weekly Report (MMWR) 63(SS2)*, 1–21.

Clifford, T. & Minnes, P.J. (2013) "Logging on: Evaluating an online support group for parents of children with autism spectrum disorders." *Journal of Autism and Developmental Disorders 43*, 1662.

Colby, S.L. & Ortman, J.M. (2015) "Projections of the size and composition of the U.S. population: 2014 to 2060: Population estimates and projections." US Census Bureau, 25-1143. Retrieved on May 19, 2017 from www.census.gov/content/dam/Census/library/publications/2015/demo/p25-1143.pdf .

Dieker, L.A., Voltz, D., & Epanchin, B. (2001) "Wingspread Conference: Guiding principles for preparing teachers to work with diverse learners." *Division of International Special Education and Services Newsletter 11*, 3, 4–5.

Dyches, T., Wilder, L., Sudweeks, R., Obiakor, F., & Algozzine, B. (2004) "Multicultural issues in autism." *Journal of Autism and Developmental Disorders 34*, 2, 211–222.

Elder, J., Ayala, G., Cambell, N., Slymen, D., *et al.* (2005) "Interpersonal and print nutrition communication for Spanish dominant Latino populations: Secretos de la buena vida." *Health Psychology 24*, 1, 49–57.

Flippin, M. & Crais, E.R. (2011) "The need for more effective father involvement in early autism intervention: A systematic review and recommendations." *Journal of Early Intervention 33*, 1, 24–50.

Fry, R. & Passel, J.S. (2009) "Latino children: A majority are U.S.-born offspring of immigrants." Retrieved on January 14, 2017 from http://pewhispanic.org/files/reports/110.pdf.

Hauser-Cram, P., Cannarella, A., Tillinger, M., & Woodman, A. (2013) "Disabilities and Development." In R.M. Lerner, A. Easterbrooks, & J. Mistry (vol. eds) *Handbook of Psychology, Vol. 6 , Developmental Psychology* (2nd ed.). Hoboken, NJ: Wiley.

Heller, T., Miller, A.B., & Hseih, K. (1999) "Impact of a consumer-directed family support program on adults with developmental disabilities and their family parents." *Family Relations 48*, 419–427.

Hoeft, K.S., Rios, S.M., Pantoja Guzman, E., & Barker, J.C. (2015) "Using community participation to assess acceptability of 'Contra Caries,' a theory-based, promotora-led oral health education program for rural Latino parents: A mixed methods study." *BMC Oral Health 15*, 103.

Huey, S.J., Jr. & Polo, A.J. (2008) "Evidence-based psychosocial treatments for ethnic minority youth." *Journal of Clinical Child and Adolescent Psychology 37*, 1, 262–301.

Iland, E.D., Weiner, I., & Murawski, W.W. (2012) "Obstacles faced by Latina mothers of children with autism." *Californian Journal of Health Promotion 10*, 25–36.

Kasari, C., Lawton, K., Shih, W., Barker, T.V., et al. (2014) "Caregiver-mediated intervention for low-resourced preschoolers with autism: An RCT." *Pediatrics 134*, 1, e72–e79.

Krug, D.A., Arick, J.R., & Almond, P.J. (1993) *Autism Screening Instrument for Educational Planning: Second Edition (ASIEP-2)*. Austin, TX: Pro-Ed.

Kuhn, J.C. & Carter, A.S. (2006) "Maternal self-efficacy and associated parenting cognitions among mothers of children with autism." *American Journal of Orthopsychiatry 76*, 4, 564–575.

Lorig, K., Ritter, P., & Gonzalez, V. (2003) "Hispanic chronic disease self-management: A randomized community based trial." *Nursing Research 52*, 361–369.

Machalicek, W., Lang, R., & Raulston, T. (2015) "Training parents of children with intellectual disabilities: Trends, issues, and future directions." *Current Developmental Disorders Reports 2*, 110–118.

Magaña, S., Li, H., Miranda, E., & Paradiso de Sayu, R. (2015) "Improving health behaviors of Latina mothers of youths and adults with intellectual and developmental disabilities." *Journal of Intellectual Disability Research 59*, 397–410.

Magaña, S., Lopez, K., Aguinaga, A., & Morton, H. (2013) "Access to diagnosis and care among Latino children with ASDs." *Intellectual and Developmental Disabilities 51*, 3, 141–153.

Magaña, S., Lopez, K., & Machalicek, W. (2017) "Padres en Acción: A psycho-educational intervention for Latino parents of children with autism spectrum disorder." *Family Process 56*, 1, 59–74.

Magaña, S., Lopez, K., Paradiso de Sayu, R., & Miranda, E. (2014) "Use of Promotoras de Salud in Interventions with Latino Families of Children with IDD." In R. Hodapp (ed.) *International Review of Research in Developmental Disabilities, 47*. London: Academic Press.

Magaña, S., Parish, S.L., & Son, E. (2016) "Functional severity and Latino ethnicity in services for children with autism spectrum disorder." *Journal of Intellectual Disability Research 60*, 424–434.

Magaña, S. & Smith, M. (2006) "Psychological distress and well-being of Latina and non-Latina white mothers of youth and adults with an autism spectrum disorder: Cultural attitudes toward coresidence status." *American Journal of Orthopsychiatry 76*, 3, 346–357.

Mandell, D.S., Wiggins, L.D., Carpenter, L.A., Daniels, J., et al. (2009) "Racial/ethnic disparities in the identification of children with autism spectrum disorders." *American Journal of Public Health 99*, 3, 493–498.

Matos, M., Bauermeister, J.J., & Bernal, G. (2009) "Parent–child interaction therapy for Puerto Rican preschool children with ADHD and behavior problems: A pilot efficacy study." *Family Process 48*, 2, 232–252.

McCabe, K., Yeh, M., Lau, A., & Argote, C.B. (2012) "Parent–child interaction therapy for Mexican Americans: Results of a pilot randomized clinical trial at follow-up." *Behavior Therapy 43*, 606–618.

McIntyre, L.L. (2013) "Parent Training to Reduce Challenging Behavior in Children and Adults with Developmental Disabilities." In R.P. Hastings & J. Rojahn (eds) *International Review of Research in Developmental Disabilities: Challenging behavior.*. San Diego, CA: Academic Press/Elsevier.

Miranda, J., Bernal, G., Lau, A., Kohn, L., Hwang, W., & LaFromboise, T. (2005) "State of the science on psychosocial interventions for ethnic minorities." *Annual Review of Clinical Psychology 1*, 1, 113–142.

Nevill, R.E., Lecavalier, L., & Stratis, E.A. (2016) "Meta-analysis of parent-mediated interventions for young children with autism spectrum disorder." *Autism*, 1–15.

Oono, I.P., Honey, E.J., & McConachie, H. (2013) "Parent-mediated early intervention for young children with autism spectrum disorders (ASD)." *The Cochrane Database of Systematic Reviews 30*, 4, CD009774.

Parra-Cardona, J., Rubén, B., Deborah, S., Cris, M., *et al.* (2017) "Examining the impact of differential cultural adaptation with Latina/o immigrants exposed to adapted parent training interventions." *Journal of Consulting and Clinical Psychology 85*, 1, 58–71.

Postorino, V., Sharp, W.G., McCracken, C.E., Bearss, K., Burrell, T., Evans, A.N., & Scahill, L. (2017) "A systematic review and meta-analysis of parent training for disruptive behavior in children with autism spectrum disorder." *Clinical Child and Family Psychology Review 20*, 4, 391–402.

Radloff, L.S. (1977) "The CES-D scale: A self-report depression scale for research in the general population." *Applied Psychological Measurement 1*, 3, 385–401.

Rashid, S., Carcel, C., Morphew, T., Amaro, S., & Galant, S. (2014) "Effectiveness of a promotora home visitation program for underserved Hispanic children with asthma." *Journal of Asthma 52*, 5, 478–484.

Ratto, A.B., Reznick, S., & Turner-Brown, L. (2016) "Cultural effects on the diagnosis of autism spectrum disorder among Latinos." *Focus on Autism and Other Developmental Disabilities 31*, 4, 275–283.

Ravindran, N. & Myers, B.J. (2012) "Cultural influences on perceptions of health, illness, and disability: A review and focus on autism." *Journal of Child & Family Studies 21*, 311–319.

Reinschmidt, K.M., Hunter, J.B., Fernández, M.L., Lacy-Martínez, C.R., de Zapien, J.G., & Meister, J. (2006) "Understanding the success of promotoras in increasing chronic disease screening." *Journal of Health Care for the Poor and Underserved 17*, 256.

Robertson, R.E., Sobeck, E.E., Wynkoop, K., & Schwartz, R. (2017) "Participant diversity in special education research: Parent-implemented behavior interventions for children with autism." *Remedial and Special Education 38*, 5,259–271.

Robins, D.L., Fein, D., & Barton, M. (1999) *The Modified Checklist for Autism in Toddlers (M-CHAT).* Self-published.

Schieve, L.A., Boulet, S.L., Blumberg, S.J., Kogan, M.D., *et al.* (2012) "Association between parental nativity and autism spectrum disorder among US-born non-Hispanic white and Hispanic children, 2007 National Survey of Children's Health." *Disability and Health Journal 5*, 1, 18–25.

Schopler, E., Reichler, R.J., DeVellis, R.F., & Daly, K. (1980) "Toward objective classification of childhood autism: Childhood Autism Rating Scale (CARS)." *Journal of Autism and Developmental Disorders 10*, 1, 91–103.

Schreck, K.A., Karunaratne, Y., Zane, T., & Wilford, H. (2016) "Behavior analysts' use of and beliefs in treatments for people with autism: A 5-year follow-up." *Behavioral Interventions 31*, 4, 355–376.

Schulze, P.A., Harwood, R.L., Schoelmerich, A., & Leyendecker, B. (2002) "The cultural structuring of parenting and universal developmental tasks." *Parenting: Science and Practice 2, 2*, 151–178.

Snowden, L.R., Hu, T.W., & Jerrell, J.M. (1999) "Emergency care avoidance: Ethnic matching and participation in minority-serving programs." *Community Mental Health Journal 31*, 463–473.

Strauss, K., Mancini, F., SPC Group, & Fava, (2013) "Parent inclusion in early intensive behavior interventions for young children with ASD: A synthesis of meta-analyses from 2009 to 2011." *Research in Developmental Disabilities 34, 9*, 2967–2985.

Tran, A., Ornelas, I.J., Kim, M., Perez, G., Green, M., Lyn, M.J., & Corbie-Smith, G. (2014) "Results from a pilot promotora program to reduce depression and stress among immigrant latinas." *Health Promotion Practice 15*, 3, 365–372.

Wainer, A.L., Hepburn, S., & McMahon Griffith, E. (2017) "Remembering parents in parent-mediated early intervention: An approach to examining impact on parents and families." *Autism 21*, 1, 5–17.

West, E.A., Travers, J.C., Kemper, T.D., Liberty, L.M., Cote, D.L., McCollow, M.M., & Stansberry Brusnahan, L.L. (2016) "Racial and ethnic diversity of participants in research supporting evidence-based practices for learners with autism spectrum disorder." *Journal of Special Education 50*, 3, 151–163.

WestRasmus, E.K., Pineda-Reyes, F., Tamez, M., & Westfall, J.M. (2012) "Promotores de salud and community health workers: An annotated bibiliography." *Family Community Health 35*, 2, 172–182.

Wilder, L.K., Dyches, T.T., Obiakor, F.E., & Algozzine, B. (2004) "Multicultural perspectives on teaching students with autism." *Focus on Autism and Other Developmental Disabilities 19*, 2, 105–113.

Williamson, A.A., Knox, L., Guerra, N.G., & Williams, K.R. (2014) "A pilot randomized trial of community-based parent training for immigrant Latina mothers." *American Journal of Community Psychology 53*, 1–2, 47–59.

Zuckerman, K.E., Sinche, B., Mejia, A., Cobian, M., Becker, T., & Nicolaidis, C. (2014) "Latino parents' perspectives of barriers to autism diagnosis." *Academic Pediatrics 14*, 3, 301–308.

Chapter 6

EFFECTIVE DELIVERY OF PCIT WITH CHILDREN WHO HAVE AN INTELLECTUAL AND DEVELOPMENTAL DISORDER

Susan G. Timmer, Brandi Hawk, and Anthony J. Urquiza

ABSTRACT

In this chapter, we describe how an evidence-based treatment for children with disruptive behavior disorders, Parent–Child Interaction Therapy (PCIT), has been provided to children on the autism spectrum (ASD) and with intellectual and developmental disabilities (IDD). We describe both how PCIT is provided to typically developing children and how the intervention was tailored for use with children with ASD and IDD, particularly when their functioning was low. On the whole, studies reported positive outcomes for families with children diagnosed with ASD or IDD. These positive outcomes fell into categories of expected (e.g., improvement in parent skills and child behavior problems), and unexpected (e.g., adaptability, shared positive affect) positive outcomes. PCIT is practiced and implemented widely within community mental health centers. However, there is some thought that community mental health therapists, who are most likely to provide PCIT to young children with ASD and IDD, do not have sufficient understanding of atypical child development or the specific needs of this population. With increasing numbers of children with ASD and IDD accessing community mental health services, it will be important to provide training to therapists to help them recognize atypical development and understand how to provide the most effective ways to work with these children.

Keywords: autism; intellectual or developmental disabilities; Parent–Child Interaction Therapy; PCIT; parent coaching, parenting intervention

Parent–Child Interaction Therapy (PCIT; Eyberg & Robinson, 1982) is a dyadic parenting intervention (i.e., parent-mediated intervention) designed to teach therapeutic parenting skills to caregivers with young children, 2 to 7 years of age, who have high levels of disruptive behaviors such as aggression, defiance, oppositional behavior, and angry outbursts (e.g., temper tantrums). This age limitation is thought to reflect developmental rather than chronological age, such that older children with a developmental age of 7 or younger would also be appropriate referrals for PCIT (Solomon *et al.*, 2008). Children across many diagnostic categories may present with these types of disruptive, externalizing behaviors. For example, the *Diagnostic and Statistical Manual of Mental Disorders, 5th edition* (*DSM-5*; American Psychiatric Association, 2013) includes externalizing behaviors as symptoms of not only oppositional defiant and conduct disorders, but also as symptoms of neurodevelopmental disorders (e.g., Attention Deficit Hyperactivity Disorder or ADHD), bipolar disorders, depressive disorders, and trauma and stressor-related disorders. PCIT can be provided to children in any diagnostic category as long as disruptive behaviors are a feature of their mental health symptomology.

Theoretical foundation

PCIT, developed by Sheila Eyberg (Eyberg & Robinson, 1982), is one of several programs that emerged from Constance Hanf's lab at Oregon Health Sciences University in the late 1960s. Hanf's two-phase model was founded on the principles of operant conditioning, believing that through strategic social reinforcement, it would be possible to change caregivers and children to modify maladaptive parent–child interactions (Reitman & McMahon, 2012). As with this earlier model, PCIT focuses on increasing discrete behaviors such as the parent's positive attention to the child, but it, additionally, incorporates the attachment theory (Ainsworth *et al.*, 1978; Bowlby, 1969) belief in the importance of maternal warmth and responsiveness, as well as the work of Axline (1947) and Guerney (1964), which promotes nondirective parental warmth and acceptance (Eyberg, 2004). While emphasizing the power of positive attention, PCIT also assumes that healthy parenting is authoritative, with clear communication and firm limit setting, consistent with Baumrind's work (1966, 1967). Using an *in vivo* "coaching" paradigm, Eyberg broke down these more abstract skills into discrete parts, or specific verbalizations, which were behaviors that she could easily teach parents and easily quantify. Discrete behaviors such as praise, reflective statements, and descriptions focused on the child's behavior, when combined together, generated greater nurturing, warmth, and responsiveness, as well as the skills needed for managing children's difficult behavior (such as selective attention, positive reinforcement for compliance), encouraged more authoritative parenting. Eyberg's PCIT was built on the belief that coaching parents to speak in specific ways and perform specific parenting skills was a more effective way to change their behavior than psychoeducational, modeling, or role play techniques common in other parent training programs.

Model description

Parent–Child Interaction Therapy (PCIT) is a 14–20-week, manualized intervention (Eyberg & Robinson, 1983) provided by Master's or doctoral level therapists primarily in community mental health settings and private practices (i.e., outpatient) as "individual therapy" nationwide, indeed worldwide. Originally, PCIT was a clinic-based intervention. However, PCIT can be provided wherever the caregiver and child can play together. More recently, therapists have begun to provide therapy in families' homes to improve community access to services. As a side note, moving therapeutic services into clients' homes has some cost benefits related to reductions in room use and increased capacity. At the same time, therapists providing services in home cannot see as many clients as clinic-based therapists because their caseloads need to accommodate time for driving to clients' houses. PCIT's underlying model of change is similar to that of other parent training programs: through positive parenting and behavior modification skills, the parents themselves become the agent of change in reducing the child's behavior problems. However, unlike other parenting-focused interventions, PCIT incorporates both parent and child in the treatment sessions and uses live, in-the-moment, therapist coaching for an individualized approach to changing parents' and children's behavior in their interactions with each other.

PCIT is conducted in two phases. The first phase focuses on enhancing the parent–child relationship (Child-Directed Interaction or CDI), and the second on improving child compliance (Parent-Directed Interaction or PDI). Both phases of treatment begin with an hour of didactic training, followed by sessions in which the therapist coaches the parent during play with the child in order to attain a predetermined level of mastery of the skills taught. Parents are taught and practice specific skills of communication and behavior management with the child during one-hour sessions once a week. The PCIT therapist attempts to make the parent the most important adult to the child in the therapy session. In the clinic, therapists coach parents from an observation room behind a two-way mirror, via a "bug-in-the-ear" receiver that the parent wears (Figure 6.1). Although wearing the earpiece can be awkward at first, most parents report feeling comfortable with the earpiece and with coaching after the first one or two coaching sessions. In homes, the therapist coaches the parent in a low voice and outside of the child's line of sight. In home or clinic, the therapist provides the parent with feedback on their use of the skills and their effects on the child in real time. In addition to practicing these skills during treatment sessions, parents are asked to practice "special play" with the child every day for five minutes.

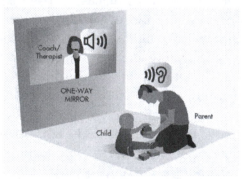

Figure 6.1 PCIT therapy room and observation room diagram—how therapist coaching works with a "bug-in-the-ear" headset and earpiece

In CDI (typically, 7–10 sessions based on length of time to mastery), parents are coached to follow their child's lead in play by describing their activities, reflecting their appropriate verbalizations, and praising their positive behavior. The skills that parents learn during this phase of treatment are represented in the acronym PRIDE, which stands for: Praise, Reflection, Imitation, Description, and Enjoyment. Additionally, parents are taught to avoid asking questions, giving commands, or making negative or critical statements, and, instead, are taught to utilize selective attention, actively ignoring non-dangerous negative behaviors. The following is an example of CDI coaching:

> (Parent and child have a bin full of interlocking plastic blocks (like LEGO®) to play with at a table in a clinic's therapy room. The therapist is watching from an adjacent observation room and talking to the parent through the "bug-in-the-ear" system.)

> *Therapist: Describe what Teddy is doing with his hands.*

> Child: (picks blue blocks out)

> Parent: You put all of the blue blocks on the table.

> *Therapist: That was a great behavioral description!*

> Child: Yes, I'm going to make a big blue barn.

> Parent: Oh…you're going to make a big blue barn.

> *Therapist: You got it! That was a perfect reflection of what Teddy said. This tells him you are paying attention to what he is doing. It also makes him more mindful of what he is saying and doing, which will help him focus.*

> Child: And I'm going to make a red barn, too!

> *Therapist: You make a red barn, too, Mom.*

> Parent: That's a great idea! I'm going to make a red barn, just like you.

> *Therapist: Great imitating! Look at him smile! You're teaching him a lot about how to play with others nicely.*

Child: Okay, you build yours right here, and the cow will go in it.

Therapist: Teddy is playing very gently with the toys today. And so creative!

Parent: Teddy, you are so creative with these blocks. You know just what to do!

Child: Yeah!

Therapist: Nice labeled praise, Mom.

In the example, it can be seen that the therapist alternates between leading (and sometimes redirecting) the parent, following the parent, and giving brief psychoeducation such as interpreting children's behavior and explaining the meaning and long-term effects of using the skills. These coaching strategies gently lead parents to try out, practice, and incorporate these skills into the fabric of their parenting.

By the end of CDI, parents generally have shifted from rarely noticing their child's positive behavior to more consistently attending to or praising appropriate behavior. When caregivers master the skills taught in CDI by demonstrating that they can give 10 behavior descriptions (e.g., "It looks like you are building a big wall"), 10 reflections (i.e., repeating back or paraphrasing the child's words), and 10 labeled praises (e.g., "You are doing a great job playing so gently with these toys"), with fewer than three instances of asking a question, giving a command, or criticizing the child in a five-minute assessment, they then move to the second phase of treatment.

In PDI (typically 7–10 sessions), therapists train parents to give effective commands (i.e., clear, simple, direct, and developmentally appropriate), maximizing the likelihood of child compliance. Parents participating in PCIT traditionally learn a specific method of using timeout for dealing with noncompliance. Parents may also be taught "hands-off" strategies (e.g., removal of privileges) if indicated due to physical difficulties with timeout (e.g., caregiver is physically unable to move the child) or to the child preferring to be isolated. These strategies are designed to provide caregivers tools for managing their children's behavior, while helping them avoid using physical power, focusing instead on using positive incentives and promoting children's emotional regulation. The following script is an example of PDI coaching:

(Parent and child are playing with blocks in a clinic's therapy room. The therapist is watching from an adjacent observation room and talking to the parent through the "bug-in-the-ear" system.)

Therapist: It is now time to clean up the toys. Tell Teddy to put the blocks back in the box.

Parent: Teddy, it's time to clean up. Can you put the blocks back in the box? [Ineffective command—question leaves open an option for not complying]

Child: (continues playing with the blocks) I'm not done yet.

Therapist: Make your command direct.

Parent: Please put the blocks back in the box, Teddy.

Therapist: That was a perfect direct command. Now Teddy knows exactly what he is supposed to do.

Child: Ohhhh…well… I'm not taking this apart… (Teddy whines, but starts to put a couple of blocks in the box)

Therapist: Now Teddy is putting the blocks away like you told him.

Parent: Thank you for listening, Teddy!

Therapist: Excellent praise…very specific. Teddy loves it when you recognize that he is being good!

Child: Look at this, Mom! (showing Mom the LEGO® horse) He's jumping around into the box.

Therapist: Teddy stopped listening, so start counting silently to five.

Parent: (quietly, under breath) One…two…three…four…five.

Child: The horse is really frisky, Mom!

Therapist: Give the timeout warning.

Parent: If you don't put the horse in the toy box, you'll have to go to timeout.

Therapist: Perfect! Start counting again.

Parent: (quietly, under breath) One…two…

Child: Awwwwww… (slams the horse into the box)

Therapist: Just ignore that. He put the horse in the box.

Parent: Great decision to put the horse in the box. When you listen, you don't have to go to timeout!

Therapist: That was BEAUTIFUL, Mom! Wow! And now he's putting the rest of the toys away a little more quickly.

As in CDI, the PCIT therapist alternates between leading, following, and explaining to the parent. However, unlike CDI, in PDI sessions, the therapist is more corrective, never ignoring mistakes, particularly in the midst of a child's timeout or timeout refusal. During these mini-crises, the therapist may give the parent the words to say, or prompt the parent with the beginning of a well-practiced phrase to keep the parent on track. Therapists coach parents to recognize and provide appropriate responses for the child's behavior (e.g., recognizing and providing praise for compliance; recognizing and ignoring minor inappropriate behavior—such as whining). As parents acquire these PCIT skills, therapists give fewer directives and instead use the coaching time to describe and praise the positive parenting they see, making connections between this behavior and the bigger picture of parenting and child development. These same coaching techniques are used in clinic via the "bug-in-the-ear" and in home with the therapist physically in the room. Regardless of the coaching method, the therapist ensures that the parent gives all directives so that the child learns to comply with the parent rather than the therapist.

Mastery of behavior management skills during PDI is achieved when therapists observe that caregivers are able to use the behavior management strategies that they were taught effectively. Specifically, mastery is attained when 75% of parent's commands are effective (i.e., direct, children comply), and when parents report children's problem behaviors as falling below the borderline range on the intensity scale of the Eyberg Child Behavior Inventory (i.e., below a raw score of 114). By the end of PDI, the process of giving commands and obtaining compliance is predictable and safe for parents and children.

Increasing predictability and safety in families is thought to help reduce the drama often associated with obtaining compliance.

An additional important element of PCIT coaching involves shifting parent responses and cognitions about child behavior. While coaching, therapists often provide supplemental information about the child's behavior in order to correct or minimize distortions in parent cognitions (especially negative or hostile cognitions). An example of this kind of coaching is illustrated in the following exchange:

(Child is coloring with a marker and paper. In the process of coloring, the child accidentally moves the marker off the paper and draws on the table.)

Therapist: (notices that the child has colored on the table and the parent is irritated about the child drawing on the table) Oh… that happens all of the time. It is common for a child of his age to accidently draw on the table. The marker washes off the table easily—so, no harm done. As soon as he starts to draw on the paper, give him a labeled praise for drawing on the paper.

Child: (starts to draw on the paper again) I am drawing a truck.

Parent: That is an awesome truck [Praise]; and you are doing a great job drawing on the paper! [Praise]

Therapist: Awesome specific praise, Dad! He wasn't misbehaving by drawing on the table. He is just not old enough to always draw on the paper. Now you've starting teaching him that it's good to draw on the paper.

Through the process of coaching, therapists can give parents immediate and accurate feedback about the child's behavior. We argue that when the therapist whispers into the parent's ear, a different view of the child's behavior—a different interpretation of the child's intent—the therapist "interrupts" the parent's previously held negative attribution about the child's behavior. Over time, parents' views of their children shift from primarily negative to recognizing, acknowledging, and accepting the child's many positive qualities.

Empirical support for PCIT with oppositional, defiant children

There have been numerous studies demonstrating the efficacy of PCIT for reducing child disruptive behavior problems, including oppositional defiance, attention difficulties, and hyperactivity (Eisenstadt et al., 1993; Eyberg, 1988; Eyberg & Robinson, 1982). Positive effects have been maintained for up to six years post-treatment (Hood & Eyberg, 2003). In addition, treatment effects have been shown to generalize to the home (Boggs, Eyberg, & Reynolds, 1990), school settings (McNeil et al., 1991), and to untreated siblings (Eyberg & Robinson, 1982). There is also research indicating that PCIT yields positive treatment outcomes with individuals from different cultural and language groups, including Spanish-speaking families (McCabe et al., 2005), Chinese-speaking families (Leung et al., 1999), and African-American families (Fernandez, Butler, & Eyberg, 2011).

While numerous studies demonstrated the value of PCIT with oppositional and defiant children, Urquiza and McNeil (1996) argued that some (if not many) of the trauma symptoms exhibited by child victims of violence and maltreatment, including emotional dysregulation, attention problems, and temper tantrums, were consistent with the disruptive behaviors of children in PCIT studies. In the last decade, research findings have shown positive outcomes with maltreating parent–child dyads (Chaffin et al., 2004; Timmer et al., 2005) and children exposed to domestic violence (Timmer et al., 2008). These positive outcomes may be related to PCIT decreasing parents' negative affect and coercive control and encouraging greater positive affect and discipline strategies.

Empirical support for PCIT with children on the autism spectrum or with intellectual or developmental disabilities

Therapists in community mental health agencies estimate that approximately 21% of their caseloads consist of children suspected of having an autism spectrum disorder (ASD) or with ASD diagnoses (Brookman-Frazee, Taylor, & Garland, 2010). However, most of these children were first referred for behavioral services and were subsequently diagnosed with ASD. Children who were first diagnosed with ASD or intellectual or developmental delays (IDD) and were later identified as having disruptive behaviors were less likely to receive community mental health services because they were already connected to developmental disability services and school-based systems that provide ASD- or IDD-specific services (Brookman-Frazee *et al.*, 2012). Instead, parents report that for the most part, their ASD children tended to be referred for mental health services because of their behavior problems before the children received their diagnosis of ASD (Brookman-Frazee *et al.*, 2012).

In general, parents preferred ASD- or IDD-specific services to community mental health services (Brookman-Frazee *et al.*, 2012). Indeed, Brookman-Frazee and colleagues (2012) interviewed 23 parents of children with ASD and reported that one of the most common challenges that parents of children with ASD mentioned in working with community mental health providers was their lack of knowledge about ASD and its specific challenges. Unfortunately, ASD- or IDD-specific services may not be available to all children, nor may they be sufficient for their needs. Children with ASD or IDD who also have extremely disruptive behaviors may subsequently be referred for mental health services, particularly if they interfere with the children's ability to profit from the ASD- or IDD-focused intervention or their school programs (Brookman-Frazee *et al.*, 2012). One parent interviewed by Brookman-Frazee and colleagues (2012) described the feeling that mental health services were their last best hope:

> it has been suggested several times to me by different therapists that weekly outpatient therapy really isn't the thing for a child with autism. And I do have a tendency to agree with that at times, but this is all he has right now. I wish there was something more specific for children like him. (p.539)

It is clear that community mental health therapists should receive more training in working with ASD and IDD populations and specifically in treatments that are effective for treating these children. To accomplish this goal, research must demonstrate whether current treatments, such as PCIT, are effective for these populations and whether specific ASD or IDD adaptations to treatments are useful for improving treatment effectiveness. Unfortunately, possibly because parents of children with ASD or IDD prefer not to engage in community mental health treatments such as PCIT, much of the empirical support for using PCIT with children diagnosed with ASD or IDD are single-case research designs or randomized trials with small samples. Nevertheless, these studies suggest that PCIT can be an effective intervention for children with ASD or IDD.

PCIT and high-functioning ASD

Researchers investigating the efficacy of PCIT among high-functioning children with ASD in a small randomized controlled trial reported improved adaptive behavior in children, increases in shared positive affect between parents and children, and decreases in numbers of behaviors parents perceived to be problems (Solomon *et al.*, 2008). A case study (Armstrong & Kimonis, 2013) and a single-case research design study with four subjects (Hatamzadeh, Pouretemad, & Hassanabadi, 2010) investigating the effects of PCIT with slightly younger high-functioning children with ASD reported significant decreases in the frequency of problem behaviors. These studies demonstrate the feasibility of attaining such outcomes in this population.

PCIT and IDD

Bagner and Eyberg (2007) demonstrated the effectiveness of PCIT with a cognitively lower-functioning population of children. In their study, young children (3–6 years old) with intellectual and developmental disabilities (IDD) and comorbid oppositional defiant disorder ended treatment with reductions in disruptive behavior problems and increases in observed child compliance. In a single-case research design study with three young children (3–4 years of age) of varying levels of cognitive functioning and symptoms, Masse and his colleagues (2016) reported reduced levels of aggression and noncompliance from pre- to post-PCIT, as did Zlomke, Jeter, and Murphy (2017), in a small open trial ($n = 17$) of 2–8-year-old children with autism or Asperger's diagnoses, or with a diagnosis of Pervasive Developmental Disorder. Both Agazzi, Tan, and Tan (2013) and Lesack and colleagues (2014) conducted case studies on the effectiveness of PCIT for 5–7-year-old boys with ASD and developmental delays (e.g., limited communication skills). Both sets of researchers reported improvements in children's problem behaviors and increased skill acquisition in parents.

Adjustments to PCIT for the ASD and IDD populations

Disruptive behaviors are common among children with ASD and IDD, varying in expression primarily by the developmental age of the child (e.g., Gadow *et al.*, 2004). In an examination of an administrative database, Mandell and colleagues (2005) found that approximately 40% of children with ASD were referred for mental health services in a community mental health setting because of their disruptive behaviors. Hence, many therapists are likely to receive referrals for children on the autism spectrum and with IDD that specifically seek treatment for disruptive behaviors. Knowing that PCIT is a highly verbal and interaction-based intervention that depends on the child placing a high value on social reinforcers (e.g., positive attention) in order to be effective, one might imagine that this intervention might not be suitable for all such children without some adaptation. For example, it is possible that the intervention might not be effective with children who share little joint attention with caregivers, do not understand or respond to verbal commands, or do not value their parents' positive attention without adapting the protocol.

In order to determine whether adaptations to PCIT are necessary for the ASD or IDD populations, it is important to distinguish between treatment *adjustments* (i.e., minor changes that stay within the standard PCIT structure) and *adaptations* (i.e., major changes to the structure of PCIT). PCIT is both a highly manualized and a highly individualized intervention, allowing space for therapists to adjust treatment to target specific child concerns. There is a clear structure to the intervention, a specific manner of observing caregiver and child behaviors and of documenting treatment progress, and specific information that must be taught at predetermined times. At the same time, therapists adjust how they present the information, nuances of coaching (e.g., timing, energy level, focus of coaching statements), and the toys and activities for coaching based on the specific needs of each parent–child dyad. Thus, many child behavior-focused adjustments maintain the structure and content of treatment (e.g., identifying imitation as an opportunity for joint attention). In contrast to these adjustments, Eyberg (2005) defined treatment *adaptations* as "changes in the structure or content of established treatments…when aspects of the standard treatment are not feasible or sufficient in the new population" (p. 200). Thus, PCIT adaptations either add new material or modify the structure of the treatment and/or individual sessions, while adjustments make changes to content without disrupting its general structure.

General adjustments to PCIT

The children described in the research looking at the effectiveness of PCIT with children diagnosed with ASD and IDD varied in age and cognitive functioning. However, the researchers did not make major *adaptations* to the model, instead finding that making minor *adjustments* within the PCIT structure was adequate to address the needs of children with ASD and IDD (Table 6.1). In fact, Masse *et al.* (2016) and Lesack *et al.* (2014) pointed out that PCIT is flexible enough to allow therapists to tailor coaching to the needs of the family, and that these tailored approaches did not meet the criteria that Eyberg (2005) described. For example, Masse *et al.* (2016) point out that when children have problems "using their words" to get what they want, and grab a toy, scream, yell, or tantrum, parents are typically taught to ignore the inappropriate attempt to get their way but to attend to any appropriate communication. This strategy is useful for "typical" PCIT clients and useful for ASD and IDD clients. Additionally, Masse *et al.* (2016) note that behaviors of special interest to parents of ASD children such as eye contact or imitation can be coached, monitored, and "shaped" using positive attention in the same way that a PCIT therapist would for behaviors like playing with toys gently or sharing.

Table 6.1 Comparison of PCIT provided to typically developing (TD) children and possible strategies for children with ASD or IDD

PCIT Strategy	Strategies used for TD Child	Possible modifications for Child with ASD or IDD
Pre-treatment		
15-minute Behavioral Observation	Standard	Standard
Child Directed Interactions		
Teach PRIDE skills & avoids	Standard	Reflect vocalizations that have communicative intent (not stereotypic vocalizations) and add behavioral descriptions after reflections in minimally verbal children
Teach selective attention	Standard	Do not ignore self-injurious behavior (e.g., head banging)
Toys for coaching	Construction and/or imagination toys without clear directions	Observe level of child's engagement in play with parent. Decide whether to: 1. Use restricted interests to increase interest in play; or, 2. Avoid restricted interests to reduce perseveration and increase interaction
Focus of coaching	Gentle, calm, concentrating, sharing	Gentle, calm, concentrating, sharing plus eye contact, joint attention, joint play, flexibility
Coaching parent statements	Targeted to child's comprehension level	Brief, simple statements, repetition-targeted to child's comprehension level
Parent Directed Interactions		
Teach direct commands	Commands to complete necessary tasks and to perform positive opposites of negative behaviors	Commands to complete necessary tasks and to perform positive opposites of negative behaviors
Teach timeout	3 min + 5 sec quiet	Start with duration of time that child will tolerate (discuss with parents), gradually increase to no more than 3 min + 5 sec quiet

PCIT Strategy	Strategies used for TD Child	Possible modifications for Child with ASD or IDD
Teach timeout back-up strategy	Back-up room for 1 min + 5 sec quiet or removal of privilege	Two-chair hold;* back-up room often not recommended
Coach commands	One direct command to complete a task	Before commands are given, "cue" child by making a bid for child's attention (e.g., Kevin!), combined with command to "Look at me," pair non-verbal cues with verbal commands, use fewer commands
Coach response to noncompliance	Coach timeout: immediately after command, begin counting, give one warning, then put child in timeout for failure to comply	Use "hand-over-hand" instead of warning for children with IDD to teach compliance to individual commands before resorting to timeout;** coach timeout: immediately after command, begin counting, give one warning, then put child in timeout

* According to Hembree-Kigin & McNeil (1995), the "two-chair hold" technique is a technique that can be used when the child escapes timeout. In such a situation, the child would be taken to a second, adjacent chair and the parent would restrict the child's movement for no longer than 45 seconds by crossing the child's arms across their chest. After the brief hold, the parent would then take the child back to the original timeout chair to complete the timeout.

** With the "hand-over-hand" technique, the parent places their hand over the child's hand and guides their hand to help the child comply with a command (e.g., "Put the block in the box").

Similarly, in the Parent Directed Interaction (PDI) phase of PCIT, Bagner and Eyberg (2007) noted that they used a strategy of giving a command incompatible with an undesired behavior to stop that undesired behavior, which is a strategy commonly used for typically developing children with disruptive behaviors, but can be extended to undesirable behaviors in ASD children. For instance, the therapist might coach the parent to give the command, "Please hold my hand," to control elopement, an undesired behavior. When the child complies with this command, the parent would be coached to praise the child for listening and then enthusiastically redirect attention to a distracting alternate activity or conversation. Although use of functional assessment (Iwata et al., 1994) and descriptive assessment (Freeman, Anderson, & Scotti, 2000) is not part of PCIT, therapists observe how children respond to direct commands and consequences in session, and each week parents report how children respond to direct commands and consequences at home. Thus, specific commands and consequences can be assessed for effectiveness and adjusted, if necessary.

Despite maintaining the overall integrity of the format of PCIT, all authors tailored the way in which they coached parents and set up play situations to meet their clients' special developmental needs. Bagner and Eyberg (2007) noted that in order to build on emerging cognitive skills, such as color identification, they might coach the parent to identify colors in the positive parenting skills they practiced. For example, the therapist would coach the parent to say, "You picked a red crayon. You're coloring the balloon red. I like your big red balloon!" (Bagner & Eyberg, 2007, p.427), coaching the parent to teach in brief comments by describing the child's behavior and praising the child's accomplishments, borrowing from the approaches of Lovaas' (1987) Discrete Trial Training (DTT) procedures and the Koegels' (2006) Pivotal Response Treatment (PRT) approach for children with autism. Masse *et al.* (2016) used Bagner and Eyberg's strategies, repeating concepts like teaching colors across different positive verbalizations, and coached the parent to use short sentences with longer pauses so as to allow a more severely delayed client enough time to generate sentences and speak.

Restricted interests and toy selection

In several of the studies, children's restricted interests affected their ability to engage in play with their parents. The researchers thus made *adjustments* within the standard PCIT model related to toy selection, without needing to make major *adaptations* to the model. For example, Agazzi *et al.* (2013) described a 7-year-old boy, K., who repeatedly resisted play with parents by arching his back away from the play during the PCIT session in the clinic and at home, which derailed parent–child play. The therapist in this case, together with the parents, identified a "preferred" toy from home, which they thought would engage K. in play and reduce resistance to play. The preferred toy was one of his restricted interests, but, nevertheless, allowed K. and his parents more opportunity to play together, and for parents to master the "CDI skills" (i.e., positive parenting). When the family entered PDI (the behavior management phase), the parents were coached to give a direct command to put away the preferred toy and pick a different toy to play with, using all the positive parenting skills that they had learned in order to reinforce K.'s compliance.

While using a preferred toy was useful in Agazzi *et al.*'s (2013) case, Lesack *et al.* (2014) had to avoid the highly stimulating, battery-operated toys preferred by the 5-year-old Kevin in their case study as he perseverated on eliciting lights and sounds to the detriment of social interaction. The researchers chose instead to use more typical PCIT toys such as blocks and Mr. Potato Head. Similarly, when working with children with high-functioning ASD, Solomon and her colleagues (2008) observed that when children's preferred toys (e.g., Thomas the Tank Engine) were excluded from the PCIT room, children developed interests in other toys and became less fixated on previously preferred toys.

In short, the goal for the PCIT therapist in the first phase of treatment is to provide opportunities for parents and children to play together, so that the parent can learn positive parenting skills and the child can learn to enjoy the parent's positive attention. Children's symptoms, stereotypies, and restricted interests at times challenged the therapists' abilities to attain this goal. Therapists considered the effects of their toy selection on children's behavior and their treatment goals. They did not automatically select typical PCIT toys but chose the toys that would best help the child and parents meet their goals.

Special strategies for handling low cognitive functioning and restricted language in CDI

Typically, one of the positive parenting skills that PCIT therapists coach parents to use with young, preverbal children is to reflect or imitate any of their children's appropriate sounds and verbalizations (e.g., reflect "ah" or elaborate the child's "ba" with "ball"). However, it is difficult to train parents to reflect children's speech if the child does not speak. The low level of expressive communication exhibited by a child with ASD and IDD required some adjustments to coaching strategies for one researcher. Lesack *et al.* (2014) reported that the subject of their study entered PCIT with little vocal communication, and the vocalizations that he uttered were largely without communicative intent. They noted that certain sounds (e.g., "ah") represented multiple items (e.g., car, ball, garage). The therapist chose to elaborate on the typical strategy for preverbal children in order to increase the child's social communication. The therapist decided to coach the parent only to reflect vocalizations "with apparent and appropriate communicative intent (e.g., requests and engagement in joint attention)" (Lesack *et al.*, 2014, p.72) and to have the parent ignore stereotypic vocalizations. The therapist also implemented a strategy for interpreting and elaborating on the sounds the child used to reference objects by adding a behavioral description. As an example, if the child said "ah" as he was reaching for a ball, then the parent would repeat "ah" and add, "you said ball" (Lesack *et al.*, 2014). These strategies, which likely resemble interventions designed to increase social communication in children with ASD and IDD, are slight adjustments of strategies that PCIT therapists might use with typically developing preverbal children as part of the overall goal of establishing the parent's positive attention as reinforcing.

Special strategies for handling low cognitive functioning and restricted receptive language in PDI

Children's cognitive functioning and level of receptive language generated a need for caution in PDI coaching in several of the studies. Both Lesack *et al.* (2014) and Masse *et al.* (2016) described the need to use a "cueing" command before giving a target command. Lesack *et al.* (2014) reported using the child's name as a bid for attention before giving a command, as in "Kevin, sit here" (p.73). Masse *et al.* (2016) cued their most delayed client by first giving the child a command to "look at me." Both studies also reported working out a system to improve the likelihood that the children understood their parents' commands so that they would not confuse noncompliance with lack of comprehension. Masse *et al.* (2016) reported pairing verbal commands with physical cues to perform the command (e.g., pointing at the chair while saying, "Please sit on the chair"). The pairing of verbal or physical cues with target commands likely has a slight effect on the structure of PCIT, and the focus is on teaching the parent to give appropriate and effective commands to support child compliance.

Lesack *et al.* (2014) used a more elaborate three-step strategy of teaching the commands and the parent's desired reactions before giving consequences for noncompliance, using verbal commands, gestural cues, and modeling the appropriate reaction while restating the command (i.e., the compliant behavior) if the child did not comply within five seconds. Following this, the caregiver would restate the original command, wait five seconds for the child to comply, then use "hand-over-hand" to "guide" the child in the compliant behavior. This strategy for teaching how to comply with commands is similar to the strategy that McNeil and Hembree-Kigin (2010) recommend using when teaching compliance to children younger than 24 months. For a typically developing child, this strategy can be a fairly quick and effective way to teach about compliance, which the child will generalize to other situations. For children with severe delays, this strategy might be slow moving, though possibly essential to fulfill PCIT's behavior management treatment goals. Possibly because of this, Lesack *et al.* (2014) reported limiting the direct commands that the parents gave the child to the management of two safety-related behaviors. While this might seem a rather slight effort to a person providing discrete trials trainings, a PCIT therapist's goal is to train parents so that they can implement effective strategies on their own. Training the child to comply with two important commands would give parents sufficient opportunity to master the parenting skill and still maintain the brief structure of PCIT.

Timeout as a behavior management tool for children with ASD and IDD

PCIT uses the timeout as its primary form of discipline in PDI. Timeout in PCIT lasts for three minutes plus five seconds of silence, using a "back-up room" when children "escape" timeout, according to Eyberg's protocol (Eyberg & Funderburk, 2011). The timeout has been the subject of considerable controversy in recent years. Some cite the considerable empirical evidence supporting the use of timeout to help reduce the frequency of oppositional and disruptive behaviors (e.g., Quetch *et al.*, 2015), and others decry the emotional toll that the timeout process takes on children (e.g., Siegel & Bryson, 2014). Apart from this controversy, there is the belief that the PCIT timeout should not be used with children under 2 because they are not likely to have the executive functions necessary to understand the cause and effect of misbehavior and negative consequences (McNeil & Hembree-Kigin, 2010). Because assessing developmental age is more complicated for children who may have ASD and IDD, one way to ensure that children are old enough for PCIT behavior management is to provide PCIT only to high-functioning children or to constantly assess and analyze children's functional behavior (e.g., reactions to their parent's behavior) while they are in CDI.

Two of the studies on PCIT with children with ASD and IDD reported difficulties implementing timeout with this population, both with the timeout process itself as well as the back-up to timeout, in cases of escape. Agazzi *et al.* (2013) reported no problems in using timeout (and back-up) in the clinic. However, in the home, K.'s parents had difficulty in finding a space for timeout back-up where they could leave him without worrying about his safety, which decreased the effectiveness of the timeout. The case that Lesack *et al.* (2014) described (that had required elaborate teaching of commands) also required some tailoring of the timeout process because of the client's low cognitive functioning. First, the therapist limited the direct commands that the parents were to give to the child to just two safety-related commands in order to limit dangerous behavior in the home. Because of this, timeout was only given to the child for noncompliance if he failed to comply with either of these two important commands. Having noticed that the child rarely sat in a chair at the best of times for more than two minutes, the therapist and parents foresaw failure in a three-minute timeout. Instead, they chose to increase the child's ability to sit on a timeout chair by initially requiring only one minute with two seconds of quiet, working gradually towards longer periods of sitting in timeout. This practice of gradually increasing the length of timeouts is common for therapists providing PCIT to 2-year-olds, who have limited understanding of the meaning of the timeout (Dombrowski, Timmer, & Zebell, 2008). McNeil and Hembree-Kigin (2010) recommend that clinicians make the decision to provide PDI to 2–3-year-olds on a case-by-case basis, as there is considerable variability in cognitive development in this age group. Similar individualized consideration should be given to providing PDI to children with developmental disabilities.

Timeout escape among children with ASD and IDD

According to the Eyberg and Funderburk (2011) PCIT protocol, if the child refuses to take or escapes from timeout, the parent must put them in a timeout room (also called "back-up room") for one minute plus five seconds of quiet and then return the child to the timeout chair. In the clinic, a back-up room is a small, empty room connected to the therapy room via a half door. When a back-up room is not feasible, parents are taught to take the toys and leave the therapy room while the therapist continues to monitor the child's behaviors via the one-way mirror. In a standard PCIT protocol, parents are asked to choose a space in their own homes to use as a back-up for timeout that is childproofed and fairly barren (e.g., large closet, laundry room). It is important that therapists help parents to consider safety concerns (e.g., outlets, sharp or heavy objects, glass). Additionally, parents are instructed to avoid using timeout at home until the child has successfully completed a timeout in the clinic. In this way, children experience their first back-up room within the highly controlled clinic environment, and parents gain experience using timeout and back-up rooms appropriately before using them at home.

However, a PCIT therapist working with a very young child (under 30 months, per McNeil & Hembree-Kigin, 2010), a child who would respond to seclusion with fear or anxiety, or a child who preferred social seclusion would not use a back-up room for timeout escape, but would instead use removal of privileges or natural consequences to encourage the child to take the timeout (Dombrowski *et al.*, 2008). In one study (Lesack *et al.*, 2014), the therapist and parents felt that it was inappropriate to put the child in a timeout room because of his preference for being alone and the danger (to himself and the light bulbs in the room) of leaving him unattended. Although this technique is no longer included in the PCIT protocol, the researchers decided to resurrect a strategy from PCIT's past called "the two-chair hold" (Hembree-Kigin & McNeil, 1995). Using this procedure, the therapist directed the parents to escort the child to a second chair if he refused to sit in the first chair, and essentially hold him in the chair for 30 seconds (plus 2 seconds of quiet). After completing the required time in the second chair, the child would be escorted back to the first timeout chair, where he would need to sit for one minute (plus 2 seconds of quiet). The therapist's options in this case situation were limited by the child's low cognitive functioning and his extremely dangerous and destructive behavior. In this case situation, the therapist was assessing the frequency and effectiveness of this strategy every time it was implemented in order to ensure that the negative attention obtained from the 30 seconds of "holding" did not become reinforcing, and that it was not dangerous for the parents (parents' arms are much closer to children's teeth in the holding chair). Lesack *et al.* (2014) reported that the holding chair was used in 5 out of 15 of the child's PDI sessions, but only once in the last five sessions. As timeout began to be possible with the child not escaping it, his behaviors also began to improve according to parent-reported measure of disruptive behaviors (Lesack *et al.*, 2014).

Summary

Overall, studies' results suggested that the social relationship and communication skills and behavior management strategies taught to parents in PCIT were effective in improving the disruptive behaviors of children with ASD or IDD. While researchers claimed to maintain fidelity to the protocol of PCIT, they did make adjustments to the way in which they provided the intervention to accommodate children's varying cognitive abilities, restricted interests, and emotional lability. The underlying message of most of the research was the need for ongoing descriptive assessment of child behavior and the assessment of the effectiveness of the different skills for the child in treatment. Additionally, it should be pointed out that the children in the studies had received developmental assessments in order to determine qualification for the different studies. However, developmental screenings are not automatically conducted with children referred for mental health services, or there may be a gap in providers' knowledge of child development. When treating children with ASD or IDD, an assessment or screening conducted by a knowledgeable provider may be critical. Without an understanding of the developmental underpinnings of a child's behavior, a therapist could interpret a child's behavior as simply "oppositional" rather than recognizing the influence of ASD or IDD, which we know from the studies discussed here, requires a slightly different approach.

PCIT implementation

In recent years, federal and state agencies that fund mental health services have emphasized the importance of using evidence-based treatments (Timmer *et al.*, 2015). Possibly in response to this, requests for training have increased and PCIT training is available nationwide by a variety of providers using different training modalities. Unlike other intensive programs that work with children diagnosed with ASD or IDD (e.g., Applied Behavioral Analysis (ABA)), training to be a PCIT therapist is limited to licensed or licensable mental health therapists (Master's and doctoral level). That is not to say that paraprofessionals who do not meet these criteria cannot be trained to provide PCIT effectively and with fidelity, only that they are not considered to be PCIT "therapists," billing services as "individual therapy." PCIT providers who are not therapists may provide these services as "rehabilitation." As training in PCIT is primarily available in only a handful of clinical psychology programs and is generally not offered in clinical Master's programs (e.g., social work, marriage and family therapy), most mental health therapists are likely to receive PCIT training only once they have completed their degrees and are working in a community mental health agency.

It is difficult to know how far and deep PCIT has spread into county and community mental health systems, or how well ensconced PCIT programs are in sites that have received training because there is no national standard way of assessing PCIT implementation. We know that the Substance Abuse and Mental Health Services Agency (SAMHSA) provided McNeil and her team with six years of funding, beginning in 2008 to train therapists in Delaware in PCIT. Additionally, First 5 LA recently provided funding to the UC Davis PCIT Training Center to provide PCIT training to licensable or licensed mental health therapists in up to 100 Los Angeles County Department of Mental Health-contracted agencies over a five-year period beginning in 2012 (Timmer *et al.*, 2015). If these two large-scale projects are any indication of the appeal of PCIT to funding agencies, it is likely that PCIT has increased its visibility across the country. From writings on implementation science and reports of implementation efforts (e.g., Herschell *et al.*, 2015; Timmer *et al.*, 2015), we also have a good sense of the factors that contribute to successful PCIT program implementation and sustainment. These factors affecting implementation are related to PCIT's training process and structure, the physical and technical setup needed for the standard practice of PCIT, its administrative support and program needs, and the information management and data feedback needs of the practice.

PCIT training

PCIT was developed by Eyberg in the late 1970s, and had been largely the property of university-based clinical psychology laboratories until the late 1980s, when Cheryl McNeil, trained by Eyberg at the University of Florida, began pushing the training envelope by training different populations of professionals who worked with children. While at the Oklahoma Health Sciences Center, she trained therapists in child guidance centers, Indian Health Centers, foster parent agencies, and therapists in community mental health settings (including UC Davis CAARE Center) to provide PCIT (McNeil, 2016, personal communication). Over the next ten years, largely because of her efforts as well as those of her Oklahoma colleagues (e.g., Chaffin *et al.*, 2004), PCIT began to gain some traction as an effective treatment for traumatized children as well as the population for which it was originally designed, children with disruptive behavior problems (Eyberg & Robinson, 1982). Once PCIT was listed as among the best practices for treating abused children (i.e., Kauffman Best Practices Final Report, 2004) and was endorsed by the National Child Traumatic Stress Network, the demand for training expanded. It should be noted that, although the need for evidence-based treatments to treat maltreated children very likely propelled PCIT into a larger arena of providers, training on child development and the effects of trauma on children, though discussed during PCIT training, has largely been adjunct to and not part of the PCIT training. In fact, requirements for PCIT training reflected in the National Training Guidelines below are fairly general, allowing the different PCIT trainers to train in their own way. These guidelines for training are still the basis of various certification requirements:

1. At least 40 hours of didactic training in basic PCIT skills (which can include 10 hours of online training) by a PCIT

trainer as well as continued training in advanced PCIT skills (e.g., how to coach effectively).

2. Consultation and supervision from a PCIT trainer throughout treatment implementation.

3. Certification by a PCIT trainer that the trainee has an understanding of how to score and interpret assessment measures, reliably code using DPICS (Dyadic Parent Child Interaction Coding System), conduct didactic sessions, and coach parents to mastery of CDI and PDI skills.

4. Successfully complete two cases, including demonstrating that the parents met CDI and PDI mastery and that the child's scores on standardized behavioral measures have improved (PCIT International, 2013).

On average, it takes trainees approximately one year to accomplish these requirements, although since completing training depends on the trainee successfully completing two cases, the timing varies by their access to clients. Trainers work closely with trainees to make sure the trainees understand and can confidently execute the PCIT protocol. Trainers emphasize that PCIT is assessment driven: at every treatment session, therapists must conduct behavioral observations and collect information about the intensity of children's behavior problems (see Table 6.2). In order to complete a case successfully, therapists must make sure that parents achieve predetermined mastery criteria in CDI and PDI before moving forward in treatment and report their children's behavior problems within normal limits before graduation. Research suggests that PCIT trainers are proficient in the art of training, which is important when trainees devote so much time and energy to training (e.g., Timmer *et al.*, 2015). Timmer and her colleagues, reporting on countywide training in Los Angeles County, noted that trainees learning to provide PCIT in community mental health agencies reported positive outcomes with their clients, even when they only completed the first part of treatment.

Table 6.2 Sample session checklist used by a UC Davis PCIT trainer to insure that the trainee conducts PCIT effectively and with fidelity

ToT Session	Checklist
Check-in:	
Thanked caregiver for coming to session	
Homework collected, reviewed, discussed barriers to completion if applicable	
Discussed objectives and goals (related to child behaviors) for session	
Plan for the session	
Kept to about 10 min of check-in without sacrificing warmth	
Coding:	
Lead in statement given	
Reliable coding	
Gives feedback to caregiver	
Give coaching strategy for session, connect with session plan	
Coaching:	
Uses 3 levels of coaching	
Sufficient quantity (e.g., not too quiet or too talkative)	
Good timing (e.g., waits for good moment to speak)	
Appropriate pace (e.g., speed—not too slow or too fast)	
Appropriate tone (e.g., warm, affirming)	
Coached to stated objectives of session	
Stayed focused on stated strategy of session (e.g., not sidetracked by parent–child interaction from moment to moment)	
Used exercises to achieve coaching goals if needed	
Gave warning (1, 2, 5 minute) before end of session	
PDI coaching only:	
Gives primarily direct commands	
Gives gentle corrections when needed	
Coaches command–comply–praise sequence	
If timeout is needed, follows timeout sequence	
If back up is needed (e.g., removal of privileges), discusses importance of enforcing consequence	
Closing the session:	
Reviews accomplishments of session related to child behaviors	
Shows graph of parent progress, connect with treatment goals	
Gives homework, connect with parent performance and treatment goals	
Asks if caregiver will be able to come to session next week	
Tells caregiver plan for next week	

With respect to therapists learning to provide PCIT to children with ASD or IDD, much of the treatment provided in the studies described in this chapter was conducted by clinical psychology graduate students under the supervision of clinical faculty who were licensed psychologists (e.g., Bagner & Eyberg, 2007; Budd *et al.*, 2011; Masse *et al.* 2016) or by newly PCIT-trained licensed psychologists with expertise in ASD and IDD under the supervision of a PCIT trainer (e.g., Lesack *et al.*, 2014; Solomon *et al.*, 2008). However, in his chapter on providing PCIT to children with ASD, Masse (2010) recommends that trained PCIT therapists wait until they are quite experienced before attempting to treat children with ASD using PCIT. Although no one has explicitly addressed the training of therapists who provide PCIT to children with IDD, Masse's (2010) recommendations likely apply to this population as well. Given the complexity of some of the cases described in this chapter, some expertise (or consultation from someone with expertise) in working with ASD and/or IDD populations seems to be indicated.

Factors promoting PCIT implementation: ToT model

When the National Training Guidelines were first developed, trainers agreed that therapists needed to complete a minimum of four PCIT cases in order to be eligible to train others. The concept of training to train (ToT) was developed in an effort to increase the likelihood that a PCIT program could be sustained in an agency setting over time. The value of having a ToT in a community mental health agency is clear when the high rate of workforce turnover is considered (Paris & Hoge, 2010). UC Davis CAARE Center recommends training a cohort of four therapists (with at least one of the trainees being licensed) to increase the likelihood that at least one person will still be working at the agency after two years and be able to train new PCIT therapists (UC Davis PCIT Training Center, 2016). In Los Angeles County over the course of a five-year PCIT training project to create a sustainable network of PCIT providers in the county, the UC Davis PCIT training team added training and consultation related to increasing their trainees' *training* skills. They developed a ToT Manual to support this work, teaching skills like coach coding, judging competence, how to prepare trainees for their PCIT sessions, calculating DPICS coding reliability, and documentation of training progress. Other trainers in the PCIT community have also begun to conduct training workshops on the art of training in PCIT (e.g., 2015 PCIT International Conference, Pittsburgh, PA), recognizing that training is a key component of promoting fidelity and quality treatment provision in the field of child mental health.

There are concerns about the effects of the ToT model on the fidelity of PCIT practice. McNeil and Hembree-Kigin (2010) state that:

> Just as a picture that gets photocopied and then recopied loses its clarity, there is danger that the recipient of third or later generation training will learn a fuzzy form of PCIT that does not look like the original.... The 'photocopied' PCIT may not be as effective as the original, which could eventually undermine the reputation of PCIT and its status as an evidence-based intervention. (p.429)

Possibly in an attempt to manage the potential for ToTs to dilute the effectiveness of PCIT, at least two of the main groups conducting PCIT training have instituted certification processes for trainers. In spite of feeling a need to monitor PCIT performance more closely, research has shown that second- and third-generation trainees reported the same strength of outcomes as those reported in research studies, suggesting that it is possible to continue to provide effective treatment across trainee generations using the ToT model (Urquiza, Timmer, & Girard, 2011) without substantial supervision from any oversight group. However, special attention should be paid to treatment fidelity when an empirically based parenting intervention is provided to a population of children with special needs and special coaching considerations. Trainers could potentially teach concepts and/or coaching strategies that are not within the PCIT protocol but that are beneficial for children with ASD or IDD. With time and training conducted by third- and fourth-generation trainees, it is possible that the intervention would not be recognizable as PCIT, even though it might work marvelously in this population.

Implementation considerations: Physical space and equipment

The practice of PCIT typically requires installation of audio and video equipment, and a two-way mirror to facilitate remote coaching of the parent from a separate, usually adjacent room (see Figure 6.1). As technology has improved, this setup has also allowed for variations on room setups. Wide-angle, high-resolution camera equipment has made it easy to coach parents from a nearby room without having to install a two-way mirror. It is even technologically possible to receive training while providing treatment in home settings. The audio/visual equipment and the need to use two separate spaces (observation room and therapy room) when conducting a PCIT session make these programs cost intensive. However, equipment and space also make the training process easier because trainers can advise their trainees *in the moment,* either by using a co-therapy model or mentoring model via telehealth. While it is possible, even common, for therapists to provide PCIT in the same room as the parents, as they do when providing PCIT in home settings, it is advisable even in these settings to make the parent–child dyad the "star of the show," supporting the parent's role as the agent of change. The therapist should remain in the background and be as unobtrusive as possible, with the parent getting as much practice with the skills as possible while under the therapist's supervision. While an agency considering pursuing training in PCIT will have to consider the space and equipment-related costs of this intervention, using space and technology in this way has been shown to contribute to the effectiveness of training and treatement.

Core PCIT implementation components

Although important, implementing an evidence-based treatment (EBT) requires more than simply setting up rooms, getting the right toys, signing on willing and capable trainees, and training those therapists to be able to provide a treatment. Implementation science tells us that being able to provide an EBT on an ongoing basis requires a broad organizational infrastructure and collaborative processes both internally and outside the organization in the community. Successful implementation requires a *facilitative administration,* a core implementation component that supports therapists' ability to provide PCIT with fidelity (Fixsen *et al.*, 2005), along with *decision support data systems*, and an *ongoing coaching, consultation, and evaluation of staff* as they provide the treatment.

Facilitative administrations and PCIT implementation

Agency leadership may be enthusiastic at the prospect of incorporating a new practice into their palette of services for their population, but it is not likely that they have considered the fact that PCIT takes more time to provide, if concerned about fidelity, than treatment as usual. Apart from needing time to meet with other PCIT providers at least monthly to discuss difficult cases and practice DPICS coding, it takes time to prepare for treatment sessions and document client accomplishments like parent skill acquisition and child behavior problems. For atypical populations of children, therapists may need to review videotapes of sessions in order to check on children's responses to different situations and PCIT skills. If the team is treating children in special need populations like ASD or IDD, regular team meetings are even more critical. These meetings can be a forum for exchanging information and ideas about how to make PCIT work in atypical situations. In short, therapists' productivity may decrease somewhat, but they may have better client retention, and may observe more positive outcomes.

Data systems that support good decision-making and PCIT implementation

When implementing any EBT, providers need to be conscious of their ability to replicate the protocol effectively. Having systems in place to capture that information is useful both for providers to evaluate their own fidelity and effectiveness, and for clinical and administrative managers, who need the feedback to know whether their efforts to support the EBT have been effective. In our experience, few agencies have data systems in place for these purposes. At best, agencies have a system for scoring standardized assessments, but these are rarely returned quickly enough to help therapists make treatment-related decisions. Possibly for this reason, Los Angeles County Department of Mental Health implemented an "Outcome Measures Application" and requires therapists to enter client scores on required standardized assessments when providing an EBT. Recognizing that therapists had difficulty scoring and using information from standardized assessments, the UC Davis PCIT training team provided their Los Angeles County agencies with a Microsoft Access database to help therapist score and store the results of required assessments (Timmer *et al.*, 2015). In PCIT, there are specific indicators that the intervention is being provided effectively: attrition rate and the timing of attrition, parents' skill acquisition, and the intensity of children's behavior problems. As a rough indicator, we might hypothesize (based only on experience and no data) that when more than half of the clients drop out of treatment, when parents' skills fall below 70% of mastery at mid- and/or post-treatment assessments, and when there is no change in the level of children's behavior problems, it might be worth examining PCIT program fidelity and supports. If an agency is providing PCIT to a substantial percentage of children with special needs, then the management and providers should pay close attention to outcomes, and also track successful tailoring strategies.

Conclusion

In this chapter, we described how an evidence-based treatment for children with disruptive behavior disorders, PCIT, has been provided to children with ASD and IDD. We described both how PCIT is provided to typically developing children and how the intervention has been tailored for use with children with ASD and IDD, particularly when their functioning was low. Studies described slightly adjusting the standard protocol when children were high functioning, primarily centering on toy choice and how to handle play related to restricted interests. Studies relating how PCIT was provided to lower functioning children described more extensive adjustments to the protocol, incorporating strategies from more traditional interventions for children with ASD and IDD (e.g., DTT, PRT), focusing on teaching the child about commands and consequences in order to ensure that the child understood commands and that the parent could distinguish between oppositional behavior and lack of comprehension. These adjustments that are done for lower functioning children do not completely depart from the scope of PCIT. However, they have the potential to shift the focus of treatment from promoting high-quality dyadic interactions (i.e., through parents acquiring specific positive parenting skills and the brief use of behavior management skills) to a concentrated focus on child comprehension and performance (i.e., through discrete trial techniques). This shift could transform treatment to be more similar to DTT or PRT than to PCIT. On the whole, studies reported positive outcomes for families with children diagnosed with ASD or IDD. These positive outcomes fell into categories of expected positive outcomes (e.g., improvement in parent skills and child behavior problems) and unexpected positive outcomes (e.g., adaptability, shared positive affect).

PCIT has been implemented and is now practiced widely within community mental health centers, with trainers and funders sharing an understanding of the importance of sustaining the practice in organizations. It is necessary to identify specific core implementation factors that can help sustain PCIT. There is some thought that community mental health therapists, who are most likely to provide PCIT to young children with ASD and IDD, do not have sufficient understanding of atypical child development or the specific needs of this population. With increasing numbers of children with ASD and IDD accessing community mental health services, it will be important to provide training to therapists in order to help them recognize atypical development and understand how to provide the most effective ways in which to work with these children.

References

Agazzi, H., Tan, R., & Tan, S.Y. (2013) "A case study of Parent–Child Interaction Therapy for the treatment of autism spectrum disorder." *Clinical Case Studies* 12, 6, 428–442.

Ainsworth, M.D.M., Blehar, M.C., Waters, E., & Wall, S. (1978) *Patterns of Attachment.* Hillsdale, NJ: Erlbaum.

American Psychiatric Association (2013) *Diagnostic and Statistical Manual of Mental Disorders* (5th ed.). Arlington, VA: American Psychiatric Publishing.

Armstrong, K. & Kimonis, E.R. (2013) "Parent–Child Interaction Therapy for the treatment of Asperger's disorder in early childhood: A case study." *Clinical Case Studies* 12, 60–72.

Axline, V. (1947) *Play Therapy.* London: Ballantine Books.

Bagner, D.M. & Eyberg, S.M. (2007) "Parent–Child Interaction Therapy for disruptive behavior in children with mental retardation: A randomized controlled trial." *Journal of Clinical Child & Adolescent Psychology* 36, 418–429.

Baumrind, D. (1966) "Effects of authoritative parental control on child behavior." *Child Development 37*, 4, 887–907.

Baumrind, D. (1967) "Child care practices anteceding three patterns of preschool behavior." *Genetic Psychology Monographs 75*, 1, 43–88.

Boggs, S., Eyberg, S., & Reynolds, L.A. (1990) "Concurrent validity of the Eyberg Child Behavior Inventory." *Journal of Clinical Child Psychology 91*, 1, 75–78.

Bowlby, J. (1969) *Attachment and Loss: Vol. 1. Attachment.* New York: Basic Books.

Brookman-Frazee, L., Baker-Ericzen, M., Stadnick, N., & Taylor, R. (2012) "Parent perspectives on community mental health services for children with autism spectrum disorders." *Journal of Child and Family Studies 21*, 533–544.

Brookman-Frazee, L., Taylor, R., & Garland, A. (2010) "Characterizing community-based mental health for children with autism spectrum disorders and disruptive behavior problems." *Journal of Autism and Developmental Disorders 40*, 10, 1188–1201.

Budd, K., Hella, B., Bae, H., Meyerson, D., & Watkin, S. (2011) "Delivering Parent–Child Interaction Therapy in an urban community clinic." *Cognitive and Behavioral Practice 18*, 502–514.

Chaffin, M., Silovsky, J., Funderburk, B., Valle, L.A., *et al.* (2004) "Parent–Child Interaction Therapy with physically abusive parents: Efficacy for reducing future abuse reports." *Journal of Consulting and Clinical Psychology 72*, 3, 500–510.

Dombrowski, S., Timmer, S.G., & Zebell, N.M. (2008) "Parent–Child Attunement Therapy for Toddlers: A Behaviorally-Oriented, Play-Based Parent Training Model." In C. Schaefer (ed.) *Play Therapy for Very Young Children.* Lanham, MD: Jason Aronson.

Eisenstadt, T., Eyberg, S., McNeil, C., Newcomb, K., & Funderburk, B. (1993) "Parent–Child Interaction Therapy with behavior problem children: Relative effectiveness of two stages and overall treatment outcome." *Journal of Clinical Child Psychology 22*, 42–51.

Eyberg, S. (1988) "PCIT: Integration of traditional and behavior concerns." *Child and Family Behavior Therapy 10*, 33–46.

Eyberg, S.M. (2004) "The PCIT story—Part One: The conceptual foundation of PCIT." *The Parent–Child Interaction Therapy Newsletter 1*, 1, 1–2.

Eyberg, S.M. (2005) "Tailoring and adapting Parent–Child Interaction Therapy for new populations." *Education and Treatment of Children 28*, 197–201.

Eyberg, S.M. & Funderburk, B. (2011) Parent–Child Interaction Therapy Protocol. Available from PCIT-International, www.pcit.org.

Eyberg, S.M. & Robinson, E.A. (1982) "Parent–Child Interaction Therapy: Effects on family functioning." *Journal of Clinical Child Psychology 11*, 130–137.

Eyberg, S.M. & Robinson, E.A. (1983) "Conduct problem behavior: Standardization of a behavioral rating scale with adolescents." *Journal of Clinical Child Psychology 12*, 347–354.

Fernandez, M.A., Butler, A.M., & Eyberg, S.M. (2011) "Treatment outcome for low socioeconomic status African American families in Parent–Child Interaction Therapy: A pilot study." *Child and Family Behavior Therapy 33*, 1, 32–48.

Fixsen, D.L., Naoom, S.F., Blase, K.A., Friedman, R.M., & Wallace, F. (2005) *Implementation Research: A Synthesis of the Literature* (FMHI #231). Tampa, FL: University of South Florida, Louis de la Parte Florida Mental Health Institute, The National Implementation Research Network.

Freeman, K.A., Anderson, C.M., & Scotti, J.R. (2000) "A structured descriptive methodology: Increasing agreement between descriptive and experimental analyses." *Education and Training in Mental Retardation and Developmental Disabilities 35*, 1, 55–66.

Gadow, K.D., DeVincent, C.J., Pomeroy, J., & Azizian, A. (2004) "Psychiatric symptoms in preschool children with PDD and clinic and comparison samples." *Journal of Autism and Developmental Disorders 3*, 4, 379–393.

Guerney, B., Jr. (1964) "Filial therapy: Description and rationale." *Journal of Consulting Psychology 28*, 4, 304–310.

Hatamzadeh, A., Pouretemad, H., & Hassanabadi, H. (2010) "The effectiveness of Parent–Child Interaction Therapy for children with high functioning autism." *Procedia Social and Behavioral Sciences 5*, 994–997.

Hembree-Kigin, T.L. & McNeil, C.B. (1995) *Parent-Child Interaction Therapy*. New York: Plenum.

Herschell, A.D., Kolko, D., Scudder, A., Taber-Thomas, S., *et al.* (2015) "Protocol for a statewide randomized controlled trial to compare three training models for implementing an evidence-based treatment." *Implementation Science 10*, 133.

Hood, K. & Eyberg, S. (2003) "Outcomes of Parent–Child Interaction Therapy: Mothers' reports of maintenance three to six years after treatment." *Journal of Clinical Child and Adolescent Psychology 32*, 412–429.

Iwata, B.A., Dorsey, M.F., Slifer, K.J., Bauman, K.E., & Richman, G.S. (1994) "Toward a functional analysis of self-injury." *Journal of Applied Behavior Analysis 27*, 197–209.

Kauffman Best Practices Final Report (2004) "Closing the quality chasm in child abuse treatment: Identifying and disseminating best practices." Retrieved on January 30, 2018 from https://depts.washington.edu/hcsats/PDF/kauffmanfinal.pdf.

Koegel, R.L. & Koegel, L.K. (2006) *Pivotal Response Treatments for Autism: Communication, Social, & Academic Development*. Baltimore, MD: Paul H. Brookes Publishing.

Lesack, R., Bearss, K., Celano, M., & Sharp, W.G. (2014) "Parent–Child Interaction Therapy and autism spectrum disorder: Adaptations with a child with severe developmental delays." *Clinical Practice in Pediatric Psychology 2*, 1, 68–82.

Leung, C., Tsang, S., Heung, K., & You, I. (1999) "Effectiveness of Parent–Child Interaction Therapy (PCIT) in Hong Kong." *Research on Social Work Practice 19*, 3, 304–313.

Lovaas, O.I. (1987) "Behavioral treatment and normal educational and intellectual functioning in young autistic children." *Journal of Consulting and Clinical Psychology 55*, 3–9.

Mandell, D.S., Thompson, W.W., Weintraub, E.S., DeStefano, F., & Blank, M.B. (2005) "Trends in diagnosis rates for autism and ADHD at hospital discharge in the context of other psychiatric diagnoses." *Psychiatric Services 56*, 1, 56–62.

Masse, J. (2010) "Autism Spectrum Disorders." In C. McNeil & T. Hembree-Kigin (eds) *Parent–Child Interaction Therapy*. New York: Springer.

Masse, J.J., McNeil, C.B., Wagner, S., & Quetsch, L.B. (2016) "Examining the efficacy of Parent–Child Interaction Therapy with children on the autism spectrum." *Journal of Child and Family Studies 25*, 2508–2525.

McCabe, K.M., Yeh, M., Garland, A.F., Lau, A.S., & Chavez, G. (2005) "The GANA program: A tailoring approach to adapting Parent–Child Interaction Therapy for Mexican Americans." *Education and Treatment of Children 28*, 111–129.

McNeil, C.B., Eyberg, S.M., Eisenstadt, T.H., Newcomb, K., & Funderburk, B. (1991) "Parent–Child Interaction Therapy with behavior problem children: Generalization of treatment effects to the school setting." *Journal of Child Clinical Psychology 20*, 140–151.

McNeil, C.B. & Hembree-Kigin, T.L. (2010) *Parent–Child Interaction Therapy*. New York: Springer.

Paris, M. & Hoge, M.A. (2010) "Burnout in the mental health workforce: A review." *Journal of Behavioral Health Services and Research 37*, 4, 519–528.

PCIT International (2013) Training Requirements for Certification as a PCIT Therapist. Retrieved on January 30, 2018 from www.pcit.org/therapist-requirements.html.

Quetch, L., Wallace, N., Herschell, A., & McNeil, C. (2015) "Weighing in on the time-out controversy: An empirical perspective." *Clinical Psychologist 68*, 4–19.

Reitman, D. & McMahon, R.J. (2012) "Constance 'Connie' Hanf (1917–2002): The mentor and the model." *Cognitive and Behavioral Practice 20*, 1, 106–116.

Siegel, D.J. & Bryson, T.P. (2014) "'Time-outs' are hurting your child." *Time*, September 23. Retrieved on January 15, 2018 from www.time.com/3404701/discipline-time-out-is-not-good.

Solomon, M., Ono, M., Timmer, S., & Goodlin-Jones, B. (2008) "The effectiveness of Parent–Child Interaction Therapy for families of children on the autism spectrum." *Journal of Autism and Developmental Disorders 38*, 1767–1776.

Timmer, S.G., Urquiza, A.J., Forte, L.A., Boys, D.K., Quick-Abdullah, D., Chan, S., & Gould, W. (2015) "Filling potholes on the implementation highway: Evaluating the implementation of Parent–Child Interaction Therapy in Los Angeles County." *Child Abuse & Neglect, Special Issue on Implementation 53*, 40–50.

Timmer, S., Urquiza, A., Zebell, N., & McGrath, J. (2005) "Parent–Child Interaction Therapy: Application to physically abusive and high-risk dyads." *Child Abuse & Neglect 29*, 825–842.

Timmer, S., Ware, L., Zebell, N., & Urquiza, A. (2008) "The effectiveness of Parent–Child Interaction Therapy for victims of interparental violence." *Violence & Victims 25*, 486–503.

UC Davis PCIT Training Center (2016) PCIT ToT Training Manual. University of California, Davis.

Urquiza, A.J. & McNeil, C. (1996) "Parent–Child Interaction Therapy: An intensive dyadic treatment for physically abusive families." *Child Maltreatment 1*, 2, 134–144.

Urquiza, A.J., Timmer, S.G., & Girard, E. (2011) *Dissemination of Parent–Child Interaction Therapy: Test of a ToT Training Model*. Poster presented at the 2011 Global Implementation Conference, Washington, DC.

Zlomke, K., Jeter, K., & Murphy, J. (2017) "Open-trial pilot of Parent–Child Interaction Therapy for children with autism spectrum disorder." *Child & Family Behavior Therapy 39*, 1–18.

Chapter 7

A PARENT EDUCATION PROGRAM DESIGNED TO ENHANCE THE DEVELOPMENTAL GROWTH OF INFANTS AT-RISK FOR AUTISM

Ronit M. Molko and Kate Guastaferro

ABSTRACT

Siblings of children diagnosed with autism spectrum disorder (ASD) and children showing signs of developmental delay are at elevated risk for developing ASD or developmental delays and should be screened during infancy to identify any delays and to receive early intervention. This chapter describes a pilot study conducted to examine if an intervention, provided as soon as early signs of developmental delay were detectable, would alter the developmental trajectory of infant and toddler siblings of children diagnosed with autism or infants and toddlers determined to be at-risk for an emerging developmental delay. The Infant Catch-Up Program taught parents behaviorally based strategies to promote the development of critical developmental skills (e.g., gesturing, babbling, or responding to their name). The prediction was that if parents can promote a developmentally stimulating environment, an autism diagnosis may be prevented, or the intensity and duration of intervention may be decreased. This chapter presents the overall model, with an emphasis on fidelity measurement, results of a pilot trial, and future dissemination directions.

Keywords: autism spectrum disorder (ASD); individuals at risk for ASD; infant/toddler; developmental delay; parent-delivered interventions; play and imitation; early intervention; parent education program

Autism spectrum disorder (ASD) is most commonly diagnosed in children between the ages of 18 months and three years. However, there are often indications of atypical development during the early stages of infancy (i.e., 3–6 months), signifying the potential for the emergence of a developmental disorder (Fombonne, 2003; Johnson, Myers, & the Council on Children with Disabilities, 2007; Paul *et al.*, 2011; Ritvo *et al.*, 1989; Sandlin *et al.*, 2014). Early signs of autism in infants include a lack of eye contact, joint attention, gesturing, or responsiveness to his or her name, or the sound of a familiar voice. Other indicative deficits include difficulty in visually tracking objects, engaging socially or sharing expressions, babbling or cooing, and delays in motor development, such as rolling over or pushing up (Barbato & Dissanayake, 2009; Sandlin *et al.*, 2014; Zwaigenbaum *et al.*, 2005).

Siblings of children diagnosed with autism have an 18–20% chance of developing ASD or developmental delays; by 4 years old, 35% of siblings who did not develop ASD developed autism behaviors and delays in reaching their developmental milestones (Ozonoff *et al.*, 2011; Newschaffer *et al.*, 2012). By comparison, the same autistic behaviors and delays are seen in less than 18% of 3-year-olds from families previously unaffected by autism. Because the presence of an older sibling with ASD is a significant predictor of an ASD outcome, infants who have older siblings with autism should be carefully monitored and screened early in development to identify at-risk signs and provide intervention as early as possible (Ozonoff *et al.*, 2011). As risk factors for autism are identified at increasingly younger ages, it is possible to introduce intervention early that may reduce the lifetime challenges and costs of necessary interventions for the child and family. Thus, it is imperative to provide a developmentally appropriate and family-friendly intervention program for these children and their families (Messinger *et al.*, 2013; Newschaffer *et al.*, 2012).

The early years, and even months, of infant development are critical. The brain is still developing at birth and experiences in the first years of life have critical and long-lasting effects on the child's abilities to learn and regulate their environment. Brain development is strongly influenced by the quality of the relationships and environmental exposures, such that the architecture, wiring, and functioning of the brain may be affected (Gopnik, Meltzoff, & Kuhl, 1999; National Scientific Council on the Developing Child, 2004, 2007; Reis, Collins, & Berscheid, 2000). Infants are born with an abundance of neurons in their brains that form neural networks based on experiences. In the first few years of life, more than a million neural connections are formed every second. Each time an infant experiences something for the first time, a strong neural connection is formed. If this experience is repeated, the connection is reactivated and becomes strengthened. Conversely, if the experience is not repeated, the connection is pruned and eventually, in the absence of repeat experience, is removed.

The ability of the brain to change in response to life experiences is at its prime during the first five years of life and slowly decreases with age. During infancy and childhood, there is significant loss of neural pathways as the brain shapes what it needs in order to function. The earlier neural connections are made through repeated appropriate learning experiences, the stronger those connections become as the brain consolidates neural pathways and structures (National Scientific Council on the Developing Child, 2007; Twardosz & Lutzker, 2010). For children with developmental delays, or children at-risk for developing a delay, this understanding of brain plasticity is especially relevant. Children with developmental delays experience neural connections that do not support effective communication and social interaction.

Interaction between a child and significant others in his/her life (parents, caregivers, family members) is essential in developing these neural connections. As infants interact more with their world by gesturing, babbling, making eye contact, demonstrating joint attention, and showing facial expressions, they receive increased responses from the adults in their environment. It is this back-and-forth process of interaction that is fundamental to the development of the wiring of the brain (National Scientific Council on the Developing Child, 2004, 2007). There is a critical need for parent training programs to specifically focus on teaching parents strategies and activities in which to engage with their at-risk children so as to stimulate brain development and the development of critical communication and social skills.

Research shows that infants exposed to stimulation engaging their bodies and senses which allows them to explore and experience their environments, especially through active play, show increased brain development (Norwegian University of Science and Technology, NTNU, 2017). In addition, children make significantly better gains with parent and caregiver involvement than when intervention is provided without parental involvement. Research with autistic children demonstrated that when parents are involved in intervention and received training, outcomes were improved for their children, including an improved understanding of communication skills and language, as well as a decrease in the severity of autism characteristics (Oono, Honey, & McConachie, 2013).

In this chapter, we describe the Infant Catch-Up Program, an intensive parent education program for parents of children identified at-risk for autism. The Infant Catch-Up Program is designed specifically for parents of children determined to be at-risk for autism or a developmental delay, but without a formal diagnosis. The goal of the Infant Catch-Up Program was to determine whether a parent-delivered intervention implemented at the first signs of an emerging developmental delay, could change the trajectory of child development and reduce the need for intensive early intervention. The program introduces the concept of providing multiple sources of stimulation to the infant, using a behavioral approach. Parents and caregivers are trained in how to interact with their children in this manner during typical family routines such as bathing, diaper changing, feeding, playtime, and bedtime. This chapter includes findings from a pilot of the Infant Catch-Up Program designed to assess the efficacy of the program in a natural setting. Participants were infants and toddlers who were showing signs of developmental delay based on an assessment by the regional center which funded the intervention. Of the 28 participants, 16 children had an older sibling with a diagnosis of ASD. As the pilot was not an experiment, data from these two groups of children are not compared. Parent fidelity of implementation of the program is discussed as well as the developmental gains made by the children. We review anecdotal information reflecting whether the children went on to participate in early intervention and how many reached a typical developmental trajectory.

Description of the model

The Infant Catch-Up Program was developed by Autism Spectrum Therapies (AST), a national provider of premier evidence-based interventions to children with autism and their families. AST, founded in 2001 in California by Ronit Molko and William Frea, provides services to children on the autism spectrum with a particular focus on individualizing treatment, supporting the needs of the entire family, and providing services in the natural environment in order to allow for the greatest learning and generalization opportunities. AST, now a division of the Learn It Systems family of companies, provides services in homes, in schools, and in the community, on a national level to support the development of age appropriate skills, promote independence and support the autism community.

The Infant Catch-Up Program curriculum is comprised of a total of 64 teaching strategies. These strategies include, but are not limited to: promoting eye contact during play or to request an item; promoting the use of distal pointing; prompting appropriate manipulation of objects; promoting responses to social praise (i.e., smiling and clapping); teaching parents to use reinforcement to encourage expressive language; and teaching parents how to promote social skill such as imitating actions during music and songs. These teaching strategies are based on the principles of applied behavior analysis (ABA) developed to teach parents to facilitate social-communicative interactions in their children. Strategies taught to parents as part of the Infant Catch-Up curriculum incorporate naturalistic strategies such as those developed in the Natural Language Paradigm (NLP), Pivotal Response Treatment (PRT), and developmentally based strategies (Casby, 2003; Koegel, Koegel & McNerney, 2001; Koegel, O'Dell, & Koegel, 1987; Wetherby & Prizant, 2001). These models of intervention focus on the essential aspects of child development such as motivation, responsivity to multiple cues, self-management, and social initiations. In addition, this naturalistic and child-centered approach creates an environment in which individuals are successfully motivated and maximizes learning opportunities through natural activities, such as those of daily living.

In addition, components from parent-education programs designed for parents of typically developing children were incorporated. Specifically, the planned activities training skills from

SafeCare®, an evidence-based parent support program, were borrowed in the development of the parent–child interaction component of the Infant Catch-Up Program (Gershater-Molko, Lutzker, & Wesch, 2003). Planned activities training teaches parents how to prepare for activities in advance (e.g., setting up supplies for bath time) and engage children in activities (e.g., telling the child a new activity will begin within a specified amount of time). In addition, the planned activities training skills emphasize the importance of making purposeful eye contact, touching children affectionately, and communicating clearly, including the praise of desired behaviors (Harrold et al., 1992; Huynen et al., 1996). The measurement of child behaviors consists of behaviors such as attending, verbalizations, affect, imitation, and following instructions. The concepts were adapted and incorporated into the Infant Catch-Up Program curriculum.

Training details

The overarching goal of the Infant Catch-Up Program is to ensure that the infant's environment provides the optimal level of stimulation in critical areas of child development so as to move the child to a typical developmental trend. Infants and toddlers with identified or potential delays who met California State regional center eligibility criteria are referred to the Infant Catch-Up Program. Although the program teaches parents directly, progress is measured for both parents and their children. At the completion of the program, it is expected that the *parents* will have learned to: (1) identify appropriate goals for their child based on developmental milestones; (2) identify their child's progress toward reaching developmental milestones; and (3) utilize parent/child interaction techniques to encourage skill development through playtime activities and daily family routines. The primary outcome, however, is accelerated development of the infant or toddler as the goal of the program is to teach parents strategies to stimulate their children, teach specific skills and enhance development.

The Infant Catch-Up Program targets some of the core areas associated with autism relevant to infant development such as joint attention, symbol use and gestures, and reciprocal interactions within the natural daily routines of the family (e.g., mealtime, bathing, playtime, transitions between activities, etc.). Joint attention, a critical skill in infant development, is when the shared focus of two individuals is on one object or event. One individual alerts the other to an object using eye contact or gazing, or another non-verbal indicator. For example, an infant might draw her mother's attention to a picture in a book by looking at the picture, looking at her mother, and looking back at the picture. In this way, the baby draws her attention to the object and when she looks at it, there is a mutual understanding that they are both interested in, and sharing enjoyment of, the same object or activity. Joint attention is a critical foundation for social, cognitive, and language development that should emerge at about 9 months. In the preceding example, the objective of her eye contact is social because she wants to show what she is looking at to someone else, in this case, her mother. It is important that children learn to initiate and respond to joint attention as this builds the foundation for many critical social and communicative skills. Gestures and symbol use are intentional motor activities such as pointing, or the use of a symbol, whereby the child communicates with others or understands another person's communication. In this program, symbol use/gesture goals focused on teaching the child skills such as imitation of sounds, pointing to show or comment, and functional play with toys.

The program incorporates the teaching of these skills to the children by their parents to enhance their development using reciprocal interactions and play. The goal is to equip parents with strategies and techniques to set the occasion for specific skill development within each domain of child development (expressive language, receptive language, cognitive development, social/emotional development, adaptive/self-help, fine motor and gross motor skills). Parents learn to better capture their infant's attention, create frequent opportunities for social-communicative interactions, motivate responses, and follow through with teaching opportunities. The expectation is for parents to become experts at using these strategies and at engaging their child during activities of daily living. It is expected that the child will make more frequent eye contact, demonstrate joint attention, and will increase the number of communicative utterances, as well as demonstrate enhanced development as measured by the standardized tests administered.

Case Study: Jack

To illustrate how the Infant Catch-Up Program may be implemented, we examine a case study of Jack (full procedural details follow in the subsequent section). Jack was 14 months old when he and his family were referred to AST. Jack lived at home with his parents and three older siblings, one of whom was previously diagnosed with autism. Jack's assessment scores showed that his expressive language skills were at a 3-month level; receptive language skills were at a 9-month level; social/emotional scores showed a 9-month level; and adaptive/ self-help skill scores showed an 8-month level of functioning. His scores for cognitive functioning were at a 16-month level of functioning, slightly above his chronological age, therefore showing no cognitive delay; developmental delay does not imply cognitive deficit. At the start of intervention, Jack was primarily non-verbal and was inconsistent with his reciprocal exchanges and responses. He exhibited fleeting eye contact, did not exhibit joint attention, and engaged minimally with others.

The Infant Catch-Up Program behavior interventionist began by reviewing infant and toddler development with Jack's parents, focusing on the typical milestones for a 14-month-old child and discussing the identifiable gaps in skills between a typically developing 14-month-old and Jack's current skills. The interventionist explained that the intention of the program was to catch Jack up chronologically such that his level of functioning matched his chronological age.

Jack's mother was the primary participant in the program. Specific program goals were developed after initial assessment to teach the requisite skills by teaching the mother strategies to encourage age-appropriate communication, social interaction, joint attention, and self-help skills. In addition, the interventionist reviewed the family's typical daily routine and identified specific opportunities when Jack's mother could practice these techniques and strategies. Some of the strategies taught to Jack's mother included:

- choosing developmentally appropriate toys

- following the child's lead

- responding to the child's initiations

- providing clear instructions

- providing appropriate feedback and consequences

- using a prompt hierarchy; and

- providing opportunities for choice-making, such as choosing between two books to read, or choosing between two or three different food items during snack time.

For example, during diaper changing, Jack's mother was shown how to engage him in a game of peekaboo to stimulate eye contact and playful social interaction. During playtime, she was taught how to stimulate joint attention by playing with a desired object or reading stories and emphasizing looking at a picture, looking at the child, and looking back at the picture. Another example of stimulating joint attention was teaching Jack to follow his mother's finger as she pointed to objects. Eventually, this was expanded to increase Jack's ability to follow point distally, from up to five feet away.

In targeting communication goals specifically, Jack was taught expressive language by imitating his mother's words. For example, his mother would say "milk" while holding his bottle and wait for him to imitate a sound before giving him access to his bottle. PRT focuses on improving children's motivation during learning by targeting preferred activities, initiations, and interests. In Jack's case, during a feeding routine when he was thirsty and wanted his bottle, his mother was taught to use this opportunity and Jack's high level of motivation to improve a core behavior such as communication. The goal is to say the word "milk" while showing Jack the bottle and wait for him to make an utterance that approximates the desired word. Immediately, upon a functional utterance (not a whine or cry, for example) Jack was given access to the milk, a natural reinforcer. As this process continued, Jack's utterances were shaped to approximate the desired word. As Jack's interests changed, so did the focus of the program and the goals. Once the feeding routine was completed, Jack's mother was shown how to transition to a play routine and follow Jack's lead as he demonstrated interest in a toy or activity. The program would then move on to playing with the toy, and the target skills would be taught using that preferred toy or activity.

With regard to self-help skills, Jack's mother was taught how to prompt him to pick up a piece of food and feed himself. Prompting involved giving Jack small pieces of a highly preferred food on a plate. If he did not reach for the pieces himself, his mother was shown how to use a system of prompting whereby she assisted Jack in learning to perform the skill, picking up food and feeding himself, independently. Prompts can be physical, verbal, or gestural in nature. Along with the prompting procedure, Jack's mother was shown how to reinforce correct responses. As Jack acquired the skill, the prompt was slowly faded out, ensuring that he was using the skill correctly.

Jack's mother was extremely receptive to the strategies and to learning the program. She demonstrated inde- pendence in the implementation of many of the strategies. His developmental gains were assessed after 90 days of the Infant Catch-Up Program, as required by the funding source, the regional center. Jack was now 17 months old, had expressive language scores scattered between 6 and 9 months (an increase of 3–6 developmental months), receptive language at 12 months (an increase of 3 developmental months), social-emotional scores at 19 months (an increase of 10 developmental months), and adaptive functioning/self-help skills at 16 months (an increase of 8 developmental months). Most notably, prior to intervention, Jack demonstrated a delay in social- emotional skills, but post-intervention he surpassed the age-appropriate milestones for these skills.

Evidence for the model

The Infant Catch-Up Program was evaluated through a pilot study, the services for which were funded by the Regional Center of Orange County in southern California. The 21 regional centers in California are nonprofit private corporations that contract with the Department of Developmental Services to provide and coordinate services and supports for individuals with intellectual and developmental disabilities. Regional centers contract with vendors, such as AST, to provide services to individuals who meet eligibility criteria for state funding. In California, infants and toddlers from birth to 36 months may be eligible for early intervention services "if they meet one of the following criteria through a documented evaluation of their functioning:

- have a developmental delay of at least 33% (as demonstrated by scores from assessment measures) in one or more areas of either cognitive, communication, social or emotional, adaptive, or physical and motor development including vision and hearing; or

- have an established risk condition of known etiology, with a high probability of resulting in delayed development; or

- be considered at high risk of having a substantial developmental disability due to a combination of biomedical risk factors of which are diagnosed by qualified personnel."

Cal. Code Regs. tit. 17, § 58822 (2018)

When parents, or medical care providers, or other professionals, become concerned about a child's development, they are referred to their local regional center for an evaluation. The results of the evaluation determine eligibility for services. Each family is assigned a regional center case manager, who determines suitability for specific programs, makes referrals, and continues to supervise and case manage the client. When the child turns 3 years of age, funding for some of the targeted goals (such as communication and other skills that are categorized as academic goals) transfers to the school districts based on federal legislation. Therefore, children may exit intervention programs at their third birthday, sometimes before completing the entire program.

The goal of the pilot study was to determine if very early intervention, provided as soon as early signs of developmental delay were detectable, would alter the developmental trajectory of infants and toddlers, thereby preventing the diagnosis of autism or decreasing the intensity and duration of intervention required long term. In this section, we describe the provision of the model in the field and results of the initial evaluation. The provision of the Infant Catch-Up Program was initially funded as a four-month parent training program, with the option of an additional 90 days of funding if approved by the regional center.

Participants
Parents and children
Participants were parents of 28 infants, aged between 6 months and 15 months, identified as having significant developmental delay, or who were identified as being at-risk for a diagnosis of autism and/or a developmental disorder. Of these infants, 16 had an older sibling with autism who was receiving intensive behavioral intervention, thereby placing them at higher risk for developing ASD. In most cases, the mother was the primary parent participating in the training.

Providers
The Infant Catch-Up Program was designed to be delivered by a behavior interventionist. The requirement to be employed by AST as a behavior interventionist was a Bachelor's degree in child development, psychology, or a related field, as well as experience working with infants and young children with autism. Upon employment, each behavior interventionist was required to complete 40 hours of didactic training and pass an examination of the learned content. In addition, staff were required to role play under observation and then shadow (work alongside) intermediate or advanced interventionists in the home working with AST clients. Behavior interventionists were required to meet an assessment of competency on behavior management strategies, ABA techniques, and professionalism. Examples of the competencies for professionalism included timeliness, appearance, communication and collaboration with team members and families, documentation of client data, and protection of privacy.

Procedure

Once the regional center conducted its assessment and determined that a child met eligibility requirements for intervention, the regional center team, along with the family, would develop an Individual Family Service Plan (IFSP), mapping out the child's goals and early intervention services, as well as how these services would be provided. This is a requirement of Part C of IDEA (Individual with Disabilities Education Act), which is a federal grant program that assists states in operating early intervention programs for young children with intellectual and developmental disabilities. Upon referral from the regional center case manager, AST conducted its own assessment, including a detailed parent interview as well as an observation of the child and parents in the natural home environment. If the child was determined to be eligible for the Infant Catch-Up Program, the parents would be assigned an interventionist who would visit their home two to four times per week.

The goals outlined in each child's IFSP, along with the Catch-Up curriculum, were the basis for the family's program. The interventionist identified the specific strategies to be taught, and individualized the Program based on the developmental goals for the child, and family routines. The IFSP goals developed by the regional center team generally focused on the following four areas of development: joint attention, reciprocal interactions, symbol use/gestures, and self-help skills. The Infant Catch-Up Program strategies to be taught were identified after initial observation and assessment of the child, developed according to the program curriculum and integrated into the four categories of child development as described in the IFSP. By way of example, if the IFSP goal was "Jack will increase his amount of interaction during play," some of the program goals would be to teach joint attention and increase eye contact during an activity or requesting an item. If the client already possessed some of the 64 strategies that comprised the program curriculum, that client's program was modified to fit that client's needs.

Intervention sessions were conducted two to four days per week for one-and-a-half to two hours per session, following a general time-limited curriculum, as the program was only funded for four months, with the option of an additional 90 days of funding if requested by AST. Intervention began with providing basic education to parents about typical developmental milestones and reviewing the assessment of their child's current skill levels. This was particularly relevant for parents whose first child was diagnosed with autism, as they had not experienced typical verbal and social child development with those children. Lesson plans targeting specific skill deficits were administered to parents in subsequent sessions. The program consisted of 64 specific strategies that parents were to learn to complete the program. If a parent demonstrated existing competence and mastery of one or more strategies, those strategies were eliminated from the program.

Each session followed a similar structure: (1) checking in with the parent; (2) a structured teaching segment; (3) an unstructured play segment; (4) debriefing with the parent; and, (5) a weekly homework assignment. The structure of the sessions was determined by individual family routines, so that the caregiver could learn how to implement strategies functionally throughout the day. At the beginning of each session, the interventionist would check in on how the family was faring in general and whether the parent had completed the homework. Quantitative data were not collected on homework completion; instead, parent involvement, participation, and acquisition of strategies was measured in terms of fidelity of implementation of the strategies during observed sessions. During the structured teaching segment, the interventionist would begin with a didactic presentation of a strategy to improve a specific skill (e.g., using a clear discriminative stimulus, such as "point to book," when communicating, using the prompting hierarchy, and facilitating peer interaction among siblings). The interventionist would then model the strategy or skill just discussed with the child as the parent observed. Next, the behavior interventionist guided the parent's practice of the strategy, and then observed the parent implementing the strategy independently. The interventionist provided reinforcement and any necessary constructive feedback, and the parent repeated the practice of correct and appropriate implementation until it was performed consistently.

These strategies were taught during natural family routines according to each family's daily structure of activities and following the child's lead and initiation. For example, if the baby showed interest in a toy, the interventionist and parent engaged in that activity, teaching the strategies for play, communication, and social interaction at that time. When the baby needed a diaper change, the parent was shown how to incorporate appropriate strategies into that routine. The program focused on routines of daily living such as bathing, diapering, playtime, and feeding. Because PRT requires that parents follow the child's lead and initiations, guidelines for engaging infants and toddlers were reviewed and suggestions for play activities were offered if parents were unable to generate their own ideas for play and interaction. At the end of each session, parents were assigned weekly activities as homework to conduct with their children. Homework assignments might include "playing peekaboo once each day during diapering" or sitting with the child on the floor for six minutes twice a day and engaging in play to practice imitation by playing with musical toys, drums, cars, and trains. Homework was reviewed at the subsequent week's session during the opening check-in conversation.

Children and their parents exited the Infant Catch-Up Program when their skill base met age-appropriate levels and their development matched that of a typically developing child of the same age. Some families did not complete the entire program for various reasons, including inability to progress through the entire curriculum in the timeframe that the program was funded, moving away, because their child was transitioned into a more intensive early intervention program sooner, or because their child stopped being eligible for service due to regional center age regulations.

Measures
Parental progress toward program goals
Parent progress was measured on weekly home activities (e.g., bathing, diapering, feeding, playtime) using a fidelity of implementation rating system. Parents were rated on the 64 curriculum strategies in which they had been trained. A five-point rating system was used to assess parent mastery of independence in implementing each of the strategies introduced into the program. A score of zero was ascribed if the parent had received no training on the strategy. A score of one was ascribed if the parent was introduced to the strategy. A score of two was ascribed if the parent implemented the strategy with guided feedback from

the therapist. A score of three was ascribed if the parent demonstrated independence in implementation of the strategy in targeted routines. A score of four was ascribed if the parent demonstrated independence in implementation across generalized routines. Skills were considered mastered if the parents received a score of three or four on each strategy. If parents demonstrated competency on any of the strategies at baseline, these were excluded from the training curriculum and considered mastered/independent. The measures for each of the strategies that were learned were reported to the funding source in the requisite reports. For the purposes of anonymity in the pilot study, the measures are reported in percentages, reflecting the percentage of the total strategies learned, as well as the percentage mastered (a score of three or four) of the strategies learned.

Child developmental assessments

Child progress was measured in terms of progress toward IFSP goals, progress toward program goals and progress toward developmental milestones. Initial developmental assessments conducted by the Regional Center upon referral to AST were used as the baseline levels for each child. Each child was assessed on expressive language skills, receptive language skills, cognitive skills, and social/emotional skills using the Developmental Assessment of Young Children (DAYC) and Rossetti Infant–Toddler Language Scale (Rossetti, 2006). The DAYC was developed for children from birth to five years of age to assess development across five domains of developments: Cognitive, Communication, Social-Emotional, Physical Development, and Adaptive Behavior (Voress & Maddox, 2013). The Rossetti Infant–Toddler Language Scale identifies preverbal and verbal language development issues in children from infancy through the age of 3 (Rossetti, 2006). Behavior interventionists at AST conducted follow-up assessments after approximately 90 days of program participation to assess developmental gains. These developmental assessments served as the primary outcome of interest. Recommendations for future programming were made based on the assessment data and progress toward program goals. Pending review and outcomes of the follow-up assessments, the regional center funded an additional 90 days of the Infant Catch-Up Program.

Results

Results from the pilot are presented in aggregate to preserve participant anonymity. When possible, information about the number of participants meeting a specific outcome is described. The results that follow are descriptive; given that this was a pilot study, no statistical inferences are presented.

Participants

Twenty-eight children and their parents participated in the pilot study. The average child age at enrollment in the study was 11.2 months (range: 6 to 15 months). Sixteen children were siblings of a child diagnosed with ASD, but other risk factors included premature birth, multiple birth, or global delays (e.g., delays in expressive and receptive language, social/emotional skills, and adaptive/self-help skills). The average program participation was 4.21 months, but ranged from 2 to 7 months. At program exit, the average chronological age of children was 15.7 months (range: 12 to 19 months).

Parent outcomes

Overall, parents mastered (i.e., learned to successfully implement) an average of 60% of the total curriculum strategies (Table 7.1). The average percentage of strategies learned from the actual number of behavioral strategies introduced was approximately 78%. The rate of progress varied, depending on individual circumstances for each family and not all strategies were introduced to all parents.

As seen in Table 7.1, not all strategies were introduced in each program (an average of 30.58%), nor did some progress beyond the early introductory phase (an average of 2.72%). The reasons for this varied. For example, one family may have received seven months of program funding while another family only received three months of funding, either because they moved away or because their child turned 3 years old and was no longer eligible for this program according to state funding regulations. Other families were transferred into more intensive early intervention programs after the 90-day follow up assessments. On average, 9.02% of the strategies scored in the guided practice phase of fidelity of implementation. An average of 20.94% and 30.70% scored in the independent ranges (independent in target ioutine and independent in generalized routine, respectively), and were considered to be mastered.

Table 7.1 Parent mastery of introduced strategies (*n* = 28)

Mean # of strategies learned	Mean
No training	30.58
Introduced	2.72
Guided practice	9.02
Independent in target routine	20.94
Independent in generalized routine	30.70
Mean % of learned strategies	60.12
Mean % of learned strategies from goals introduced	77.40

Child developmental gains

Table 7.2 shows the percent delay of each child at the start of the program and the percent delay of each child 30 days prior to exiting the program. The percent delay for expressive language decreased from a mean of 52.13% prior to entering the program to a mean of 30.34% at exit. Specifically, decreases in percent delay for expressive language skills were observed in 19 of the 28 children. Decreases in percent delay for receptive language skills were observed in 16 children, with overall decreases from a mean of 45.22% at the start of the program to a mean of 29.77% at exit. Reductions in percent delays for cognitive functioning were observed in 20 children, with overall percent decreases from a mean of 13.97% to a mean of 5.32%. Decreases in percent delay for social/emotional skills were observed in 20 children, with percent decreases from a mean of 34.78% to a mean of 11.3%.

Table 7.2 Child developmental assessment (*n* = 28)

% Developmental delay at pre-intervention	Mean
Expressive language	52.13
Receptive language	45.22
Cognitive	13.97
Social/emotional	34.78

% Developmental delay at post-intervention	Mean
Expressive language	30.34
Receptive language	29.77
Cognitive	5.32
Social/emotional	11.73

Table 7.3 depicts the number of months that each child gained developmentally from participating in the Infant Catch-Up Program. The children in the program demonstrated overall gains across all four developmental areas (expressive, receptive, cognitive, and social/emotional). The mean developmental gain was 6.9 months, with a range of gains from 1.5 to 18.5 months. Gains from each developmental domain averaged 6.9 months for expressive language, 6.8 months for receptive language, 6.7 months for cognitive functioning, and 7.3 months for social/emotional. Rapid gains were observed in 9 of the 28 children; these children demonstrated a mean of 2.8 months gain for each month in the program. Moreover, prior to exiting the program, all the children were assessed and 4 of the 9 children demonstrated that they were functioning at or above developmental age level (no developmental delay and/or exceeding developmental functioning), compared to typical children in their age group.

Table 7.3 Child developmental gains in developmental months (n = 28)

Child developmental domains	Mean
Overall developmental gain	6.99
Expressive language	6.92
Receptive language	6.88
Cognitive	6.79
Social/emotional	7.39

Program goals met
Variability in the number of IFSP goals were observed across all the children; the number of IFSP goals met ranged from 2 to 29. On average, participants met an average of 66% of their IFSP goals, with 11 children meeting at least 80% of their goals. Of the total number of participants, 7 met 100% of their IFSP goals.

Recommendations for additional intervention

Initial participation in the Infant Catch-Up Program was funded for four months. At the end of the first 90 days of the Infant Catch-Up Program, interventionists collected and reviewed developmental assessment data, child progress towards meeting IFSP goals, and parent progress on implementation of behavioral strategies and made recommendations for further intervention. The funding source required that this occurred at 90 days so that the families would be given 30-days' notice if funding was going to terminate. If recommendations were made for continued intervention, the regional center either funded an additional 90 days of Infant Catch-Up Program (thereby funding a total of seven months in the program) or funded a more intensive early intervention program.

It was recommended that the participants discontinue receiving intervention if they were functioning at their chronological age. Two of the participants met exit criteria for the Infant Catch-Up Program and were not referred for additional services as their follow-up scores showed that they were functioning at or above age level in all developmental domains as compared to typically developing peers. Alternatively, if the assessment scores showed that the child was still functioning below their chronological age developmentally, a referral was made for additional services. Participants were either funded for an additional three months of the Infant Catch-Up Program, referred to the AST intensive early intervention program, referred to a center-based program, or referred to another vendor, depending on parental request, circumstances, and best fit for continued intervention. The rest ($n = 26$) of the children continued to receive additional services, including moving on to intensive early intervention programs. Of these, 36% exited early intervention programs once the child achieved age-appropriate levels across all developmental domains. Ten children discontinued early intervention services before turning 3 years old and only one child transitioned to a school district's special education program after age 3. Some of the participants transitioned to other vendors and their progress beyond their participation in the Infant Catch-Up Program was not reported back to AST.

Conclusion

This early intervention model utilizes ABA methodology, incorporates family members, is conducted in the natural environment, provides education regarding typical development, and includes data collection on both parent and child performance. Preliminary data collected on the Infant Catch-Up parent education program for infants at-risk for autism indicate that, in general, parents were able to learn to independently implement the strategies taught during specific routines, and to some extent, generalize those strategies to other routines as well. Children who participated in the program demonstrated gains in all developmental areas. Although many continued to receive intensive early intervention following completion of the infant program, almost half of these children had met developmental criteria for their age by 3 and only one child was in a special education classroom. Long-term outcome data of infants participating in this type of program will need to be collected to evaluate its impact as the initial stage of intensive early intervention. In this case, long-term data were not available to AST. For consistency, it would have been beneficial if the regional center continued to collect follow-up data on these children to evaluate their long-term outcomes.

There is evidence that parent-delivered programs can be effective with children with autism and other disabilities. Training parents early to engage and interact with their children has led to gains in language, social attention, and imitation skills. Research also supports the efficacy of individualized programs. Even though the Infant Catch-Up Program taught the same set of strategies to all parents, the programs were tailored around individual family routines and structures making the programs more customized and attending to the needs of each family. Additionally, when programs are tailored to family's needs and structures parents are more likely to participate. Teaching parents to follow their children's lead and respond to their children's initiations has additional positive effects on child development.

Returning to the case study of Jack, a sibling of a child diagnosed with ASD, after completion of the Infant Catch-Up Program, Jack was referred to the AST early intervention program for intensive early intervention. The regional center funded 12 hours per week of intervention and Jack started receiving direct intervention daily for just over two hours per day. The goals of the program were to bring his developmental skills as close to his chronological age as possible. Goals targeted receptive and expressive language, social skills, and self-help skills. Jack's mother was taught skills to increase his attention, imitation, social reciprocity (such as responding to "hi" with a wave or a "hi"), pointing and gesturing, following one- and two-step instructions, taking turns, walking next to his mother without dropping to the ground or running away, playing functionally with toys, and pretend play, and so forth. At 24 months of age, Jack's expressive language scores were 18–21 months, his receptive scores were 18 months, his cognitive scores were 30 months, his social emotional scores were 30 months, his adaptive skills were 28 months. These represent impressive gains.

Due to the nature of this pilot study, it was not possible to conduct a randomized control study, the design of which would ideally assist in demonstrating the efficacy of very early intervention (see Chapter 4). Without a randomized trial, it cannot be determined at what level the participants would have scored developmentally without intervention. Despite this shortfall, this pilot study has notable strengths: the focus on relevant and meaningful outcomes; and the change in child developmental trajectory and parental mastery of strategies and techniques that can be incorporated into the families' daily lives are important contributions to the literature because it has been demonstrated that the development of infants who were later diagnosed with autism started to digress from a typical developmental trajectory as early as 6 months old. Infants with symptoms of developmental delay in the first year of life may be an especially high-risk group for developing autism. The importance of intervening early and demonstrating the positive impact of that intervention is significant.

Acknowledgments

The authors would like to acknowledge Sabrina Daneshvar, Riki Frea, William Frea, Erin McNerney, and Casey Nguyen for their contributions to the development of this program and participation in the pilot study. The assistance of Casey Nguyen and Christina Hempstead in compiling the data is especially appreciated and gratefully acknowledged.

References

Barbato, J. & Dissanayake, C. (2009) "Autism spectrum disorders in infancy and toddlerhood: A Review of the evidence on early signs, early identification tools, and early diagnosis." *Journal of Developmental & Behavioral Pediatrics 30*, 5, 447–459.

Cal. Code Regs. tit. 17, § 58822 (2018) Retrieved on 9 May, 2018 from https://www.dds.ca.gov/ProposedRegs/ES/FinalText.pdf

Casby, M. (2003) "The development of play in infants, toddlers, and young children." *Communication Disorders Quarterly 24*, 163–174.

Fombonne, E. (2003) "Epidemiological surveys of autism and other pervasive developmental disorders: An update." *Journal of Autism and Developmental Disorders 33*, 4, 365–382.

Gershater-Molko, R.M., Lutzker, J.R., & Wesch, D. (2003) "Project SafeCare: Improving health, safety, and parenting skills in families reported for, and at risk for child maltreatment." *Journal of Family Violence 18*, 377–386.

Gopnik, A., Meltzoff, A.N., & Kuhl, P.K. (1999) *The Scientist in the Crib: Minds, Brains and How Children Learn*. New York: William Morrow & Co.

Harrold, M., Lutzker, J.R., Campbell, R.V., & Touchette, P.E. (1992) "Improving parent–child interactions for families of children with developmental disabilities." *Journal of Behavior Therapy and Experimental Psychiatry 23*, 89–100.

Huynen, K.B., Lutzker, J.R., Bigelow, K.M., Touchette, P.E., & Campbell, R.V. (1996) "Planned activities training for mothers of children with developmental disabilities: Community generalization and follow-up." *Behavior Modification 20*, 406–427.

Johnson, C.P., Myers, S.M., & the Council on Children with Disabilities (2007) "Identification and evaluation of children with autism spectrum disorders." *Pediatrics 120*, 5, 1183–1215.

Koegel, R.L., Koegel, L.K., & McNerney, E.K. (2001) "Pivotal areas in intervention for autism." *Journal of Clinical Child Psychology 30*, 1, 19–32.

Koegel, R.L., O'Dell, M.C., & Koegel, L.K. (1987) "A natural language teaching paradigm for nonverbal autistic children." *Journal of Autism and Developmental Disorders 17*, 2, 187–200.

Messinger, D., Young, G.S., Ozonoff, S., Dobkins, K., *et al.*(2013) "Beyond autism: A baby siblings research consortium study of high-risk children at three years of age." *Journal of the American Academy of Child & Adolescent Psychiatry 52*, 3, 300–308.

National Scientific Council on the Developing Child (2004) *Young Children Develop in an Environment of Relationships*. Working Paper No. 1. Retrieved on January 16, 2018 from www.developingchild.harvard.edu/resources/wp1.

National Scientific Council on the Developing Child (2007) *The Science of Early Childhood Development: Closing the Gap Between What We Know and What We Do*. Retrieved on January 16, 2018 from www.developingchild.harvard.edu/resources/the-science-of-early-childhood-development-closing-the-gap-between-what-we-know-and-what-we-do.

Newschaffer, C.J., Croen, L.A., Daniele Fallin, M., Hertz-Picciotto, I., *et al.* (2012) "Infant siblings and the investigation of autism risk factors." *Journal of Neurodevelopmental Disorders 4*, 1, 1–16.

Norwegian University of Science and Technology (NTNU) (2017) "Babies exposed to stimulation get brain boost." *ScienceDaily*, January 2. Retrieved on January 16, 2018 from www.sciencedaily.com/releases/2017/01/170102143458.htm

Oono, I.P., Honey, E.J., & McConachie, H. (2013) "Parent-mediated early intervention for young children with autism spectrum disorders (ASD)." *Cochrane Database of Systematic Reviews 4.* Art. No.: CD009774.

Ozonoff, S., Young, G.S., Carter, A., Messinger, D., *et al.* (2011) "Recurrence risk for autism spectrum disorders: A Baby Siblings Research Consortium study." *Pediatrics 128*, e488–e495.

Paul, R., Fuerst, Y., Ramsay, G., Chawarska, K., & Klin, A. (2011) "Out of the mouths of babes: Vocal production in infant siblings of children with ASD." *Journal of Child Psychology and Psychiatry 52*, 5, 588–598.

Reis, H.T., Collins, W.A., & Berscheid, E. (2000) "Relationships in human behavior and development." *Psychological Bulletin 126*, 6, 844–872.

Ritvo, E.R., Jorde, L.B., Mason-Brothers, A., Freeman, B.J., *et al.* (1989) "The UCLA-University of Utah epidemiologic survey of autism: Recurrence risk estimates and genetic counseling." *American Journal of Psychiatry 146*, 8, 1032–1036.

Rossetti, L. (2006) *The Rossetti Infant–Toddler Language Scale: A Measure of Communication and Interaction.* Austin, TX: Linguisystems.

Sandlin, S., Lichtenstein, P., Kuja-Halkola, R., Larsson, H., Hultman, C.M., & Reichenberg, A. (2014) "The familiar risk of autism." *JAMA 311*, 17, 1770–1777.

Twardosz, S. & Lutzker, J.R. (2010) "Child maltreatment and the developing brain: A review of neuroscience perspectives." *Aggression and Violent Behavior 15*, 59–68.

Voress, J.K. & Maddox, T. (2013) *Developmental Assessment of Young Children* (2nd ed.). Austin, TX: PRO-ED.

Wetherby, A. & Prizant, B. (2001) *Communication and Symbolic Behavior Scales Developmental Profile* (1st ed.). Baltimore, MD: Paul H. Brookes Publishing.

Zwaigenbaum, L., Bryson, S., Rogers, T., Roberts, W., Brian, J., & Szatmari, P. (2005) "Behavioral manifestations of autism in the first year of life." *International Journal of Developmental Neuroscience 23*, 2–3, 143–152.

Chapter 8

USING ACCEPTANCE AND COMMITMENT THERAPY FOR PARENTS OF CHILDREN WITH AUTISM SPECTRUM DISORDER

Kenneth Fung, Lee Steel, Kelly Bryce, Johanna Lake, and Yona Lunsky

ABSTRACT

Acceptance and Commitment Therapy (ACT) is a behavioral intervention that enhances one's psychological flexibility, fostering acceptance, and mindfulness while increasing commitment to valued actions. This chapter reviews what is known about ACT as it relates to supporting families of children with disabilities, especially families of individuals with autism spectrum disorder (ASD). We will present our model of ACT group intervention offered to parents of children with ASD. Some key elements include: the use of experiential ACT group exercises; a mindful focus on parents' own health and well-being; and engaging parents as facilitators. In one version of our intervention, the emphasis is specifically on supporting mothers of children with ASD. Some of the observed therapeutic enabling processes included the high degree of group cohesion, the shift in roles from caregiver to care recipient, and the process of individual and collective empowerment. Based on the observed outcomes and participant feedback, we find that this model shows promise as an effective and sustainable intervention for promoting the mental health and resilience of parents with children with ASD.

Keywords: Acceptance and Commitment Therapy (ACT); mindfulness; parent health; autism spectrum disorder (ASD); group therapy

Introduction to the ACT model

Parents of children and youth with autism spectrum disorder (ASD) face a variety of challenges and experience high levels of distress (Dabrowska & Pisula, 2010; Estes *et al.*, 2009; Schieve *et al.*, 2007). While many interventions have been developed to increase parents' capacity to manage their children's behaviors, few interventions have been developed to address parents' own emotional needs. Acceptance and Commitment Therapy (ACT), one of the third wave behavioral psychotherapies (Hayes, Strosahl, & Wilson, 2012), or Acceptance and Commitment Training (ACT), an alternative term sometimes used for non-clinical populations, may be a particularly well-suited model for this. ACT fosters acceptance, one of the emotional challenges commonly experienced by parents of children with ASD. Further, ACT is a mindfulness-based behavioral intervention consistent with behavioral principles with which parents may already be familiar as a means of helping their children, as well as consonant with the increasing popularity of the idea of "mindful parenting" in the community. In this chapter, we outline the ACT model, review the evidence of its use for parents of children with ASD, and share our own experience with its use.

ACT is a transdiagnostic psychological model of health and psychopathology that has been effectively used in various clinical populations, including individuals with depression, anxiety, psychosis, and substance abuse (A-Tjak *et al.*, 2015). ACT has also been used to help decrease burnout among professionals and internalized stigma among diverse communities (Ruiz, 2010). ACT is based on Relational Frame Theory, a behavioral account of the development of human language and cognition, including how we come to construct internal meaning from our experiences and how this can shape our behaviors (Hayes, 2004). The implication is that, at its core, ACT posits that human suffering is often related to *psychological inflexibility*; that is, being "hooked" by our internal experiences, such as difficult thoughts and emotions, and resorting to avoidant or other counterproductive rule-governed behaviors. To increase one's *psychological flexibility*, ACT strives to enhance six core psychological processes: *defusion, acceptance, present moment, self-as-context, values,* and *committed action* (Hayes *et al.*, 2012).

Many key ACT exercises are designed to promote *defusion*, the capacity to relate to one's thoughts as merely thoughts, rather than to react to them as true reality. This decreases the perceived importance of one's thoughts and negates the need to dispute the content of these thoughts, as in many other types of psychological interventions. For example, whether the thoughts are about children, such as *"my child is impossible to manage"* or *"children with autism have no future,"* or about parents' own capacity, such as *"I cannot handle this"* or *"I am a terrible parent,"* they can all be treated merely as thoughts, and not something that we necessarily need to embrace or directly challenge. The latter example in particular, which links the descriptive qualifier ("terrible") and the conceptual role of being a "parent" with the self ("I") through a word that implies equivalence ("am"), can also be defused. In this instance, loosening the association of these psychological concepts with the self can potentially alleviate a sense of labeling, judgment, and guilt, while at the same time increase one's psychological flexibility about the self. The self without close attachments to these self-concepts can remain grounded and can, in fact, become *more* resilient and enduring by fostering an alternative sense of self *as context* (versus psychological *content*), the container of thoughts versus the content of thoughts, that is, to develop a sense of self as an *observer* with respect to our experience. In some ways, this approach is similar to Positive Family Intervention (PFI; Durand *et al.*, 2013), where parents learn to think differently about their own thoughts related to their child and their child's behaviour. However, in PFI, parents are essentially taught cognitive restructuring to challenge their thoughts and ultimately to change them, similar to conventional cognitive behavioral therapy. In ACT, parents put distance between themselves and their thoughts, without attempting to alter the thoughts directly.

The practice of *defusion* and *self-as-context* decreases the perceived power of negative thoughts and feelings, decreases one's rigidity in following unhelpful scripts and rules, and facilitates the process of *acceptance*, conceptualized as the willingness to experience rather than to avoid internal psychological events, including aversive thoughts and associated feelings. Further, by increasing *contact with the present moment*, parents are guided to become less entrapped by memories of past frustrations and disappointments and less threatened by worries about the future for themselves or their children. All four ACT processes described above, *defusion, acceptance, self-as-context*, and *present moment*, are consistent with the concept of mindfulness as commonly used in psychological interventions, that is, becoming aware and attentive to the present moment, inclusive of our inner experiences, nonjudgmentally from an observer stance (Fletcher & Hayes, 2005). While ACT interventions often include traditional mindfulness exercises, ACT encourages but does not require participants to be engaged in regular, formal mindfulness practice and meditation, unlike other mindfulness-based psychological interventions. This may be particularly suitable for those who are not yet fully committed to a regular meditative practice.

In addition to the central importance of mindfulness, ACT is a values-based intervention through the linked processes of *values* and *committed action*. *Values* in ACT are distinguished from goals, as the former are often expressed as descriptive qualities (e.g., being a *caring* parent), that can inform a broad sense of chosen direction in life rather than discrete goals or outcomes (e.g., "My child should graduate from high school"), that may or may not be attainable. Discussion of values not only inspires a sense of vitality and meaning, but also affords increased choice and flexibility as many potential *committed actions* may be consistent with one's chosen values. Thus, one's focus can become process-oriented rather than being overly wedded to desirable yet potentially unrealistic outcomes. Exploration of values in life domains other than parenting, such as self-care, can also contribute to the re-establishment of life-balance, often lacking among parents who are overwhelmed by a sense of responsibility in the prevalent discourse of trying to cure or defeat autism.

Evidence for the ACT model

For years, parents have been included in interventions for their children, even prior to the recent interest in mindfulness and acceptance-based therapies (Singer, 1993). However, most of the focus has been on training parents to support their children, including intensive behavioral intervention and other models. This way of working with parents neglects the struggles that parents themselves face, fails to address their mental health issues, and does not strengthen their resilience. Given the chronic demands of parenting and the reality that sometimes child interventions are not successful, parents playing the role of their own children's "therapists" may in some cases add to parents' sense of failure when gains made through interventions are not as significant as advertised. As mindful parenting was shown to benefit children with developmental disabilities, an interest emerged in applying mindfulness to caregivers (Singh *et al.*, 2007). A review of mindfulness interventions for parents of children with autism concluded that mindfulness-based interventions can have positive long-term effects on parent and child well-being, but that more research is required to tailor the delivery method to the needs of this demographic (Cachia, Anderson, & Moore, 2015). To date, most interventions studied have built upon either the work of Singh and colleagues (2007), the application of Mindfulness-Based Stress Reduction (MBSR; Bazzano *et al.*, 2013; Kabat-Zinn, 2003), or Mindfulness-Based Cognitive Therapy (MBCT; Segal, Williams, & Teasdale, 2002; van der Oord, Bögels, & Peijnenburg, 2011). The empirical study of ACT for parents is nascent.

In 2006, one of the first studies on ACT included 20 parents who participated in a two-day workshop (Blackledge & Hayes, 2006). Repeated measures prior to the intervention demonstrated that without the intervention, parents did not change in either depression or psychological acceptance. Parents reported reductions in depression after the intervention, which were maintained three months later. In addition, the parents reported increased psychological flexibility as measured by the Acceptance and Action Questionnaire (AAQ) (Hayes *et al.*, 2004). While findings demonstrate promise for the utility of ACT among parent caregivers, the study sample was small, the follow-up time was brief, and the study did not include an active treatment control group.

Since that time, different groups of clinicians have built upon this original study. Whittingham's team offered a brief ACT intervention (two two-hour sessions) to groups of parents of children with either Cerebral Palsy (Whittingham *et al.*, 2016) or Acquired Brain Injury (Brown *et al.*, 2015) prior to participating in parent education and behavior training groups called Stepping Stones Triple P (SSTP). The Whittingham and colleagues (2016) study found that parents reported reduced depression and stress, as well as improvements in their children, not seen in the intervention without ACT. The Brown and colleagues (2015) study found that parents reported reduced distress and increased psychological flexibility in the combined treatment compared to care as usual. Together, these studies demonstrate that even a very brief ACT component may be beneficial to parents of children with various disabilities when used in combination with other interventions. In 2015, a qualitative study described the impact of ACT with five mothers of children with intellectual disabilities and challenging behavior (Reid *et al.*, 2015). Prior to intervention, the mothers used avoidant coping strategies, leading to an accumulation of problems and, ultimately, to a "breaking point." Through the workshops, mothers learned more effective ways to respond to situations as well as to their own emotions. This, in combination with the unique element of support the all-mother group offered, allowed mothers to feel less stressed and more in control of their lives. Although based on a small sample, this study offered helpful insights into some of the unique benefits of an ACT approach for parents in difficult parenting situations.

An Iranian study randomly assigned 24 mothers of children with high-functioning autism to either individual counseling (treatment as usual group) or group ACT (Joekar *et al.*, 2016). They reported that mothers in the ACT group showed improvements with regard to depression and psychological flexibility and suggested that parents should receive parent-focused services such as ACT during the time that they are already bringing their children to child-focused services. In another small study, a group of researchers in India examined the effects of ACT among five mothers of children with ASD (Poddar, Sinha, & Urbi, 2015). After 10 sessions spanning over two months of treatment, mothers reported lower anxiety and depression, higher quality of life, and increased psychological acceptance.

Although it has been suggested that ACT is an important intervention for parents of children with various disabilities, few studies have been published since Blackledge and Hayes in 2006. Findings are limited due to small sample sizes and no control groups, with the exception of the Triple P study with a brief ACT component (Whittingham *et al.*, 2016). Examples of ACT as an individual and as a group intervention have been reported, and the majority of studies have focused on parents of children with ASD as opposed to other disabilities.

Full description of our ACT model
Development of our ACT intervention

Since 2010, we have run a number of ACT groups for parents of children and youth with ASD based on our previous work in adapting ACT experiential exercises for group therapy among clinical and non-clinical populations, including individuals with chronic pain, depression, anxiety, and for decreasing HIV and mental health stigma for diverse communities (Fung, 2015; Fung & Wong, 2014a, 2014b; Fung & Zurowski, 2008; 2016). The format of the parent groups that we conducted consisted of a single evening session followed by a full-day session, with a second "refresher" evening session about four weeks later. The target population was parents of school-age children and youth with ASD. Parents still seeking an ASD diagnosis were not included. The group size varied from 10 to 20 parents.

Apart from a brief didactic presentation during the first evening, most sessions consisted of group or paired experiential exercises, open sharing, and mindfulness-based exercises. Table 8.1 provides an outline of the current design of the group with a description of the core group activities. As detailed description of each activity is beyond the scope of this chapter, we will describe one activity in more detail in order to illustrate the complexity of the process and how ACT processes are experientially taught.

Table 8.1 Outline and description of ACT group core activities

Activities	Brief Description
Day 1 – Evening (5:30–9:00pm, including dinner break)	
Self-introduction	Bringing an item symbolic of themselves in some way, participants introduce themselves and their children to each other
Didactic presentation	Interactive slide presentation on: the stress of parents with children with ASD and the need to focus on parental health; an overview of the 6 ACT core processes; and the nature of an experiential workshop focusing on the parents themselves (vs. children)
Group rules & goals	Collaboratively establish group norms and goals, creating safety and united purpose
ACT matrix as a group	Use the ACT matrix to illustrate ACT core processes, including the nature of avoidance vs. value driven behaviors
Video on mindfulness	A video introduction to mindfulness from YouTube
Leaves on a stream exercise	Cognitive defusion/mindfulness exercise: through guided imagery, participants are invited to observe their thoughts on leaves floating down a stream
Closure & homework	Participants to do a mindful activity at home; close with the poem "The Guest House" by Jellaludin Rumi
Day 2 – Full Day (9:00–4:00pm, including lunch break)	
Review of homework	Sharing the experience of doing a mindful activity at home
Sweet spot	An exercise to cultivate mindfulness while touching on other ACT processes; each participant in a pair takes turns sharing a sweet moment in their lives
Video on values	A video introduction to valued actions from YouTube
Chair sculpture of suffering	An exercise in creative hopelessness, demonstrating the unavoidability of suffering as a parent of children with ASD in spite of coping efforts and introducing the alternative of acceptance
Soap bubble exercise	A mindfulness exercise, observing bubbles floating up and bursting
Paired-sharing	Each participant in a pair takes turns sharing something about themselves that they do not like, first as a story and then as a song
Video on acceptance	A video on acceptance/mindfulness from YouTube—"The Fly" by Hanjin Song
Values lists & 100th birthday	Reviewing a list of words on values and creating a short speech from a significant person at a gathering that would include these values

Bulls eye	Mapping out consistency of action with respect to one's values in four life domains on a bull's eye handout, and sharing this with the group on a large bulls eye
Group bus driver (or show video)	A group exercise to explore a participant's experience in role playing a bus driver trying to steer a bus towards her own values, while other participants, role playing as passengers, act as barriers
Group goodbye	Sharing appreciation of the group and committing to one valued action
Day 3 – Half Day – 4 weeks after Day 2 (5:30–9:00pm, including dinner break)	
Centering exercise	Brief mindfulness to ground participants
Review of homework	Participants sharing their committed action and other changes in their lives
Review of the ACT hexaflex	Review of the 6 core processes of ACT
ACT matrix	Participants are guided to fill out an ACT matrix on themselves
Raisin exercise	Mindful eating of a raisin
Le'go exercise	A Self-as-context exercise—exploring the participants' past and the "observer self" through meditation and use of construction blocks on paper plates with their names on it
Closing	Closure of the group; Invitation for self-help support group; Opportunity to say something to one another

Note: Sources and more detailed description of the exercises: Fung & Wong (2014a), Fung & Zurowski (2016), Hayes *et al.* (2012), Polk & Schoendorff (2014), Wilson & DuFrene (2009)

In the *paired-sharing exercise*, the group is first divided into pairs, with each participant seated facing one another. The facilitator describes the procedure of the exercise, and rings a bell to guide the participants through each step of the process. The participants would first start by looking at their partner mindfully in silence for a minute in preparation. Then, one participant from each pair would share something about herself that she does not like for two minutes while the partner listens without making any comments. This would be followed by another minute of silence before the roles are reversed. This first half of the exercise is ended by another minute of silence. The entire exercise is then repeated, except that the participants are asked to sing about their deficits to their partner instead of speaking. Finally, the large group is reconstituted for sharing and debriefing. The main aim of the exercise is to invite the participants to experience *defusion* in the ACT model. The experience of singing about our negative thoughts, such as our own perceived deficits, often actually alters our experience with these emotionally laden thoughts. Typically, participants giggle through their singing and report their sharing as lighter or more embarrassing in a different way, such as now being worried about their voices rather than the content of their difficulties. The minute of silence that punctuates the exercise allows a discussion of the concepts of mindfulness applied in an interpersonal relationship, that is, being able to attend to each other with compassion and without judgment, including being aware of any arising discomfort without reacting to it.

The groups were initially developed and co-facilitated by two psychiatrists (Fung and Mateusz Zurowski), with recruitment taking place through partnerships with local autism agencies and other healthcare providers. The groups took place at either the local hospital or in a community autism agency. Initial results from these groups were quite encouraging, with positive feedback from participants (Lunsky, Fung, & Zurowski, 2012). Based on clinical observation and participant feedback about the cohesive effect related to one of the facilitators (Fung) being a father with a child with ASD, we obtained research funding to run further groups specifically for mothers of children and youth with ASD with group facilitators who were themselves also parents of children with ASD. These groups were co-led and co-developed by Fung and two mothers of children with ASD (Steel and Bryce), who previously participated in the original ACT parent workshops and expressed interest in becoming involved. One of these mothers (Bryce) was a registered nurse working in the field of developmental disabilities and the other (Steel) was a family support worker in a community agency. They trained through self-study, attending a course and a workshop on ACT, and one-on-one training by the psychiatrist lead (Fung) to facilitate ACT exercises. As it was a research study, the participating mothers received a stipend to support childcare. Further modifications and refinements made to the groups included:

- creating a more welcoming ambience for sharing and creativity (e.g., holding the groups in a community space not associated with autism services; use of candles, music, poetry, and video-clips; a more cozy setting, with comfortable chairs and couches)

- adding new exercises (e.g., blowing soap bubbles as a metaphor for defusion and mindfulness)

- incorporating the use of the ACT matrix, a conceptual tool for simplifying the understanding of ACT (Polk & Schoendorff, 2014).

Clinical outcomes and group satisfaction

All groups conducted were well received and perceived to be helpful by the majority of participants. Results of our most recent series of groups specifically for mothers (n = 29) revealed a statistically significant improvement in depression and stress scores as measured by the Depression Anxiety Stress Scale (DASS-21) and in the Isolation and Health subscales of Parenting Stress Index (PSI-4) (Lunsky et al., 2017). Mothers also reported improvements in acceptance and defusion, as well as shifts in their values (Fung, Lake et al., 2018). Qualitative results were also very positive in terms of reported satisfaction and narrative feedback (Shao et al., 2016).

Therapeutic processes

In addition to the rationale involving the six underlying ACT core processes as described above, several other factors appear to have contributed to the success of the groups, including: (1) the high degree of group cohesion; (2) the shifting of roles from caregiver to care recipient; and, (3) the process of empowerment through realizing individual and group strengths.

Group cohesion

In any group therapy, group cohesion, akin to the therapeutic alliance in individual therapy, is one of the key processes that contribute to its therapeutic effects (Yalom & Leszcz, 2005). We observe that as group members, including the facilitators, share their personal experience as parents, the commonality enhances the sense of group cultural identification, mutual understanding, and trust. As ACT is grounded in a non-pathologizing theory of human suffering and the exercises are enacted nonjudgmentally with acceptance and mindfulness, the resultant open sharing of distress in mutual acceptance greatly contribute to a palpable sense of safety and group cohesion. Further, as the underlying ACT processes would equally apply to the therapist, self-disclosure is more often utilized, modeling acceptance and non-avoidance. In these particular groups, the facilitators can share their similar struggles in both process and content. Through the interactive experiential ACT exercises, participants are able to share their challenges, including: issues around accepting their children's diagnoses; managing their children's needs, behaviors, and treatments; the experience of others, including family, teachers, and the wider systems/society not understanding these difficulties; the internalized burden or guilt of not doing enough or losing temper with one's children; the incessant and sometimes wholly consuming nature of being a caregiver; the stress of re-establishing order amidst chaos and unpredictably; the multi-faceted impact on intimate relationships and all other aspects of life; and uncertainties and worries about their children's future, etc.

Shifting roles from caregiver to care-recipient

When parenting and other emotionally charged issues are raised in groups, such as how to best manage meltdowns or deal with an unsympathetic teacher, it is often tempting for participants and facilitators to jump into problem-solving and advice-giving mode, especially around parenting skills and techniques. To avoid this tendency, we made a deliberate and conscientious effort to dedicate these groups towards the health and resilience of the parents. This is carefully considered in the design of the group in order to enable this shift in roles, including: instructions for participants on how to introduce themselves to the group from the very first moments of the group; didactic presentation and group discussion about the purpose of the group with an explicit invitation to participants to focus on themselves; discussion of group rules including advice-giving; and design of each of the ACT exercises. During the actual facilitation, continuous attention by the facilitators is needed to detect any content drift towards focusing on the children and gently reorientate the focus back on the parents in a mindful and accepting way. Mindful parenting can often be a by-product and yet it is not an explicitly emphasized target to strive for nor evaluated on. Further, ACT exercises are particularly helpful to facilitate increased flexibility in roles, scripts, and behavioral repertoire through defusion exercises, perspective-taking self-as-context exercises, and, most powerfully, values and committed action exploration. Areas of personal values, needs, and aspirations that might long have been abandoned and rekindled by the group have ranged from dating and working on intimate relationships, to considering new careers, to re-establishing self-care through diet and exercise.

Individual and group empowerment

Open group sharing and the shift towards their own experience as parents enabled participants to identify in others as well as within themselves the tremendous strengths and resilience that they all possess in dealing with the multiple challenges they face. For example, being able to settle their child and make it to the group in the morning can be daunting. The fact that ACT does not focus on evaluating wrong thoughts or identifying missed solutions, while at the same time encourages not "buying into" perceived obstacles, can instill a sense of self-efficacy and renewed hope on identified values and commitment to possible actions. We have encountered many examples of empowerment in follow-up and qualitative feedback. For example, a participating mother commented:

> It [workshop] will help to build your own self-confidence by reassuring us that we are going in the right direction if our actions are congruent with our values. It helps us learn to draw strength from within even when we are in emotional pain. I even feel GOOD about my emotional distress now.

Another mother said:

> Overall I thought this was such a valuable group and I have learned to think about some of the more challenging things in my life in a very different way—a way that is extremely helpful. For example, I find myself better able to see where I get caught up in pre-existing scripts or rules about how I should respond to certain things. I am more aware of my thoughts and feelings as I am having them.

Further, the sense of collective empowerment is evidenced by mothers continuing to meet on a monthly basis after the intervention for mutual support and to practice ACT and mindfulness. This ongoing self-help group for mothers is co-facilitated by the mothers (Steel & Bryce) who co-lead our ACT groups, with other participating mothers taking turns to lead mindfulness exercises. Furthermore, other mothers have expressed interest in receiving training to become ACT group facilitators, as our two exemplary moms have done. Including mothers as facilitators has not only enhanced the clinical outcome of the groups, but has also greatly informed the research design and process. They participate fully now as members of the research and evaluation team, in addition to having become strong facilitators.

Implementation and dissemination
Challenges, limitations, and future directions

As with all interventions, ACT groups, at least as described above, may not be a fit for all parents. In particular, we found that parents within the first year of their child's diagnosis may need more informational support and practical help, and may become overwhelmed if placed in a group where others are struggling with longer-term issues. Similarly, there were a few parents who appeared to be expecting a more traditional didactic, problem-solving approach, and/or parenting skills-type workshop. For these parents, a modified approach or other interventions may be more suited. Time commitment can also be a challenge for some parents. The time, location, and the ability to provide childcare support are all factors that need to be considered. This is one of the reasons why we chose to structure the intervention as a shorter and more intense group experience so as to ease the requirement of organizing ongoing childcare. Finally, some specific exercises may not be equally appreciated or liked by everyone in the group. For example, some participants may be reluctant to use singing as a form of defusion technique. Offering alternatives (e.g., using a different voice or reciting a poem) in these cases may be helpful. We also found that some participants actually grew to more fully appreciate the exercises when they experienced them a second time or when they reflected on them or practiced them after the group (e.g., mindfulness exercise).

With the encouraging results of our groups, we are looking at ways of scaling up the capacity to offer such groups to more parents. The model of having parents as co-facilitators has not only added benefits as described above, but it also serves as a means towards wider dissemination, capacity building, and sustainability. More research needs to be conducted to determine the exact type and amount of training required, as well as the scope and range of ACT exercises that can be run by lay parent facilitators, particularly in the absence of experienced clinicians.

Another area of research is the sequential combination of ACT with other types of workshops, including workshops focusing on child intervention and parenting skills. The integrated approach of ACT with SSTP, as described above, is an example of this, although their ACT intervention was limited to only two sessions (Brown *et al.*, 2015; Whittingham *et al.*, 2016). It would be interesting to compare the effects of that approach to one where ACT is more fully implemented, followed by a skills-based intervention with a child focus, especially if the latter can be tailored and modified to be consistent with ACT principles. Finally, the optimal means of supporting long-term use of ACT skills to sustain the resilience of parents needs to be investigated. This may take the form of structured self-help groups, intermittent ACT booster workshops, or combinations of these. The use of technology, including videoconferencing or mobile apps, may also be employed as a way of connecting parents to resources and to one another, given the challenges of organizing time to connect without their children present.

Conclusion

Our efforts on delivering ACT to parents of children and youth with ASD add to the emerging literature on the benefits of parent-focused interventions for parents of children with disabilities. Indeed, it is feasible to deliver ACT to parents. Recruitment and retention for such brief intervention models may be less challenging than longer-term interventions, and the participating parents had improved clinical outcomes and reported high satisfaction. Our evaluation and the work of others reviewed in this chapter suggest that the ACT model is a promising brief intervention model to strengthen parental mental health. One of the other unique contributions of our work is the use of parents as facilitators. The parent experience may not be as seamlessly integrated in other intervention models that do not include self-reflection and disclosure, mindfulness, and acceptance in the way that ACT does. Clearly, parent participants appreciated joining with parent facilitators who had "walked in their shoes," and this may impact group cohesion in a positive way, particularly when the intervention is so brief. Going forward, it will be important to continue to develop, refine, and evaluate these types of interventions because of the vital role that parents play in the lives of their children. Involving families in the development and delivery of family-based interventions is crucial to help develop a family-centered practice agenda in our field.

References

A-Tjak, J.G.L., Davis, M.L., Morina, N., Powers, M.B., Smits, J.A.J., & Emmelkamp, P.M.G. (2015) "A meta-analysis of the efficacy of Acceptance and Commitment Therapy for clinically relevant mental and physical health problems." *Psychotherapy and Psychosomatics 84*, 1, 30–36.

Bazzano, A., Wolfe, C., Zylowska, L., Wang, S., Schuster, E., Barrett, C., & Lehrer, D. (2013) "Mindfulness Based Stress Reduction (MBSR) for parents and caregivers of individuals with developmental disabilities: A community-based approach." *Journal of Child and Family Studies 24*, 2, 298–308.

Blackledge, J.T. & Hayes, S.C. (2006) "Using acceptance and commitment training in the support of parents of children diagnosed with autism." *Child & Family Behavior Therapy 28*, 1, 1–18.

Brown, F.L., Whittingham, K., Boyd, R.N., McKinlay, L., & Sofronoff, K. (2015) "Behaviour research and therapy." *Behaviour Research and Therapy 73*, C, 58–66.

Cachia, R.L., Anderson, A., & Moore, D.W. (2015) "Mindfulness, stress and well-being in parents of children with autism spectrum disorder: A systematic review." *Journal of Child and Family Studies 25*, 1, 1–14.

Dabrowska, A. & Pisula, E. (2010) "Parenting stress and coping styles in mothers and fathers of pre-school children with autism and Down syndrome." *Journal of Intellectual Disability Research 54*, 3, 266–280.

Durand, V., Hieneman, M., Clarke, S., Wang, M., & Rinaldi, M. (2013) "Positive family intervention for severe challenging behavior I: A multisite randomized clinical trial." *Journal of Positive Behaviour Intervention 15*, 3, 133–143.

Estes, A., Munson, J., Dawson, G., Koehler, E., Zhou, X.H., & Abbott, R. (2009) "Parenting stress and psychological functioning among mothers of preschool children with autism and developmental delay." *Autism 13*, 4, 375–387.

Fletcher, L. & Hayes, S.C. (2005) "Relational frame theory, acceptance and commitment therapy, and a functional analytic definition of mindfulness." *Journal of Rational-Emotive & Cognitive-Behavior Therapy 23*, 4, 315–336.

Fung, K. (2015) "Acceptance and Commitment Therapy: Western adoption of Buddhist tenets?" *Transcultural Psychiatry 52*, 4, 561–576.

Fung, K.P. & Wong, J. (2014a) "ACT to reduce stigma of mental illness: A group intervention training manual on Acceptance and Commitment Therapy." (Unpublished manuscript.)

Fung, K.P. & Wong, J. (2014b) "Using ACT to address HIV/AIDS stigma in ethnoracial communities." Presented at the 12th Association for Contextual Behavioral Science (ACBS) World Conference, Minneapolis.

Fung, K.P. & Zurowski, M. (2008) "ACT vs CBT groups for treatment of chronic pain in Toronto." Presented at the Acceptance and Commitment Therapy Summer Institute IV, Chicago.

Fung, K.P. & Zurowski, M. (2016) "Chair Sculpture of Suffering Exercise." In A. Peterkin & P. Brett-McLean (eds) *Keeping Reflection Fresh: Top Educators Share Their Innovations in Health Professional Education*. Kent, OH: Kent State Press.

Fung, K., Lake, J., Steel, L., Bryce, K., & Lunsky, Y. (2018) "ACT processes in group intervention for mothers of children with autism spectrum disorder." *Journal of Autism and Developmental Disorders*. Advance online publication, doi 10.1007/s10803-018-3525-x.

Hayes, S.C. (2004) "Acceptance and commitment therapy, relational frame theory, and the third wave of behavioral and cognitive therapies." *Behavior Therapy 35*, 4, 639–665.

Hayes, S.C., Strosahl, K., & Wilson, K.G. (2012) *Acceptance and Commitment Therapy: The Process and Practice of Mindful Change*. New York: Guilford Press.

Hayes, S.C., Strosahl, K., Wilson, K.G., Bissett, R., *et al.* (2004) "Measuring experiential avoidance: A preliminary test of a working model." *Psychological Record 54*, 553–578.

Joekar, S., Farid, A.A.A., Birashk, B., Gharraee, B., & Mohammadian, M. (2016) "Effectiveness of Acceptance and Commitment Therapy in the support of parents of children with high-functioning autism." *International Journal of Humanities and Cultural Studies 2*, 4, 2763–2772.

Kabat-Zinn, J. (2003) "Mindfulness-based interventions in context: Past, present, and future." *Clinical Psychology: Science and Practice 10*, 2, 144–156.

Lunsky, Y., Fung, K., Lake, J., Steel, L., & Bryce, K. (2017) "Evaluation of Acceptance and Commitment Therapy (ACT) group intervention to improve health and wellbeing of mothers of individuals with autism spectrum disorder." *Mindfulness*. Advance online publication, doi 10.1007/s12671-017-0846-3.

Lunsky, Y., Fung, K., & Zurowski, M. (2012) "Acceptance and commitment therapy (ACT) for parents of youth with autism spectrum disorders: Preliminary findings." Presented at the International Association for the Scientific Study of Intellectual Disabilities (IASSID) World Congress, Halifax, Canada.

Poddar, S., Sinha, V.K., & Urbi, M. (2015) "Acceptance and commitment therapy on parents of children and adolescents with autism spectrum disorders." *International Journal of Educational and Psychological Researches 1*, 3, 221–225.

Polk, K.L. & Schoendorff, B. (2014) *The ACT Matrix: A New Approach to Building Psychological Flexibility across Settings and Populations*. Oakland, CA: New Harbinger Publications.

Reid, C., Gill, F., Gore, N., & Brady, S. (2015) "New ways of seeing and being: Evaluating an acceptance and mindfulness group for parents of young people with intellectual disabilities who display challenging behaviour." *Journal of Intellectual Disabilities 20*, 1, 5–17.

Ruiz, F. (2010) "A review of Acceptance and Commitment Therapy (ACT) empirical evidence: Correlational, experimental psychopathology, component and outcome studies." *International Journal of Psychology and Psychological Therapy 10*, 1, 125–162.

Schieve, L.A., Blumberg, S.J., Rice, C., Visser, S.N., & Boyle, C. (2007) "The relationship between autism and parenting stress." *Pediatrics 119*, S114–S121.

Segal, Z.V., Williams, J.M.G., & Teasdale, J.D. (2002) *Mindfulness-Based Cognitive Therapy for Depression: A New Approach to Preventing Relapse*. New York: Guilford Press.

Shao, Y.W., Abou Chacra, M., Heifetz, M., Lake, J., Bryce, K., Fung, K., & Lunsky, Y. (2016) Feedback from a parent-led workshop for mothers of children with Autism Spectrum Disorder, November.

Singer, G. (1993) "When It's Not So Easy to Change Your Mind: Some Reflections on Cognitive Interventions for Parents of Children with Disabilities." In A.P. Turnbull (ed.) *Cognitive Coping, Families, and Disability*. Baltimore, MD: Paul H. Brookes Publishing Co.

Singh, N.N., Lancioni, G.E., Winton, A.S.W., Singh, J., Curtis, W.J., Wahler, R.G., & McAleavey, K.M. (2007) "Mindful parenting decreases aggression and increases social behavior in children with developmental disabilities." *Behavior Modification 31*, 6, 749–771.

van der Oord, S., Bögels, S.M., & Peijnenburg, D. (2011) "The effectiveness of mindfulness training for children with ADHD and mindful parenting for their parents." *Journal of Child and Family Studies 21*, 1, 139–147.

Whittingham, K., Sanders, M.R., McKinlay, L., & Boyd, R.N. (2016) "Parenting intervention combined with Acceptance and Commitment Therapy: A trial with families of children with cerebral palsy." *Journal of Pediatric Psychology 41*, 5, 531–542.

Wilson, K.G. & DuFrene, T. (2009) *Mindfulness for Two: An Acceptance and Commitment Therapy Approach to Mindfulness in Psychotherapy*. Oakland, CA: New Harbinger Publications.

Yalom, I.D. & Leszcz, M. (2005) *The Theory and Practice of Group Psychotherapy* (5th ed.). New York: Basic Books.

The Contributors

Mallory Brown, PhD is a licensed psychologist as part of a growing group practice in Phoenix, Arizona. Mallory provides outpatient evaluation and treatment services to families with children with developmental disabilities and other behavioral health needs. She also provides second opinion school evaluations and collaborates with local schools to best support her clients' needs across settings. Mallory's areas of clinical and research interest include children with intellectual and developmental disabilities (IDD), parent training for families with young children with IDD, and prevention, intervention, and home–school collaboration for children with or at-risk for behavioral health needs.

Kelly Bryce is a mother of three wonderful children. Her two teenage boys are in high school and both have intellectual disabilities and autism. She is a registered nurse at Surrey Place Centre, Toronto, and helps children with medical issues related to their disabilities. Kelly has always been a spiritual person and, despite challenges and responsibilities, remained optimistic and grateful. However, she became so totally consumed with the care and attention that her children needed that she started to slip into a space where she was beginning to become a stranger to herself. Being very aware of this feeling, she became increasingly more anxious and easily overwhelmed. It started to affect her other relationships and interfere with her ability to juggle all of life's demands, but, most importantly, her ability to nurture herself. This is where Acceptance and Commitment came in.

Shelley Clarke, MA, BCBA is an associate in research and a faculty member within the Florida Center for Inclusive Communities, located at the College of Behavioral and Community Sciences, University of South Florida-Tampa. She has been involved in conducting PBS-applied research for over twenty years. During this time, she has worked in home, school, and community environments, using a collaborative approach to facilitate the use of evidence-based practices in order to address challenging behavior and issues related to improved quality of life. Her efforts in this area have resulted in over 30 peer-reviewed publications and four book chapters. Her major interests include conducting empirical applied research studies, practice-based coaching, PBS, early childhood, and collaboration with families and schools to promote success for children.

V. Mark Durand, PhD is Professor of Psychology at the University of South Florida St. Petersburg. Mark has more than 125 publications. His books include two textbooks on abnormal psychology that have been translated into 10 languages and used at more than 1000 universities world-wide. His other books include the multiple national award-winning *Optimistic Parenting: Hope and Help for You and Your Challenging Child*. He was named a 2014 Princeton Lecture Series Fellow and received the 2015 Jacobson Award for Critical Thinking from the American Psychological Association (APA). In 2019, Mark will serve as President of Division 33 (Intellectual and Developmental Disabilities/ASD) for APA.

Kenneth Fung, MD is the proud father of his 13-year-old son with ASD and ADHD. Kenneth is also Staff Psychiatrist and Clinical Director of the Asian Initiative in Mental Health Program at the Toronto Western Hospital, University Health Network, and Associate Professor with Equity, Gender, and Populations Division at the Department of Psychiatry, University of Toronto. His academic interests include both cultural psychiatry and psychotherapy, especially Cognitive Behavioral Therapy (CBT) and Acceptance and Commitment Therapy (ACT). Since 2005, he has experience in adapting ACT for diverse mental health problems, ethnic populations, and non-clinical applications through his clinical work, teaching, and community-based research. Kenneth is one of the founding members and past Chair of the Ontario

Chapter of the Association of Contextual Behavioral Science (ACBS) and a member of the Diversity Committee of ACBS.

Kate Guastaferro, PhD is Assistant Research Professor at the Methodology Center at the Pennsylvania State University. Her research focuses on the development, optimization, evaluation, and dissemination of multicomponent behavioral interventions using the multiphase optimization strategy (MOST). Substantively, Kate's focus is on the prevention of child maltreatment, with an eye toward co-occurring risk factors, such as parental substance use and mental health. She received her Master's and doctorate in Public Health from Georgia State University under the mentorship of Dr John R. Lutzker and a Bachelors of Arts in Anthropology from Boston University.

Brandi Hawk, PhD earned her doctorate in Clinical and Developmental Psychology from the University of Pittsburgh, where she studied the impact of institution-wide caregiver interventions on the development of young children reared in institutions in the Russian Federation. She is currently a licensed psychologist at the Child and Adolescent Abuse Resource, Evaluation, Diagnostic, and Treatment Center (CAARE Center) within the Department of Pediatrics, University of California (UC) Davis Children's Hospital. Brandi is also a co-developer of PC-CARE, a brief parenting intervention for children with behavioral problems. Current research interests include the evaluation of PC-CARE, and its integration into primary care, as well as the effectiveness of dyadic interventions in the treatment of trauma and disruptive behavior disorders.

Emily Iland, MA is an award-winning author, advocate, film-maker, researcher, and leader in the field of autism. As the mother of a young man with autism, she brings personal experience and insight to her professional roles. Emily is an educational consultant and adjunct professor in the Department of Special Education at California State University, Northridge. She is in high demand as a bilingual trainer and presenter in the US and abroad on almost every topic related to autism. Her many projects include curriculum and program development for autism awareness, safety, reading comprehension, inclusion, and equity.

Brittany Lynn Koegel, PhD received her BA in Psychology and a PhD in Special Education. Her dissertation focused on improving prosody in adolescents and adults with ASD through the use of self-management. She currently presents trainings worldwide on Pivotal Response Treatment. Additionally, Brittany has conducted trainings on reducing behavior problems in school settings. She has published chapters and articles on improving communication and socialization in children, adolescents, and adults with ASD and has presented her work at conferences throughout the United States and abroad. Brittany is currently researching a Trainer-of-Trainers model for more rapid dissemination of PRT in public schools as well as university and community clinics. She also regularly serves as a reviewer for scientific journals.

Lynn Kern Koegel, PhD is Clinical Professor at the Stanford University School of Medicine. She and her husband, Robert, are the developers of Pivotal Response Treatment, which focuses on motivation. The Koegels have published extensively and have been the recipients of many awards, including the first annual Children's Television Workshop Sesame Street Award for "Brightening the Lives of Children," the first annual Autism Speaks award for "Science and Research," and the International ABA award for "Enduring Programmatic Contributions in Behavior Analysis." In addition, Lynn appeared on ABC's hit show *Supernanny*, working with a child with autism. The Koegels' work has also been showcased on ABC, CBS, NBC, PBS, and the Discovery Channel. The Koegels are the recipients of many state, federal, and private foundation gifts and grants for developing interventions and helping families with autism spectrum disorder.

Robert L. Koegel, PhD is Senior Researcher in the Department of Psychology and Behavioral Sciences at Stanford University. Robert has focused his career in the area of autism, specializing in language intervention, family support, and school integration. He has published over 200 articles and papers relating to the treatment of autism, and is the founding editor of the *Journal of Positive Behavior Interventions*. Models of his procedures have been used in public schools and in parent education programs throughout the United States and in other countries. He has trained many health care and special education leaders in the US and abroad. Robert and Lynn Koegel are the developers of Pivotal Response Treatment, an empirically supported treatment for autism.

Johanna Lake, PhD is a psychologist by training and is currently a fellow at York University and the Centre for Addiction and Mental Health at York. Her clinical and research interests are broadly focused on the health and well-being of individuals with developmental disabilities. Currently, Johanna is involved in a project studying and delivering cognitive behavioral therapy to children with neurodevelopmental disorders. She is particularly interested in how this therapy affects change in child emotion regulation and parent co-regulation. She is also interested in supporting caregivers of individuals with autism spectrum disorder using Acceptance and Commitment Therapy (ACT).

Kristina Lopez, PhD is Assistant Professor in the School of Social Work at Arizona State University, Phoenix. Kristina earned a PhD from the University of Michigan in Social Work and Psychology. She is an expert in Latino children with autism spectrum disorders (ASD) and their families. She has practiced with children and youth with ASD and provided parent education to parents raising children with ASD. Her research interests include disparities in age of diagnosis and service receipt among racial and ethnic minority groups, the impact of ASD on families, the development and implementation of culturally informed autism intervention for Latino families, and ecological and socio-cultural perspectives of Latinos raising children with ASD.

Yona Lunsky, PhD is a clinical psychologist in the field of intellectual disability and autism. She is currently a senior scientist at the Centre for Addiction and Mental Health and Professor in the Department of Psychiatry at the University of Toronto, where she directs a research program focused on health and developmental disabilities (www.hcardd.ca). She has a particular interest in mental health promotion for individuals and families.

John R. Lutzker, PhD founded the Mark Chaffin Center for Healthy Development in the School of Public Health at Georgia State University (GSU), Atlanta. He is a distinguished university professor and expert in residence at GSU. He has published over 180 articles and eight books. Among his awards is the Outstanding Research Career Award from the American Professional Society on the Abuse of Children. John is on the editorial boards of five professional journals. He has been interviewed on *Morning Edition* of National Public Radio, ABC's *Good Morning America*, and served as a consultant for *60 Minutes* on CBS.

Wendy Machalicek, PhD, BCBA-D is Associate Professor in Special Education in the Department of Special Education and Clinical Sciences at the University of Oregon, Eugene, and a Board Certified Behavior Analyst at the doctoral level. Her scholarship focuses on the assessment and treatment of developmental delays and challenging behavior for children with autism spectrum disorders and related developmental disorders with specific emphasis on parent and teacher training, and the use of telecommunication technology to deliver interventions at a distance to address inequities in service delivery.

Sandy Magaña, PhD, MSW holds the Professorship in Autism and Neurodevelopmental Disabilities at the Steve Hicks School of Social Work, University of Texas at Austin. Sandy's research focus is on the cultural context of families who care for persons with disabilities across the life course. She has received funding for her research from the National Institute of Mental Health (NIMH), National Institute on Aging (NIA), National Institute of Child Health and Human Development (NICHD), and National Institute on Disability, Independent Living, and Rehabilitation Research (NIDILRR). Sandy's current focus is on identifying racial and ethnic disparities, and pathways from identification to diagnosis to evidence-based treatment for underserved children with autism spectrum disorder and their families.

Laura Lee McIntyre, PhD is Professor and Head of the Department of Special Education and Clinical Sciences and Associate Director of the Child and Family Center at the Prevention Science Institute at the University of Oregon, Eugene. Laura is interested in early identification and treatment of childhood developmental and behavioral problems, including autism spectrum disorder. Over the past 15 years, she has worked in the areas of prevention and early intervention of behavior and mental health problems in children with developmental disabilities. Her research has been funded by the National Institutes of Health and the US Department of Education and emphasizes working with families, schools, and healthcare systems to promote positive outcomes for children with developmental disabilities and their families.

Melissa A. Mello, MEd is a project manager for the TEAMS Study and an ESDM certified therapist and trainer at the University of California Davis MIND Institute. She has been working with children with autism for the past 12 years in a variety of settings, including as a special education teacher and early interventionist delivering one-on-one intervention in community-based programs. For the past nine years, Melissa has been supervising early intervention programs as a Clinical Manager, using behaviorally based, empirically validated methods to ensure that children with autism are improving their behavior, language, and social skills at home and in the classroom. Melissa has a Master's degree in Special Education from San Francisco State University and is a Board Certified Behavior Analyst.

Ronit M. Molko, PhD is the founder and principal of Empowering Synergy Inc, and advises investors and service providers in the behavioral healthcare field, with a special focus on services to individuals with autism and developmental disabilities. Ronit co-founded and scaled Autism Spectrum Therapies, which grew into one of the largest multi-state providers of premier, evidence-based behavioral interventions for individuals on the autism spectrum. Her mission is to ensure that service providers and investors incorporate best practices, with a focus on individualized, family-focused ABA interventions delivered in the natural environment to support meaningful long-term outcomes. Ronit is a licensed clinical psychologist in the states of California and Washington, a Board Certified Behavior Analyst, and a graduate of Harvard Business School's Owners/President Management program.

Sally J. Rogers, PhD is Professor at the University of California Davis MIND Institute and specializes in conducting developmental and treatment research into autism and other developmental disorders and in working with children with developmental disabilities and their families, especially young children with autism. She studies early developmental processes, including imitation, social-communicative behavior, development of motor skills, language, and social interaction patterns. She is currently focused on developing and improving treatments for early autism using the Early Start Denver Model. Her clinical interests include evaluation of cognitive, behavioral, social, emotional, and adaptive functioning; early intervention for children with autism; and developing treatment and educational interventions for persons with autism of all ages, and social skills groups for adults with autism. Sally has written extensively in her field, authoring numerous articles and books and developing training videos.

Lee Steel is the proud parent of two adult children. Her eldest son was diagnosed at 3 years of age with ASD. As a coordinator with Extend-A-Family, Lee brings her firsthand experience to provide advocacy, support, and hope to other parents whose children have been diagnosed with a developmental disability. Prior to joining Extend-A-Family four years ago, Lee was the parent liaison at the Autism Research Unit, Hospital for Sick Children, for 11 years. Lee is honored to be part of this research and to be trained as a co-facilitator for the ACT workshops for parents.

Julia Strauss, MEd candidate is Graduate Assistant within the Vanderbilt Kennedy Center at Vanderbilt University. She has been involved in multiple empirical research studies across her undergraduate and graduate studies. During this time, Julia has provided Applied Behavior Analysis services in the home, school, and clinical settings. Along with research on positive family intervention and positive behavior supports (PBS) training for families of children with challenging behavior, the research projects that she has been involved in evaluate the effectiveness of applied interventions to support the social and academic development of students with disabilities. Her work has resulted in three published papers and multiple presentations at national conferences.

Meagan R. Talbott, PhD is Postdoctoral Fellow at the University of California Davis MIND Institute. She received her doctorate from Boston University. She has been conducting research on parent–child interactions and early communication development in infants and toddlers with ASD for more than 10 years.

Susan G. Timmer, PhD is Research Scientist at the CAARE Diagnostic and Treatment Center and Managing Director of the PCIT Training Center at University of California Davis Children's Hospital. She is also a faculty member of the Human Development Graduate Group at UC Davis, and Clinical Associate Professor in the Department of Pediatrics at the UC Davis Children's Hospital. Susan was a co-developer of the PCIT for Traumatized Children Web Course (https://pcit.ucdavis.edu) and co-developer of PC-CARE, a brief parenting intervention for children with behavioral problems. Her research focuses on evaluating the effectiveness and implementation of PCIT and PC-CARE. She also investigates the effects of maltreatment on children, and parent–child relationship processes in the context of children's experience of maltreatment.

Anthony J. Urquiza, PhD is a clinical psychologist, Professor in Pediatrics, and Director of both the CAARE Center and PCIT Training Center at the UC Davis Children's Hospital. The CAARE Center provides medical evaluations, psychological assessments, and a range of mental health treatment services, primarily for abused and neglected children. During the last two decades, Anthony has overseen the implementation of an adaptation of Parent–Child Interaction Therapy (PCIT) for families involved in child welfare systems (i.e., physically abusive families, foster families, adoptive families) receiving services in community mental health clinics. Under his leadership, the PCIT Training Center has trained more than 130 community mental health agencies throughout the United States and internationally. He is currently involved in a large-scale training and PCIT implementation project in Los Angeles County.

Subject Index

Author Index